Mastering OpenShift

Deploy, Manage, and Scale Applications on Kubernetes

Robert Johnson

Published by HiTeX Press

For permissions and other inquiries, write to:
P.O. Box 3132, Framingham, MA 01701, USA

Contents

Introduction

OpenShift has established itself as a leading open-source platform for automating the deployment, scaling, and management of applications. Standing on the shoulders of Kubernetes, OpenShift provides an enterprise-grade solution that simplifies the complexities of orchestrating containerized applications. As organizations continuously seek efficiency in their deployment pipelines and resilience in their application infrastructure, OpenShift emerges as an indispensable tool that merges the robustness of Kubernetes with additional capabilities tailored for enterprise needs.

This book, "Mastering OpenShift: Deploy, Manage, and Scale Applications on Kubernetes," is designed to impart both foundational knowledge and practical skills required to harness the full potential of OpenShift. Whether you are a software developer, system administrator, or IT professional, this guide will equip you with the necessary insights and techniques to effectively deploy, manage, and scale applications using OpenShift.

The content is meticulously organized to cater to readers new to OpenShift, as well as those looking to deepen their proficiency. We begin by providing an overview of the fundamental concepts of Kubernetes and how OpenShift enhances and extends these capabilities. Subsequent chapters delve into various aspects of getting started with OpenShift, such as installation, using the command line interface, and creating projects. You will learn how to confidently navigate through the OpenShift architecture and understand its components, allowing you to effectively deploy applications and manage resources.

Additionally, this guide will explore advanced topics such as scaling applications, implementing robust security practices, managing networking configurations, and optimizing storage solutions within the OpenShift environment. Building on this foundation, the book further examines automation strategies with OpenShift Pipelines and provides actionable insights into managing complex deployments and overcoming common troubleshooting challenges.

Throughout this book, we prioritize a structured, fact-based approach to present OpenShift's features and best practices. By maintaining a focus on clarity and precision, our aim is to provide a resource that is comprehensive in scope, yet approachable for individuals at various stages of their cloud-native journey.

In closing, "Mastering OpenShift" seeks not only to educate but also to serve as a reference that professionals can depend on as they design and maintain sophisticated application architectures. As OpenShift continues to evolve, embracing new technologies and methodologies, its continuous development ensures it remains at the forefront of cloud-native orchestration solutions. By immersing yourself in the content of this book, you will be well-prepared to leverage OpenShift's capabilities in your organization's pursuit of technological excellence.

Chapter 1

Introduction to OpenShift and Kubernetes

OpenShift enhances Kubernetes's renowned container orchestration capabilities with enterprise-level offerings, making it a sought-after solution for efficient application deployment and management. By expanding upon Kubernetes's robust infrastructure, OpenShift integrates vital features such as developer-friendly tools and enhanced operational controls. This chapter provides a foundational understanding of both technologies, detailing their components, benefits, versions, and use cases within enterprise environments. By setting up an initial OpenShift environment, readers will gain the essential knowledge required to navigate and utilize the platform effectively, laying the groundwork for deeper exploration into OpenShift's advanced capabilities.

1.1 Overview of Kubernetes

Kubernetes, often abbreviated as K8s, is an open-source platform designed to automate deploying, scaling, and operating application containers. Developed by Google, and now managed by the Cloud Native Computing Foundation, it is a complete ecosystem that provides the fundamental building blocks for running containerized applications. To understand Kubernetes fully, one must delve into its architecture, key concepts, operational paradigms, and associated tooling.

- **Kubernetes Architecture**

  Kubernetes operates as a cluster management system that abstracts the underlying hardware infrastructure, offering a consistent platform for application deployment. It comprises several vital components categorized primarily into the *Control Plane* and the *Worker Nodes*.

  - *Control Plane*: This centralized coordination point is responsible for maintaining the desired state for the cluster. It consists of components like the API Server, etcd (a consistent and highly-available key-value store), Controller Manager, and Scheduler. These elements work together to ensure the system's consistency and availability.

  - *Worker Nodes*: Also known as minions within the Kubernetes ecosystem, worker nodes execute the applications. Each node runs at least one Kubelet, a container runtime (such as Docker or containerd), and the Kube Proxy.

  - *Pods and Containers*: The smallest deployable units within Kubernetes are *pods*. A pod encapsulates one or more containers with shared storage and networking, representing a single instance of a running process in your application.

```
apiVersion: v1
kind: Pod
metadata:
  name: my-pod
spec:
  containers:
  - name: my-container
    image: nginx
```

- **Core Concepts**

  Kubernetes introduces several abstractions that allow developers and operations teams to manage the lifecycle and demands of containerized applications efficiently.

  - *Deployments*: This resource ensures declarative updates to applications and containers. A deployment specifies the desired state for applications, like image version, replicas, and strategies for updates.

    ```yaml
    apiVersion: apps/v1
    kind: Deployment
    metadata:
      name: nginx-deployment
    spec:
      replicas: 3
      selector:
        matchLabels:
          app: nginx
      template:
        metadata:
          labels:
            app: nginx
        spec:
          containers:
          - name: nginx
            image: nginx:1.14.2
            ports:
            - containerPort: 80
    ```

  - *Services*: Services provide stable endpoints to pods running within a cluster. They abstract the underlying details, such as IP addresses, enabling seamless interaction with the deployed applications.

  - *Namespaces*: These are utilized for organizing objects within a Kubernetes cluster. They facilitate environment-specific segmentation, resource allocation, and administration.

  - *ConfigMaps and Secrets*: ConfigMaps allow external configuration of application data, whereas Secrets store sensitive data like passwords and credentials in a secure manner.

- **Kubernetes Operational Paradigms**

  Operating Kubernetes involves understanding several paradigms and models that ensure a resilient and efficient container orchestration.

11

– *Desired State Management*: Kubernetes operates based on the desired state model. Users declare the state of the application they desire, and the control plane works to maintain this state continuously.

– *Reconciliation Loop*: This is a continuous process where the Kubernetes controllers manage the divergence between the current state and the desired state, ensuring systems become increasingly consistent.

– *Autoscaling*: Kubernetes supports horizontal pod autoscaling, which automatically adjusts the number of pod replicas based on current demand. The Horizontal Pod Autoscaler is a built-in mechanism capable of scaling based on CPU utilization metrics.

```
apiVersion: autoscaling/v1
kind: HorizontalPodAutoscaler
metadata:
  name: nginx-autoscaler
spec:
  scaleTargetRef:
    apiVersion: apps/v1
    kind: Deployment
    name: nginx-deployment
  minReplicas: 1
  maxReplicas: 10
  targetCPUUtilizationPercentage: 50
```

- **Ecosystem and Tooling**

  Kubernetes is complemented by an extensive ecosystem of tools and extensions designed to enhance its capabilities, streamline operations, and broaden its applicability.

  – *Helm*: Often referred to as the package manager for Kubernetes, Helm facilitates the management of complex Kubernetes applications. It allows for the efficient configuration, upgrade, and rollback of applications using Helm Charts.

  – *Prometheus and Grafana*: These are powerful open-source monitoring tools integrated into many Kubernetes clusters to provide insights into system health and performance metrics.

  – *Istio*: Providing service mesh capabilities, Istio manages service-to-service communications, often crucial in microservices architectures deployed within Kubernetes clusters.

- *Kubectl*: The command-line utility kubectl allows users to interact with their Kubernetes cluster, manage resources, and retrieve information about their system state.

```
# Gets a list of all pods in the default namespace
kubectl get pods

# Describes a specific deployment
kubectl describe deployment nginx-deployment

# Apply a configuration to a resource by filename
kubectl apply -f my-pod-definition.yaml
```

- **Security and Networking**

  Security and effective networking are core features baked into Kubernetes and require understanding and implementation to ensure robust deployment scenarios.

  - *Network Policies*: These define how pods communicate with each other and other network endpoints, enabling granular control over permitted connections and traffic.

  - *Role-Based Access Control (RBAC)*: Kubernetes uses RBAC to specify permissions and regulate access to its resources. This ensures that users and applications can interact only with what they have explicit permissions for, safeguarding sensitive configuration and operational parameters.

  - *Secrets Management*: Kubernetes manages secrets efficiently, allowing encrypted storage and retrieval of confidential data, such as API tokens and passwords, within pods.

```
apiVersion: rbac.authorization.k8s.io/v1
kind: Role
metadata:
  namespace: default
  name: pod-reader
rules:
- apiGroups: [""]
  resources: ["pods"]
  verbs: ["get", "watch", "list"]


---
apiVersion: rbac.authorization.k8s.io/v1
```

13

```
kind: RoleBinding
metadata:
  name: read-pods
  namespace: default
subjects:
- kind: User
  name: my-user
  apiGroup: rbac.authorization.k8s.io
roleRef:
  kind: Role
  name: pod-reader
  apiGroup: rbac.authorization.k8s.io
```

- **Multi-cloud and Hybrid Cloud Deployments**

  Kubernetes is pivotal in enabling multi-cloud and hybrid cloud deployment strategies. By providing a unified abstraction layer, Kubernetes facilitates the deployment of workloads across differing cloud providers, such as Amazon Web Services, Google Cloud Platform, and Microsoft Azure, or within a private cloud setting.

  Federation is a critical component that allows for the management of multiple clusters as a single entity, providing benefits such as improved fault tolerance, load balancing, and disaster recovery.

  The adoption of Kubernetes within these deployment models caters to contemporary demands for flexibility, resilience, and performance, contributing to its popularity as a de facto standard for container orchestration.

  While Kubernetes offers unparalleled advantages in container orchestration, its complexity necessitates a comprehensive understanding of its architecture, components, and operations. This enables organizations and developers to leverage its full potential, facilitating scalable, resilient, and efficient application deployments within a rapidly evolving technological landscape.

1.2 OpenShift as an Enterprise Kubernetes Platform

OpenShift is a robust container application platform that builds upon Kubernetes, extending its capabilities with additional enterprise-level features. It is designed to facilitate a developer-friendly and operationally sound environment for building, deploying, and managing containerized applications. This section explores OpenShift's unique attributes, enhancements over standard Kubernetes, and how it integrates into enterprise environments.

1. The OpenShift Architecture

OpenShift augments traditional Kubernetes architecture by introducing components and workflows that optimize both development and operations.

- *OpenShift Master and API Server*: The OpenShift Master includes the Controller Master and etcd, similar to Kubernetes's control plane, but also incorporates additional API endpoints for OpenShift-specific resources.

- *Nodes and Container Registry*: OpenShift nodes run containerized applications and provide resources like CPU and memory. The integrated image registry stores and serves Docker-formatted container images, allowing images to be easily managed and deployed.

- *Networking Enhancements*: OpenShift utilizes Software Defined Networking (SDN) to manage container networking processes, providing unique features like automatic DNS management and integrated router functionality for complex applications.

2. Developer Centric Enhancements

While Kubernetes provides foundational container orchestration capabilities, OpenShift extends these to improve developer productivity.

- *Source-to-Image (S2I)*: A standout feature, S2I automatically builds reproducible container images directly from source code repositories. Developers focus on coding, while OpenShift manages the intricacies of building and deploying application containers.

```
s2i build https://github.com/myrepo/myapp.git centos/python-36-centos7
    myapp:latest
```

- *Developer Tools Integration*: OpenShift includes plugins for popular Integrated Development Environments (IDEs) such as Eclipse and Visual Studio Code, alongside command-line tools for seamless integration into the developer workflow.

- *Templates and Catalogs*: OpenShift's application templates streamline common development tasks. The OpenShift Service Catalog allows developers to browse and use services from a comprehensive marketplace.

3. Operational Enhancements

OpenShift integrates several features designed to simplify operational tasks and enhance platform security.

- *Automated Operations*: Features such as automated scaling, health checks, and rolling updates minimize downtimes and maintain application availability. Operators automate the configuration, provisioning, and management of complex applications.

- *Logging and Monitoring*: OpenShift aggregates, indexes, and displays logs using the EFK stack (Elasticsearch, Fluentd, Kibana). Integration with Prometheus provides detailed metrics and alerts, ensuring operational insights.

- *Security Context Constraints*: These define the security conditions for pods, managing permissions and accessing sensitive data effectively. This feature enhances Kubernetes's security capabilities, making it enterprise-ready.

```
apiVersion: v1
kind: Pod
metadata:
  name: secure-pod
spec:
  containers:
  - name: my-container
    image: centos
    securityContext:
      runAsUser: 1000
      runAsNonRoot: true
```

4. OpenShift on Multi-Cloud and Hybrid Cloud

16

Enterprises increasingly adopt multi-cloud and hybrid cloud strategies to optimize resource use and enhance resilience. OpenShift facilitates these strategies with its flexible deployment options.

- *Consistency Across Environments*: OpenShift ensures consistent application deployment and management across on-premise and cloud environments, supporting a mix of public cloud providers including AWS, Azure, and Google Cloud Platform.

- *Centralized Management*: With OpenShift's centralized console, administrators can manage clusters and workloads across multiple environments seamlessly. This consolidation simplifies operations and provides a unified view for streamlined management.

- *OpenShift Federation*: Enabling applications to span multiple clusters or clouds, OpenShift Federation manages these environments as a cohesive system, integrating seamlessly with Kubernetes Federation.

5. Use of CI/CD Pipelines

OpenShift excels in establishing and integrating Continuous Integration and Continuous Deployment (CI/CD) pipelines, critical for modern application development.

- *Jenkins Integration*: OpenShift includes built-in integration with Jenkins, supporting pipelines as code. This facilitates the automated execution of defined build, test, and deployment stages for efficient developer workflows.

```
pipeline {
    agent any
    stages {
        stage('Build') {
            steps {
                script {
                    oc.startBuild('my-app')
                }
            }
        }
        stage('Deploy') {
            steps {
                script {
                    openshiftDeploy deploymentConfig: 'my-app'
```

```
                    }
                  }
               }
             }
          }
```

- *Tekton Pipelines*: For cloud-native CI/CD, Tekton provides a Kubernetes-native pipeline system. OpenShift integrates Tekton for creating event-driven workflows with cloud-first principles.

- *GitOps*: OpenShift embraces GitOps practices, utilizing Git as the single source of truth for application and infrastructure definitions. Tools like ArgoCD facilitate GitOps, maintaining system state through Git repositories.

6. OpenShift and DevSecOps Integration

The emphasis on shifting security left, inherent in DevSecOps practices, is evident in OpenShift's design. OpenShift integrates security measures seamlessly into development pipelines and operations.

- *Image Scanning*: Integrated scanning capabilities identify vulnerabilities in container images. Regular scans and audits ensure that only secure and compliant images are deployed, addressing common attack vectors.

- *RBAC Policies*: OpenShift enhances Kubernetes's Role-Based Access Control (RBAC) with fine-grained policies, tailoring permissions to meet stringent enterprise security standards.

- *Service Mesh and Encryption*: OpenShift Service Mesh integrates with Istio, offering advanced traffic management and security features like mutual TLS between services, supporting policy-based encryption and network observability.

7. Comprehensive User and Access Management

For enterprises, user and access management is paramount. OpenShift provides comprehensive tools for managing these concerns at scale.

- *Identity Providers*: OpenShift supports numerous identity providers, from LDAP and Active Directory to OAuth and

18

Google, ensuring flexible integration with existing enterprise identity management systems.

```
apiVersion: config.openshift.io/v1
kind: OAuth
metadata:
  name: cluster
spec:
  identityProviders:
  - name: my_ldap
    mappingMethod: claim
    type: LDAP
    ldap:
      url: ldaps://ldap.example.com/ou=people,dc=example,dc=com
      bindDN: "cn=Manager,dc=example,dc=com"
      bindPassword:
        name: ldap-bind-password
      insecure: false
```

- *Quota Management*: OpenShift enforces resource quotas and limits to control consumable resources, safeguarding fair usage and preventing abuse in shared environments.

- *Audit Logs*: OpenShift maintains comprehensive audit logs, tracking user actions and system events for compliance and troubleshooting.

OpenShift, as an enterprise Kubernetes platform, addresses the inherent complexities of container orchestration with advanced features tailored for scalability, security, and developer productivity. Its enhancements over Kubernetes help bridge the gap between development and operations teams, facilitating seamless deployment and management across diverse and complex environments. This integration into enterprise systems not only accelerates application delivery but also ensures that these applications meet rigorous standards for performance, security, and reliability.

1.3 Core Components of OpenShift

The OpenShift platform is built on top of Kubernetes and extends it with a set of components and tools that provide a comprehensive application lifecycle management experience. Understanding these core components is crucial for efficiently deploying and managing applications within OpenShift. This section delves into the roles and interactions of these components, explaining their significance in the infrastructure of OpenShift.

1. OpenShift Master

The OpenShift Master controls the entire platform cluster, managing workloads, and the overall ecosystem. It consists of several critical subcomponents that coordinate the system's operations.

- *API Server*: It exposes the Kubernetes API, interfacing with the OpenShift API tailored for enhanced features. The API server handles requests for resource definitions and updates, orchestrating interactions between different OpenShift components.

- *etcd*: An integral component that acts as a highly available key-value store, etcd is responsible for storing all cluster data, including the state and configuration of all objects, such as pods, services, and deployments.

- *Controller Manager*: It runs on the master node and manages various processes like node operations, managing state transitions, and controlling replication controllers.

- *Scheduler*: It is tasked with assigning new containers to nodes based on resource requirements and policy constraints. The scheduler ensures optimal deployment, enhancing resource utilization and efficiency.

2. OpenShift Nodes

Nodes are the infrastructure that runs containerized workloads, interfacing directly with the containers.

- *Node Management*: OpenShift nodes integrate deeply with Kubernetes nodes but include additional services optimizing application deployments. The node is responsible for launching container instances.

- *Kubelet*: The primary node agent, Kubelet ensures that containers are running within each pod. It receives PodSpecs and ensures those specified containers are running and healthy.

- *Kube Proxy*: This component runs on each node, maintaining network rules and facilitating network abstraction, managing pod-to-pod communication and services.

3. The Container Runtime and Image Registry

These components are essential for managing container images and running containers effectively in OpenShift.

- *Container Runtimes*: OpenShift supports CRI-O and Docker as primary container runtimes. These runtimes manage the lifecycle of containers, ensuring seamless execution of containerized applications while interfacing with Kubernetes components.

- *Integrated Image Registry*: OpenShift includes an integrated container image registry utilized for managing Docker-formatted images. It stores application images securely for deployments, easing image distribution across cluster nodes.

```
oc import-image my-image --from=docker.io/library/mysql:5.7 --confirm
```

4. OpenShift CLI (OC)

The OpenShift CLI (oc) is a robust command-line interface that extends Kubernetes's CLI with configuration and control features specific to OpenShift.

- *Deployment Management*: Users can interact with the OpenShift cluster, managing deployments, scaling applications, and interacting with underlying resources seamlessly.

```
# Login to an OpenShift cluster
oc login --server=https://api.openshift.example.com

# Display status of the current project
oc status

# Deploy an application
oc new-app my-image --name=my-app
```

- *Application Debugging and Monitoring*: Provides extensive functionality for monitoring application status, logs, and debugging information, ensuring operational efficiency.

5. Developer and User Portal (Web Console)

A user-friendly web-based interface provides access to OpenShift resources and functionality, complementing the CLI.

- *Resource Visualization*: It displays the cluster's resources graphically, allowing users to visualize the deployment status, logs, and metrics of applications.

- *Operational Controls*: Users can adjust configurations, manage role-based access control, and handle networking components via an intuitive dashboard, enhancing user experience and productivity.

6. Networking Infrastructure

Networking is a cornerstone of OpenShift's architecture, enhancing Kubernetes networking with sophisticated features and integrations.

- *Open vSwitch (OVS) based Networking*: OpenShift employs OVS to configure multiple distinct networking constructs such as services, routes, and pod networking. This differentiation allows for managing complex networking scenarios.

- *Routes and Services*: Routes expose services to external clients, enabling seamless traffic routing to application pods. It supports various routing strategies like edge, pass-through, and re-encrypt modes.

```
apiVersion: route.openshift.io/v1
kind: Route
metadata:
  name: my-route
spec:
  host: www.example.com
  to:
    kind: Service
    name: my-service
```

7. Storage Management

Persistent storage is crucial for stateful applications. OpenShift integrates sophisticated storage management mechanisms.

22

- *Persistent Volume Claims (PVC)*: PVCs are user requests for persistent storage resources in OpenShift. They abstract the underlying storage deployment mechanics, aligning storage requirements with application needs.

- *Dynamic Provisioning*: OpenShift supports dynamic provisioning, allowing volumes to be provisioned automatically when PVCs are created, enhancing scalability and usability in cloud environments.

8. Security and Policy Management

OpenShift security is a multi-faceted approach spanning several components, ensuring a secure environment for workload deployment.

- *Security Context Constraints (SCCs)*: SCCs apply security restrictions to pods, defining constraints on resources, user permissions, and network configurations. This ensures applications adhere to organizational security policies.

- *Role-Based Access Control (RBAC)*: An evolution over Kubernetes RBAC, OpenShift tightly integrates user and namespace management, restricting access to resources effectively as per defined policies.

9. Operator Framework

The Operator Framework in OpenShift provides a model for managing Kubernetes-native apps called Operators, encapsulating operational knowledge into code.

- *Operators*: Simplify complex application deployment by codifying administrative logic, handling everything from installation to maintenance and upgrades.

```
oc apply -f my-operator.yaml
```

10. Service Mesh Integration

OpenShift Service Mesh, an integration of Istio and Kubernetes, manages services' inbound and outbound traffic, adhering to robust security and policy enforcement guidelines.

23

- *Traffic Management*: Fine-grained controls over service communications, facilitating retries, circuit-breaking, and traffic splitting.

- *Observability and Security*: Offers comprehensive service metrics, tracing, and logging capabilities, alongside enabling mutual TLS for interservice communications.

The core components of OpenShift form a sophisticated platform that builds on the foundations of Kubernetes, enhancing deployability, usability, and manageability for enterprise environments. Understanding each component's role enables administrators and developers to fully leverage OpenShift's capabilities, fostering a productive, secure, and resilient application lifecycle management environment. As OpenShift continues evolving, it advances the intersection of DevOps and application infrastructure, supporting cutting-edge methodologies and practices in modern cloud-native environments.

1.4   Benefits of Using OpenShift

OpenShift offers a comprehensive suite of features and advantages that make it an attractive choice for enterprises seeking to deploy and manage containerized applications. As an enterprise Kubernetes platform, OpenShift provides a blend of operational efficiency, developer productivity, and enhanced security, making it a pivotal tool in modern IT infrastructures. This section examines these benefits in depth, highlighting how OpenShift addresses common challenges faced by organizations in the containerization domain.

1. Enhanced Development Experience

One of the primary benefits of using OpenShift is its focus on enhancing the developer experience. It allows developers to concentrate on writing code without worrying about the complexities of deploying and managing containers.

- *Source-to-Image (S2I)*: A unique feature of OpenShift, S2I enables developers to build and deploy applications from source code seamlessly. By automating container image creation, S2I boosts productivity and reduces time-to-market for applications.

```
s2i build https://github.com/example/repo centos/python-36-centos7
    python-app:latest
```

- *Integrated CI/CD Pipelines*: OpenShift integrates with Jenkins and supports Tekton Pipelines, providing a robust framework for Continuous Integration and Continuous Deployment (CI/CD). This integration allows for automated testing and deployment, ensuring high-quality code delivery.

```
pipeline {
    agent any
    stages {
        stage('Build') {
            steps {
                script {
                    oc.startBuild('my-app')
                }
            }
        }
        stage('Deploy') {
            steps {
                script {
                    openshiftDeploy deploymentConfig: 'my-app'
                }
            }
        }
    }
}
```

2. Scalability and Flexibility

OpenShift is designed to scale efficiently with the needs of modern enterprises, facilitating growth and resource utilization.

- *Horizontal and Vertical Scaling*: OpenShift supports both horizontal and vertical scaling, allowing for flexibility in resource allocation. By scaling pods up or out, OpenShift ensures applications maintain performance under varying loads.

- *Cluster Federation*: With support for multi-cluster management, OpenShift enables applications to span multiple clusters, offering global load balancing and resilience across environments.

3. Improved Security Model

Security is a paramount concern in container orchestration platforms, and OpenShift excels in providing a secure environment.

- *Integrated Security Mechanisms*: OpenShift incorporates security features like Role-Based Access Control (RBAC) and Security Context Constraints (SCCs) to manage permissions and isolate workloads effectively.

```
apiVersion: v1
kind: Pod
metadata:
  name: secure-pod
spec:
  containers:
  - name: my-container
    image: example-image
    securityContext:
      allowPrivilegeEscalation: false
      runAsUser: 1000
      runAsNonRoot: true
```

- *Secure Networking*: OpenShift's networking model supports TLS encryption, network policies, and integrated service meshes, fostering secure communications between microservices.

- *Compliance and Auditing*: Built-in compliance checks and audit logging help organizations meet regulatory requirements and maintain a secure operational footprint.

4. Enterprise Integration

OpenShift seamlessly integrates with existing enterprise infrastructures, enabling smooth adoption and streamlined operations.

- *Identity and Access Management*: OpenShift supports LDAP, Active Directory, and other identity providers to integrate with existing authentication systems, facilitating user management and access control.

```
apiVersion: config.openshift.io/v1
kind: OAuth
metadata:
  name: cluster
spec:
  identityProviders:
  - name: ldap_provider
    mappingMethod: claim
```

```
type: LDAP
ldap:
  url: ldaps://ldap.example.com/ou=people,dc=example,dc=com
  bindDN: "cn=admin,dc=example,dc=com"
  bindPassword:
    name: ldap-bind-password
  insecure: false
```

- *Infrastructure Agnosticism*: OpenShift can be deployed on various platforms, including on-premise data centers, public clouds, and hybrid cloud environments, providing unmatched flexibility and choice for enterprises.

5. Comprehensive Tooling and Analytics

The platform offers a plethora of tools and analytics features that are crucial for monitoring and optimizing application performance.

- *Monitoring and Logging*: OpenShift is equipped with metrics and logging stacks, often using Prometheus and the EFK (Elasticsearch, Fluentd, Kibana) stack for comprehensive monitoring and alerting.

- *Performance Optimization*: With real-time metrics and insights, OpenShift enables proactive optimization of application performance, reducing downtime and improving user experience.

6. Reduced Complexity with Operator Framework

Operators in OpenShift encapsulate operational knowledge for container applications, reducing the operational burden.

- *Custom Resource Management*: Operators automate not just the deployment but also the management tasks associated with software lifecycles, monitoring their status and executing updates.

```
oc apply -f my-operator-definition.yaml
```

- *Industry-Specific Solutions*: OpenShift's OperatorHub offers operators for various use cases, ensuring industry-specific best practices are embedded into enterprise solutions.

7. Hybrid and Multi-Cloud Capabilities

OpenShift provides the tools and frameworks needed for successful hybrid and multi-cloud environments.

- *Consistent Deployment Models*: OpenShift enables consistency in application deployment and management across diverse environments, ensuring minimal disruption and coherent operation irrespective of location.

- *Cross-Cloud Visibility and Management*: By providing a single pane of glass for multi-cloud environments, OpenShift simplifies managing and monitoring workloads across cloud providers, maximizing resource efficiency and minimizing cloud sprawl.

8. Cost Efficiency and Resource Optimization

OpenShift helps organizations optimize resource usage and reduce costs associated with infrastructure management and operations.

- *Automated Resource Management*: With automated scaling and resource allocation, OpenShift ensures that infrastructure is utilized efficiently, reducing waste and optimizing expenditure.

- *Reduced Overhead*: The platform's extensive automation of deployment, scaling, and management tasks means reduced overhead for development and operations teams, translating into cost savings for enterprises.

The benefits of using OpenShift are manifold, catering to a broad spectrum of operational and development needs. By providing a platform that integrates seamlessly with existing enterprise infrastructures and supports a wide array of deployment models, OpenShift positions itself as a versatile solution for modern container orchestration. Its ability to enhance developer productivity, bolster application security, and optimize resource utilization makes it invaluable for organizations navigating the complexities of digital transformation. As more enterprises adopt cloud-native practices, the comprehensive features and advantages of OpenShift will continue to facilitate and drive innovation at scale.

1.5 OpenShift Versions and Release History

The evolution of OpenShift has been marked by continuous innovation and adaptation to meet the dynamic needs of enterprises deploying cloud-native applications. Understanding the versions and release history of OpenShift provides insight into its technological advancements, essential features, and strategic enhancements that have shaped its deployment in modern IT infrastructures. This section explores the key milestones in OpenShift's journey, analyzing the progression from early versions to its current state-of-the-art capabilities.

- *Origin and Early Development*

  OpenShift originated as a Platform-as-a-Service (PaaS) solution, originally introduced by Red Hat around 2011. The initial offerings focused on enabling developers to deploy applications without managing the underlying infrastructure.

  - *OpenShift Origin*: Initially an open-source project, OpenShift Origin served as the community-driven upstream of OpenShift. It allowed users to deploy applications via source code in a PaaS model, supporting several programming languages through integrated cartridges.

    ```
    rhc app create python-app python-3.3
    ```

  - *Shift towards Kubernetes*: Over time, the realization of containers as the foundational technology for future PaaS frameworks led OpenShift to transition towards a Kubernetes-based platform. This pivot occurred around OpenShift v3, aligning the tool with the industry's standard for container orchestration.

- *OpenShift 3.x Series*

  The OpenShift 3.x series marked a significant transformation of the platform, establishing OpenShift as a leading Kubernetes distribution.

– *OpenShift 3.0*: Released in June 2015, OpenShift 3.0 was the first version fully based on Kubernetes, integrated with Docker as its runtime. It introduced enhanced orchestration capabilities, declarative management, and additional tools for seamless container management.

– *Network and Security Enhancements*: Throughout the 3.x series, OpenShift saw the inclusion of Open vSwitch (OVS) for advanced networking, as well as Security Context Constraints (SCCs), which improved multi-tenancy security.

– *OpenShift Container Platform (OCP)*: Starting with version 3, Red Hat's commercialization of OpenShift under the OCP banner emphasized enterprise-ready features like fine-grained RBAC policies, integrated logging and metrics, and extensions into hybrid cloud scenarios.

• *OpenShift 4.x Series*

A transformative release, OpenShift 4.x brought forth Kubernetes-native infrastructure enhancements and modern operational practices, further solidifying OpenShift's stance as an enterprise-class platform.

– *Operator Framework and Automation*: With OpenShift 4.0, the platform introduced Operators - Kubernetes-native applications that manage maintained application life cycles. This release gave birth to the OperatorHub, a marketplace for operator integration.

```
oc apply -f operator-sdk.yaml
```

– *Cluster Update Automation*: By automating cluster deployment and management tasks, OpenShift 4.x minimized operational overhead and reduced the complexity associated with maintaining production environments.

– *Machine API*: A key feature in the 4.x releases, the Machine API provided automatic provisioning and scaling of the compute resources, ensuring efficient infrastructure usage and facilitating rapid scale-out capabilities.

• *Key Milestones within OpenShift 4.x*

30

Several pivotal releases within the OpenShift 4.x series introduced groundbreaking features that steered the platform's future.

— *OpenShift 4.1*: Launched in June 2019, OpenShift 4.1 was the first production-ready release under the new 4.x architecture, aligning tightly with Kubernetes standards while offering OpenShift-specific enhancements like native image registry capabilities and improved monitoring integration.

— *OpenShift 4.3*: Furthering hybrid cloud support, version 4.3 bolstered storage and networking options, with features such as enhanced IPv6 support and integrations with Red Hat Virtualization (RHV).

— *OpenShift 4.5*: Launched in 2020, this version integrated OpenShift Virtualization, enabling both containerized applications and virtual machines to run side-by-side, further enhancing cloud-native capabilities.

- *OpenShift Shift towards Multi-Cluster and Hybrid Cloud*

The versions following OpenShift 4.5 focused intensively on multi-cloud environments, bringing unparalleled support for hybrid cloud strategies. These versions equipped OpenShift with sophisticated capabilities for cross-cloud deployment and management.

— *OpenShift 4.6*: Incorporating Advanced Cluster Manager (ACM), OpenShift 4.6 streamlined the management of Kubernetes clusters across diverse environments, supporting use cases like disaster recovery and global application policies.

— *OpenShift Plus*: As OpenShift expanded to manage workloads across multiple clouds, it introduced OpenShift Plus, combining Kubernetes management tools with DevOps security frameworks, thereby supporting complex edge and hybrid cloud dynamics.

- *Release Management and Support Cycles*

Red Hat's release management strategy for OpenShift is characterized by regular updates, ensuring rapid incorporation of new features and security patches.

- *Long-Term Support (LTS) Policy*: OpenShift follows a defined release cadence, with key versions offering extended maintenance and support, essential for enterprises requiring stability over innovation.

• *Community and Ecosystem Growth*

OpenShift's continued evolution is heavily tied to its vibrant community and vast ecosystem, each new version contributing to a larger network of partners and contributors.

- *OpenShift Commons*: This collaborative forum connects users, partners, and industry experts, sharing knowledge and driving OpenShift innovations across industries.

- *Broad Integration Facilities*: From engaging with upstream projects in the OpenShift Origin (OKD) to supporting diverse workloads with Tekton, Knative, and other cloud-native tools, OpenShift versions are marked by increased compatibility.

• *Cutting-edge Features in Latest Releases*

As OpenShift progresses, its newer versions encapsulate features that define the frontiers of container orchestration.

- *OpenShift Pipelines*: Based on Tekton, OpenShift's pipeline capabilities evolved to support cloud-native CI/CD processes, offering developer-centric integrations and security measures tailored for permanent workloads.

```
apiVersion: tekton.dev/v1beta1
kind: Pipeline
metadata:
  name: golang-build
spec:
  tasks:
  - name: build-go
    taskRef:
      name: golang-build-task
```

- *Service Mesh Advancements*: OpenShift continues exploring service mesh capabilities, integrating enhanced Istio features that refine service observability, traffic management, and policy enforcement strategies.

- *Future Trajectories and Roadmap*

  Red Hat's commitment to enhancing OpenShift reflects its dedication to addressing contemporary enterprise challenges while anticipating future trends. Emerging focuses include:

  - *Edge Computing*: As edge workloads grow, OpenShift versions increasingly incorporate edge-specific enhancements, providing nimble, lightweight deployment options for distributed environments.
  - *AI and ML Workloads*: Future OpenShift iterations aim to facilitate AI/ML life cycles, optimizing their deployment and resource requirements in hybrid cloud ecosystems.

OpenShift's version history illustrates its evolution from a static PaaS framework to a versatile, enterprise-ready Kubernetes platform. Each iteration represents strategic decisions guided by customer needs and technological innovations, positioning OpenShift as a critical enabler of digital transformation. As enterprises navigate their hybrid cloud and container journey, OpenShift's consistent growth ensures it remains at the forefront of cloud-native application paradigms.

1.6 Setting up Your OpenShift Environment

Setting up an OpenShift Environment comprises a range of tasks, from infrastructure preparation and cluster installation to configuration and deployment of applications. This section walks through the essential steps and considerations for establishing a robust OpenShift environment tailored to an organization's specific requirements, whether deploying on-premises, in the cloud, or across hybrid infrastructures. An intricate understanding of the setup process is crucial for ensuring operational success and optimal performance in production environments.

• 1. Preparing the Infrastructure

– *Hardware and Networking Requirements*: Determine the resource requirements based on projected workloads. This includes CPU, memory, and storage capacities, aligning with network configurations that facilitate high availability and load management.

– *Network Configuration*: Set up network policies, software-defined networking (SDN), and DNS configurations. Ensure that the network is segmented appropriately to accommodate OpenShift components and secure communications.

```
# Adding DNS A record for OpenShift API Server
api.openshift.example.com. IN A 192.168.1.100
```

• 2. OpenShift Installation Methods

– *OpenShift Installer*: The OpenShift Installer automates the deployment process, offering streamlined workflows for various infrastructure providers like AWS, Azure, and Bare Metal. It uses a declarative configuration model outlined in an install-config.yaml file.

```
apiVersion: v1
baseDomain: example.com
metadata:
  name: mycluster
platform:
  aws:
    region: us-west-1
pullSecret: '{"auths": {...}}'
sshKey: ssh-rsa AAAA...
```

– *CodeReady Containers for Local Development*: For developers looking to explore OpenShift locally, CodeReady Containers (CRC) provides a lightweight, single-node OpenShift cluster. It is ideal for development and testing purposes.

```
crc setup
crc start
crc console
```

- *OpenShift on OpenStack or RHV*: Organizations deploying in private cloud environments can leverage OpenShift's integration with OpenStack or Red Hat Virtualization (RHV), utilizing pre-provisioned instances for complex network and storage environments.

• 3. OpenShift Configuration

- *Cluster Administration Console*: Navigate through the OpenShift Web Console for an intuitive GUI experience. Administrators can use this to manage users, projects, roles, and policies at scale, complementing command-line actions.

- *Resource and Node Management*: Define quotas and constraints on compute resources, setting limits on pod deployment across nodes to prevent resource over-utilization.

- *Storage Configuration*: Configure persistent storage solutions like NFS, GlusterFS, or provision cloud-based storage options conforming to workload requirements.

```
apiVersion: v1
kind: PersistentVolumeClaim
metadata:
  name: claim1
spec:
  accessModes:
    - ReadWriteOnce
  resources:
    requests:
      storage: 1Gi
```

• 4. Securing Your OpenShift Cluster

- *Identity and Access Management (IAM)*: Leverage existing identity providers such as Active Directory or OAuth to enforce user authentication. Define roles and bind them to users or groups for comprehensive access control.

35

```
apiVersion: config.openshift.io/v1
kind: OAuth
metadata:
  name: cluster
spec:
  identityProviders:
  - name: ldap_provider
    mappingMethod: claim
    type: LDAP
    ldap:
      url: ldaps://ldap.example.com/ou=people,dc=example,dc=com
      bindDN: "cn=admin,dc=example,dc=com"
      bindPassword:
        name: ldap-bind-password
      insecure: false
```

- *Network Policies*: Implement network policies to control traffic between pods, namespace, or the external network, preventing unauthorized communications and lateral movements.

- *Security Context Constraints (SCCs)*: Enforce security constraints on pods to control permissions and ensure workloads are not run with elevated privileges.

• **5. Integrating DevOps Tools**

- *Jenkins for CI/CD*: Adopt Jenkins integration with OpenShift for automation of build, test, and deploy processes. Jenkins pipelines can be enhanced using OpenShift plugins to facilitate deployment actions.

```
pipeline {
    agent any
    stages {
        stage('Build') {
            steps {
                script {
                    oc.startBuild('my-app')
                }
            }
        }
        stage('Deploy') {
            steps {
                script {
                    openshiftDeploy deploymentConfig: 'my-app'
                }
            }
        }
    }
}
```

36

- *Tekton Pipelines*: For a Kubernetes-native CI/CD solution, Tekton offers a powerful alternative to Jenkins, with seamless integration with OpenShift service catalogs.

- **6. Monitoring and Logging Setup**

  - *Prometheus and Grafana*: Utilize built-in Prometheus integration for metrics collection, coupled with Grafana dashboards for visualizing performance data.

  - *Elasticsearch, Fluentd, and Kibana (EFK) Stack*: This open-source logging stack supports comprehensive log management, aiding in audit trails, debugging, and compliance reporting for OpenShift workloads.

```
apiVersion: "v1"
kind: "ConfigMap"
metadata:
  name: "fluentd"
  namespace: "openshift-logging"
data:
  fluent.conf: |-
    <source>
      @type http
      bind 0.0.0.0
      port 9880
    </source>
```

- **7. Testing and Validation**

  - *Functional Testing*: Validate application deployments, ensuring they align with deployment definitions and operate as expected.

  - *Load Testing*: Simulate real-world conditions to evaluate how the environment scales under increasing load, optimizing configurations accordingly.

  - *Security Audits*: Conduct security audits to identify vulnerabilities in network configurations, permissions, and container setups.

- **8. Advanced Configurations and Customizations**

  - *Cluster Autoscaling*: Implement cluster and pod autoscaling policies to dynamically adjust resources based on demand, thereby optimizing cost.

– *Multi-Tenancy Management*: Configure namespaces and quotas for managing multi-tenancy, ensuring fair and isolated resource usage across teams and departments.

Setting up an OpenShift environment encompasses a wide array of activities, each integral to creating a mature and efficient platform for containerized applications. Adequate preparation, installation methodologies, and configuration insights are necessary to leverage OpenShift's full potential, aligning IT operations with strategic business objectives. With careful attention to each phase of deployment, organizations can successfully navigate the complexities of their digital transformation journey, ensuring readiness for future innovations and scalability opportunities.

1.7 Common Use Cases for OpenShift

OpenShift, as an enterprise-grade Kubernetes platform, supports a variety of use cases ranging from containerized application delivery to complex multi-cloud environments. Its comprehensive feature set enables organizations to optimize workflows, enhance application performance, and streamline operations across diverse environments. This section explores prevalent use cases, underlining how OpenShift facilitates critical business objectives and addresses industry-specific requirements.

- **1. Continuous Integration and Continuous Deployment (CI/CD)** One of the hallmark use cases of OpenShift is its robust support for CI/CD, enabling developers to automate and streamline the application lifecycle, from code check-in to production deployment.

  – *Pipeline Automation*: Using Jenkins pipelines in conjunction with OpenShift, organizations can automate building, testing, and deploying applications. With OpenShift's scalable infrastructure, it supports parallel builds and deployments, ensuring efficient utilization of resources.

```
pipeline {
    agent any
    stages {
        stage('Build') {
            steps {
                script {
                    oc.startBuild('spring-petclinic')
                }
            }
        }
        stage('Test') {
            steps {
                script {
                    echo 'Running Tests...'
                    // Execute tests and store results
                }
            }
        }
        stage('Deploy') {
            steps {
                script {
                    openshiftDeploy deploymentConfig: 'spring-petclinic'
                }
            }
        }
    }
}
```

  – *Tekton Integration*: OpenShift integrates Tekton Pipelines
    for Kubernetes-native CI/CD processes, supporting cloud-
    native deployments through lightweight and modular
    build frameworks that align well with microservices
    architectures.

- **2. Multi-cloud and Hybrid Cloud Deployments** Many organizations adopt OpenShift for its ability to unify and manage
  workloads across disparate cloud environments, resulting in cohesive operational models for hybrid and multi-cloud strategies.

  – *Cross-cloud Consistency*: With OpenShift, applications can
    be consistently deployed across various cloud providers, re-
    ducing the complexity associated with managing differing
    environments and enabling seamless workload portability.

  – *Unified Management*: OpenShift's centralized manage-
    ment console provides comprehensive oversight and
    governance, simplifying policy enforcement, resource
    allocation, and cost optimization across clouds.

- **3. DevSecOps and Security Enhancement** OpenShift supports advanced DevSecOps practices, embedding security within the application lifecycle thus ensuring real-time threat mitigation.

    - *Integrating Security in Pipelines*: Built-in security checks, vulnerability scanning, and compliance enforcement in CI/CD pipelines detect and mitigate issues early in the development cycle.

    - *Comprehensive Access Controls*: Utilizing Role-Based Access Control (RBAC) and Security Context Constraints (SCCs), OpenShift ensures restricted access to resources and workloads, maintaining secure and compliant operational environments.

```
apiVersion: security.openshift.io/v1
kind: SecurityContextConstraints
metadata:
  name: restricted
allowHostDirVolumePlugin: false
allowHostIPC: false
runAsUser:
  type: MustRunAsRange
seLinuxContext:
  type: MustRunAs
```

- **4. Microservices and Application Modernization** OpenShift provides a highly conducive environment for deploying and managing microservices, facilitating application modernization initiatives essential for digital transformation.

    - *Microservices Architecture Support*: OpenShift's orchestration capabilities, along with service mesh integration, offer efficient service discovery, load balancing, and fault tolerance, essential for microservices architecture.

    - *Functionality through Containers*: By leveraging containerization, OpenShift ensures that applications can encapsulate their dependencies, enabling agility in delivering applications representing a wide range of functionalities.

- **5. Edge Computing and IoT Implementations** OpenShift offers edge computing solutions that support IoT deployments,

40

handling data processing close to the origin and providing low-latency applications.

– *Lightweight and Scalable Deployments*: OpenShift's ability to manage multi-node clusters enables localized processing at the edge, ideal for reducing bandwidth and latency in IoT applications.

```
oc label nodes <node_name> node-role.kubernetes.io/edge=
oc create -f edge-component-deployment.yaml
```

– *Disaster Recovery and Resilience*: Supporting edge-specific use cases such as autonomous vehicles and remote monitoring systems with disaster recovery features ensures continuity in critical infrastructure operations.

- **6. Application Migration and Consolidation** Organizations frequently use OpenShift to transition and consolidate applications, driven by strategic objectives like cost reduction, performance optimization, and maintenance simplification.

  – *Containerization of Legacy Applications*: By migrating legacy workloads onto OpenShift, organizations can exploit container technology's agility and scalability, enabling gradual modernization without re-architecting.

  – *Centralized Operations*: OpenShift offers a single platform for managing new and existing applications, streamlining operational workflows and reducing the complexity associated with diverse platform portfolios.

- **7. Big Data and Analytics** The scalable infrastructure of OpenShift accommodates big data workloads and advanced analytics, offering tools for processing large volumes of data efficiently.

  – *Data Processing Pipelines*: OpenShift facilitates the orchestration of complex data processing pipelines, essential for insights, analytics, and machine learning workloads.

  – *Integration with Data Services*: Through OpenShift Operators, databases and data services like Cassandra, Hadoop, and Apache Spark can seamlessly integrate, maintaining resource efficiency and optimizing analytics processing.

- **8. AI/ML Workloads and Model Deployment** The integration of AI/ML tools within OpenShift addresses computing demands and rapid deployment of models within production environments.

  - *Machine Learning Pipelines*: OpenShift supports building, training, and deploying machine learning models, benefiting from Kubernetes's elasticity to manage compute-intensive tasks adaptively.

  - *Intelligence at Scale*: Integrating OpenShift with frameworks like TensorFlow and PyTorch facilitates large-scale AI initiatives, enabling organizations to embed intelligence into their application offerings effectively.

- **9. Software as a Service (SaaS) Delivery** For SaaS vendors, OpenShift provides infrastructure that ensures reliable delivery, optimal scalability, and compliance with multi-tenancy requirements.

  - *Tenant Isolation*: Using OpenShift's namespace-based isolation ensures customer separation within shared environments, maintaining security and compliance.

  - *Autoscaling and Financial Efficiency*: SaaS platforms benefit from OpenShift's autoscaling features, ensuring applications can handle fluctuations in demand while optimizing resource usage costs.

```
apiVersion: autoscaling/v1
kind: HorizontalPodAutoscaler
metadata:
  name: saas-app-autoscaler
spec:
  scaleTargetRef:
    apiVersion: apps/v1
    kind: Deployment
    name: saas-app
  minReplicas: 2
  maxReplicas: 10
  targetCPUUtilizationPercentage: 60
```

OpenShift's versatile capabilities and enterprise-grade features empower organizations to address a wide spectrum of use cases spanning various industries. Whether modernizing legacy applications, managing distributed infrastructure, or securing critical application lifecycles, OpenShift provides comprehensive solutions tailored to organizational needs, facilitating effective transitions to cloud-native architectures while enhancing competitive advantage. As diverse industries increasingly shift toward containerization, OpenShift's ability to meet these varying demands underscores its pivotal role in modern digital ecosystems.

Chapter 2

Getting Started with OpenShift

This chapter focuses on the practical steps involved in setting up and navigating OpenShift for the first time. Readers will learn the process of installing OpenShift on various platforms, exploring both the web console and command line interface for effective management. Further, the chapter guides the creation of a project and deployment of a simple application, emphasizing initial configurations crucial for development. By leveraging tools such as Source-to-Image (S2I), users will gain insights into building container images directly from source code, preparing them to develop and deploy applications within the OpenShift ecosystem confidently.

2.1   Installing OpenShift on Your System

OpenShift serves as a robust platform designed to facilitate the deployment, management, and scaling of containerized applications. This section delves into the intricate process of installing OpenShift on various systems, offering a comprehensive examination of installation options tailored for local environments, cloud platforms, and OpenShift Online. Each installation scenario is examined meticulously to furnish users with the necessary insights for a successful setup, irrespective of the chosen environment.

Local Installation

Installing OpenShift locally is essential for users who aim to explore or develop applications in a controlled environment before migrating them to a production-grade setup. OpenShift's local installation most commonly takes advantage of the OpenShift Local (formerly CodeReady Containers) configuration, enabling a development-focused instance on personal computers.

Prerequisites

Prior to initiating the installation procedure, verify that your system meets the minimum requirements:

- **Operating System:** Compatible with recent Linux distributions, macOS, or Windows.

- **System Resources:** At least 4 CPU cores, 9 GB RAM, and 35 GB of free disk space.

- **Virtualization Support:** Ensure your machine has virtualization enabled, often configurable in the system's BIOS/UEFI settings.

- **Tools:** Install the Hypervisor (such as KVM, HyperKit, or Hyper-V) and required command line tools like curl, jq, and tar.

Installation Steps

1. **Download OpenShift Local:** Obtain the latest OpenShift Local archive suitable for your operating system from the Red Hat developers site.

2. **Extract the Archive:** Use the tar command to extract the downloaded archive. For example:

```
tar -xvf crc-linux-amd64.tar.xz
```

3. **Start OpenShift Local:** Configure and start the OpenShift instance using the CRC (CodeReady Containers) binary. The following commands initialize and start the environment:

```
./crc setup
./crc start
```

During the crc start process, a pull secret is required. It is obtainable from the same website where the OpenShift Local was downloaded.

4. **Access the Web Console:** Upon successful start, OpenShift Local offers access through a web console at https://api.crc.testing:6443. Use the login credentials provided in the CRC setup outputs.

5. **Validate the Setup:** Verify the installation by checking the OpenShift components through the Command Line Interface (CLI):

```
crc oc-env
eval $(crc oc-env)
oc status
```

Installation on Cloud Platforms

Installing OpenShift on cloud platforms allows leveraging scalable infrastructure provided by leading cloud vendors, ideal for production-level deployment. OpenShift supports diverse cloud environments, including AWS, Azure, and Google Cloud Platform (GCP). This section will detail the installation process on Amazon Web Services (AWS).

Prerequisites

Before proceeding with the installation:

- **AWS Account:** Ensure access to a configured AWS account with appropriate user permissions for resource creation.

- **AWS CLI:** Install and configure the AWS CLI on your local machine.

- **IAM Roles:** Create or identify appropriate Identity and Access Management (IAM) roles with specified policies for OpenShift deployment.

Installation Steps

47

1. **Configure AWS Environment:** Establish a virtual private cloud (VPC) with necessary subnets and security groups to host OpenShift components.

2. **Install Red Hat OpenShift Service on AWS (ROSA):** Utilize the ROSA CLI to set up your OpenShift cluster. Install the CLI using:

```
curl -o rosa https://mirror.openshift.com/pub/openshift-v4/clients/rosa/latest/rosa-
    linux.tar.gz
tar -xvf rosa-linux.tar.gz
```

3. **Create the Cluster:** Follow the ROSA command-line steps to create a cluster:

```
rosa login
rosa create cluster --cluster-name=mycluster --region=us-west-2 --compute-nodes=3
    --type=moa
```

4. **Manage the Cluster:** Use ROSA and OpenShift CLI for management:

```
rosa list clusters
oc get nodes
```

5. **Verify Cluster Deployment:** Inspect the deployment details and access through console links provided post-installation. Verify the connection and resources.

OpenShift Online

OpenShift Online, a Platform-as-a-Service (PaaS) offered by Red Hat, allows users to develop and host applications without managing the underlying infrastructure. This approach provides a quick and hassle-free mode to start using OpenShift capabilities.

Steps to Start Using OpenShift Online

1. **Visit OpenShift Online Registration:** Navigate to the OpenShift Online portal and register an account. Select a suitable plan based on organizational needs.

2. **Create a New Project:** After account activation, proceed to create a new OpenShift project through the web console's intuitive interface:

```
oc login https://api.openshift.com
oc new-project my-online-project
```

48

3. **Deploy Applications:** Utilize the S2I build process or deploy pre-built container images from trusted repositories. You can experiment with sample applications provided within the OpenShift quick-start templates.

4. **Manage and Scale:** Access the dynamic scaling and management features within the web console or with oc commands to scale workloads:

```
oc scale --replicas=3 dc/my-deployment
```

Successfully navigating the installation routes of OpenShift on different environments not only lays the foundation for developing robust applications but also enables a deepened understanding of cloud-native technologies. Users can leverage the power of virtualized, scalable platforms engineered towards reliable and swift software delivery. The nuances associated with each installation method are intrinsic to the operational capabilities OpenShift offers, thus presenting users with adaptable environments complemented by enterprise-level support for diverse computing requirements.

2.2 Navigating the OpenShift Web Console

The OpenShift web console offers an intuitive graphical interface, streamlining the management and monitoring of applications, resources, and user permissions integral to cluster operation. This section will comprehensively explore navigating the web console, facilitating heightened efficiency in utilizing various features inherent to OpenShift's design.

Accessing the OpenShift Web Console

Upon completing OpenShift installation, access the web console using a provided URL, typically https://console-openshift-console.apps.<your-domain>. Authentication methods may vary, encompassing SSO integrations, OAuth, or standard login credentials defined during the setup.

Login Process

49

Initiate access by visiting the web console URL in a browser. The login screen solicits authentication credentials, entailing user ID and password, or via token when warranted. After successful login, the user interface's landing page presents an overview of cluster health and performance metrics.

Navigating the Dashboard

The dashboard serves as the user interface's heart, providing at-a-glance insights into core metrics and systemic health. Key sections include:

- **Overview:** Upon initial login, the console presents an overview aligned with real-time analytics on cluster health, including pod counts, node utilization, and system alerts.

- **Projects:** OpenShift segregates workloads into discrete namespaces or projects. The Projects tab allows users to create, delete, and manage these projects effortlessly.

- **Search:** The robust search functionality aids in locating resources across the cluster, capable of filtering via labels or specific resource types, such as pods, nodes, or services.

Exploring Projects in Detail

Projects form the organizational cornerstone of OpenShift, encapsulating resources under specific namespaces. In depth, project pages offer insights into the following:

- **Workloads:** Comprising applications' deployment configurations, builds, and workloads' current states — comprehensive visuals allow users to ascertain deployment status swiftly.

- **Applications:** Granular views into the applications field include specific application metrics in terms of runtime throughput, request handling efficiency, and version information.

- **Builds:** This section provides an overview of current builds and history. OpenShift's integration with CI/CD pipelines becomes palpable here, allowing users to initiate new builds directly.

```
{
  "kind": "ProjectList",
  "apiVersion": "project.openshift.io/v1",
  "metadata": {
    "selfLink": "/apis/project.openshift.io/v1/projects",
    "resourceVersion": "425"
  },
  "items": [
    {
      "metadata": {
        "name": "sample-project",
        "selfLink": "/apis/project.openshift.io/v1/namespaces/sample-project",
        "uid": "d55d4039-c103-11ec-b64b-525400503f12",
        "creationTimestamp": "2023-04-10T12:34:56Z"
      },
      "spec": {
        "finalizers": [
          "openshift.io/origin"
        ]
      },
      "status": {
        "phase": "Active"
      }
    }
  ]
}
```

Resource Definitions and Management

Navigating through specific resources is paramount for efficient cluster management, informing decision-making processes on deployments, revisions, and scaling efforts. Within OpenShift, these include pod management, service orchestrations, and network policies.

Pods

Pods are the smallest deployable units in OpenShift, encapsulating one or more containers with shared storage, policies, and network. The Pod details page within the web console delineates numerous parameters:

- **Logs and Events:** Real-time diagnostics and event logs furnish profound insights into application health and anomaly detection.

- **Terminal Access:** Provides an on-demand command-line interface directly interfacing with running containers.

Navigating to a particular pod's page offers potent instruments that facilitate high-level management through real-time metrics and accessible command interfaces.

```
oc logs -f <pod-name> --namespace=<namespace>
```

Services

Defining services in OpenShift involves establishing stable endpoints for applications. The console provides capabilities to manage type and exposure style of services, such as ClusterIP, NodePort, or LoadBalancer configuration.

Networking and Routes

Configuring networking policies and routes surpasses basic service provision, dictating external access and traffic segmentation. Users can assign specific paths and domains within the Routes interface, elaborating on route status and ingress control.

Monitoring and Metrics

Comprehensive monitoring encompasses several built-in observability tools within the OpenShift console, focusing on metrics, dashboards, and alert mechanisms necessary for ensuring application performance reliability.

- **Dashboards:** Provide real-time visualizations of resource utilization, application status, and operational health at both the node and pod levels.

- **Alerts:** Users can view and set alerts based on telemetry data and resource utilization thresholds, offering proactive system management.

```
oc adm top nodes
oc adm top pods --namespace=<namespace>
```

Access Control and Role Management

Effective access control is indispensable for maintaining operational security and resource integrity within OpenShift environments. The web console provides frameworks for role-based access control (RBAC), including:

- **User Management:** Ability to add, modify, and revoke user permissions, thereby delineating access boundaries.

- **Role Assignments:** OpenShift's RBAC policy permits assignment of roles — Viewer, Editor, Admin — reflecting operational needs and security protocols.

Managing User Access

To assign roles to users, navigate the User Management section and apply role bindings accordingly through intuitive dropdown menus encapsulating user/group selections. Ensure compliance with security and operational guidelines to mitigate inadvertent access grants.

```
oc adm policy add-role-to-user edit <user-name> --namespace=<namespace>
```

Comprehensively navigating the OpenShift web console reveals an ecosystem of tools and features pivotal for proficient cluster management and operational oversight. Mastery of console navigation significantly enhances operational efficiency, ensuring alignment between resource management and organizational goals within containerized ecosystems. Through strategic exploitation of available functionalities, users can drive OpenShift operations toward optimal performance, reliability, and security outcomes.

2.3   Understanding OpenShift Command Line Interface (CLI)

The OpenShift Command Line Interface (CLI) is an indispensable tool for efficiently managing and automating diverse tasks within an OpenShift environment. This section provides an exhaustive exploration of the OpenShift CLI, examining its capabilities for administering resources, orchestrating deployments, and retrieving state information from your OpenShift cluster. Leveraging the CLI suitably can greatly enhance productivity, streamline numerous aspects of cluster management, and facilitate precise control over infrastructure components.

Installation and Configuration of OpenShift CLI

The OpenShift CLI, known as 'oc', can be installed on Linux, macOS, or Windows environments. To acquire the CLI, follow these steps:

Installation Steps

1. **Download the CLI:** Obtain the latest version of the 'oc' binary from the OpenShift releases page or your OpenShift provider. Ensure it matches your operating system's architecture.

```
curl -LO https://mirror.openshift.com/pub/openshift-v4/clients/oc/latest/linux/oc.
    tar.gz
```

2. **Extract the Archive:** Unpack the downloaded tarball and move the 'oc' binary to a directory included in your system's 'PATH', such as '/usr/local/bin'.

3. **Verify Installation:** Confirm the installation by executing:

```
oc version
```

This command should return details about the OpenShift CLI version, ensuring it aligns with your OpenShift cluster version.

Basic Concepts and Commands

Understanding the foundational syntax and command structures within the OpenShift CLI is essential for productivity. The 'oc' tool offers a streamlined gateway to interact with OpenShift resources, primarily operating on the following principles:

- **Objects:** Tangible resources within your cluster, such as pods, services, deployments, and routes.

- **Namespaces:** Logical units that segregate resources and permissions.

- **Operations:** Actions performed on resources, such as get, describe, create, delete, and update.

To illustrate standard 'oc' command usage, key examples include:

Resource Queries

Use the 'oc get' command to retrieve lists of resources. This command can target specific resource types or namespaces:

```
oc get pods
oc get services --namespace=my-namespace
```

Detailed Resource Views

The 'oc describe' command presents an in-depth view of individual resources, providing valuable insights into configurations and statuses:

```
oc describe pod my-pod
```

Advanced Resource Management Using OpenShift CLI

The 'oc' CLI enables more complex resource management tasks, facilitating a programmatic approach to operations often required in CI/CD workflows or scaling activities.

Creating and Deleting Resources

You can create deployments, services, and other resources using YAML configuration files or interactive commands:

```
oc create -f <resource-file>.yaml
oc delete deployment my-deployment
```

Updating Running Configurations

Edit resources in real time to accommodate changes without downtime — specifically useful for configuration updates across deployments:

```
oc edit configmap my-config
```

Scaling Deployments

Scale application deployments to manage workload demands using:

```
oc scale --replicas=5 deployment/my-deployment
```

Networking and Routing Commands

Handling networking tasks efficiently is a major feature of 'oc'. From defining services to creating routes, the CLI offers potent functions.

- **Service Management:** Create and manage network access, relying on commands like:

```
oc expose deployment/my-app --port=8000
```

- **Route Creation:** Establish external access routes to services, by applying:

```
oc expose svc/my-service --hostname=myapp.example.com
```

Automation and Scripting

The CLI's capability extends into scripting and automation scenarios. Bash scripts and pipelines can integrate 'oc' commands for automated OpenShift management tasks, significantly optimizing operational efficiency.

Sample Script for Automated Deployments

Deployments may often require automation, such as during CI/CD pipeline execution. Consider the following example processing:

```bash
#!/bin/bash

# Define Environment Variables
NAMESPACE="myapp"
DEPLOYMENT="myapp-deployment"
IMAGE="myapp-image:latest"

# Login to OpenShift cluster
oc login https://api.openshift.example.com --token=<my-token>

# Create namespace if not existing
oc get namespace $NAMESPACE || oc create namespace $NAMESPACE

# Set current context to the new namespace
oc project $NAMESPACE

# Update the image of the deployment
oc set image deployment/$DEPLOYMENT $DEPLOYMENT=$IMAGE

# Scale the deployment to ensure zero downtime
```

```
oc scale --replicas=2 deployment/$DEPLOYMENT

# Verify deployment status
oc rollout status deployment/$DEPLOYMENT
```

Implementing such scripts effectively reduces human error and elevates the speed of operations through coherent task execution automation.

Managing Access and Security with CLI

The 'oc' CLI is adept at managing user access rights and cluster security policies, aligning with RBAC principles described previously.

- **Role Binding:** Assign roles to users or services within specific namespaces.

```
oc adm policy add-role-to-user admin john --namespace=my-namespace
```

- **Security Context Constraints (SCC):** Manage security constraints applicable to processes within pods:

```
oc adm policy add-scc-to-user privileged user1
```

Troubleshooting and Diagnostics

Utilizing the CLI for troubleshooting enhances operational clarity. Key commands fall under status checks, log reviews, and diagnostics.

Diagnosing Cluster States

Execute diagnostic commands within the 'oc' CLI to gain insights into cluster health — an essential factor during failure or anomaly events:

```
oc adm top nodes
oc debug debug-pod
```

The accumulation of diagnostic knowledge and experience through these CLI commands equips administrators to resolve incidents effectively while improving long-term system resilience.

Embracing OpenShift CLI's versatility and breadth unequivocally translates to proficiently managing clusters of various scales, automating critical tasks and orchestrating complex operations effectively. Mastery of the CLI results in transformative infrastructure management, optimizing time, effort, and ensuring streamlined operations within cloud-native environments.

2.4 Creating Your First Project in OpenShift

Embarking on developing and deploying applications within OpenShift begins with creating a project, a fundamental organizational construct encapsulating all associated resources. Establishing a project is crucial as it segregates workloads, defines user permissions, and ensures resource quotas align with development objectives. This section provides a detailed walkthrough for creating and configuring your first project in OpenShift, introducing critical concepts and practical techniques essential for optimizing project setup and resource allocation.

Understanding OpenShift Projects

In OpenShift, a project is analogous to a Kubernetes namespace. It serves as a container encapsulating all elements associated with a particular application or microservice, including pods, services, gateways, and storage definitions. Projects streamline resource management, enforce security controls, and facilitate policy administration. Establishing a logical boundary for each application or microservice yields numerous benefits such as scalability, security isolation, and resource tracking.

Creating a New Project

Project creation in OpenShift is straightforward, comprising primarily the definition of project names and descriptions and setting up basic configuration. You can undertake this task using either the OpenShift CLI or the web console, each method offering distinct conveniences.

Using the OpenShift CLI

The 'oc' CLI provides seamless accommodation for project creation and configuration, adhering to succinct syntax essentials.

1. Login to the Cluster:

Begin by authenticating to your OpenShift cluster using:

```
oc login https://api.openshift-cluster.local:6443
```

2. Create the Project:

Execute the 'oc new-project' command, specifying a project name and description:

```
oc new-project my-first-project --description="My First OpenShift Project" --
    display-name="FirstProject"
```

Upon successful execution, the CLI confirms project creation, setting it as the active context for subsequent commands.

Using the OpenShift Web Console

For those favoring graphical interfaces, the web console offers an intuitive, user-friendly pathway:

1. Navigate to the Web Console:

Access the OpenShift web console by entering your custom URL in a web browser.

2. Initiate Project Creation:

Enter the console's Projects section and select the Create Project button, revealing a fields-formulated field requesting:

- Name: The unique project identifier (e.g., 'my-first-project').

- Display Name: A friendly descriptor enhancing readability (e.g., 'FirstProject').

- Description: A substantive narrative outlining project purposes or dispositions.

3. Create the Project:

Click Create, finalizing project instantiation and rendering the new project selectable from your dashboard's project listings.

Resource Configuration and Setup

Upon project creation, attention turns to resource configurability and orchestration. OpenShift offers a suite of administration tools ensuring projects maintain operational efficacy through scaling policies, resource limits, and quota assignments.

Defining Resource Quotas and Limits

Precise allocation of compute, memory, and storage resources sustains systemic balance and precludes excessive consumption that could impinge upon other projects. Deploy resource quotas using manifests or 'oc' commands:

```
apiVersion: v1
kind: ResourceQuota
metadata:
  name: my-project-quota
  namespace: my-first-project
spec:
  hard:
    pods: "20"
    requests.cpu: "4"
    requests.memory: "20Gi"
    limits.cpu: "10"
    limits.memory: "50Gi"
```

Apply the YAML configuration using:

```
oc apply -f resource-quota.yaml
```

Labeling and Annotation Practices

Implement resource labeling and annotation codecs to enable seamless identification, filtering, and application of policies. This is exceptionally beneficial for monitoring workflows and setting up tiered environments:

```
oc label pod my-pod app=tier-one env=production
```

Integrating CI/CD Pipelines

Projects within OpenShift support robust integration with continuous integration/continuous deployment (CI/CD) pipelines, fortifying automated software delivery processes aligning with DevOps practices.

Deploying Jenkins Pipelines

OpenShift facilitates Jenkins as a ready-integrated environment enhancing build and deployment automation. Initiate leveraging Jenkins through:

1. Instantiate Jenkins Setup in Project:

Deploy Jenkins utilizing OpenShift's predefined templates:

```
oc new-app jenkins-ephemeral
```

2. Create a Pipeline:

Add pipeline definitions using Jenkinsfile syntax to direct build and deployment sequences, simplified through OpenShift templates.

3. Secure Jenkins Access:

Retrieve Jenkins route to access UI,

```
https://jenkins-my-first-project.apps.openshift-cluster.local
```

Networking and Routing Configuration

Establishing coherent networking models between components ensures data flow integrity, enhanced through configuring services, and establishing ingress/egress controls.

Service Creation and Management

Create services to expose applications internally within a project:

```
oc expose deployment my-first-app --port=8080
oc get svc my-first-app
```

Defining External Routes

Expose services externally via HTTP/S endpoints using routes:

```
oc create route edge --service=my-first-app
```

Verify routes and secure configurations are conjunctively established within DNS to facilitate smooth operation.

Security and Compliance Principles

Enforcing security measures and compliance protocols ensures project adherence to organizational and regulatory standards stringently delineating operations.

Role-Based Access Control (RBAC)

Define access paradigms through roles and bindings — ensure precise access management by configuring individual or group entitlements:

```
oc policy add-role-to-user edit devuser --namespace=my-first-project
```

Network Policies Implementation

Secure network policies govern ingress/egress traffic and communication among pods, aiding the mitigation of security breaches:

```
apiVersion: networking.k8s.io/v1
kind: NetworkPolicy
metadata:
  name: deny-all
  namespace: my-first-project
spec:
  podSelector: {}
  policyTypes:
  - Ingress
  - Egress
```

Monitoring and Logging

Integrative monitoring and logging underpins operational resilience and yields pivotal insights essential for diagnosis and retrospective analysis.

Utilizing OpenShift Monitoring

Visualize metrics and build dashboards through Prometheus, native to OpenShift deployments, capturing key performance indicators (KPIs).

Log Aggregation with Elasticsearch

Aggregate logs to Elasticsearch indices, facilitating in-depth audits and correlated visibility across deployment artifacts:

```
oc logs -f dc/my-first-app
```

Through diligent application of configuration principles outlined, creating and optimizing your first OpenShift project sets the foundation for scalable, secure, and efficient application lifecycle management. Project-specific practices culminate in a robust development ecosystem, lending themselves to seamlessly harness inherent OpenShift capabilities and aligning infrastructure development trajectories with overarching business objectives.

2.5 Deploying a Simple Application on OpenShift

Deploying applications on OpenShift involves a series of orchestrated steps, significantly simplified by the platform's robust infrastructure. This section offers a thorough exposition on deploying a simple application on OpenShift, walking through the essential phases of build configurations, deployment definitions, and service management. By the end of this exploration, you will garner the practical competence necessary for deploying applications, while also appreciating OpenShift's underlying architecture and its strategic advantages in managing containerized applications.

Preparing the Application for Deployment

Before deployment, ensure the application is containerized or compatible with containerization principles. A simple web application, such as an Express.js or Flask app, should have its source code stored in a version control system, such as GitHub.

Assumptions for this deployment:

- The application is a basic web application stored in a public GitHub repository.

- The application requires a Dockerfile describing the build environment and runtime configuration.

Setting Up the OpenShift Environment

Ensure that the OpenShift CLI is configured and connected to a cluster instance where you have administrative privileges. Begin by logging in:

```
oc login https://api.openshift-cluster.local:6443
```

Verify your context is set to the desired project (namespace):

```
oc project my-first-project
```

Defining a Build Configuration

OpenShift builds applications using a build configuration, specifying the source and methodologies for constructing container images. There are several build strategies, including Source-to-Image (S2I), Docker, and custom builds, each catering to different requirements.

Using Source-to-Image (S2I)

S2I facilitates converting source code repositories into deployable images automatically. Define the build configuration:

```
oc new-build --strategy=source --name=myapp --binary
```

Upload the application source to the build configuration:

```
oc start-build myapp --from-dir=. --follow
```

For Docker strategy, ensure the Dockerfile resides in your source repository, followed by initiating the build:

```
oc new-build --strategy=docker --name=myapp https://github.com/user/myapp.git
```

Configuring the Deployment

Upon successfully creating the build or uploading binaries, integrate deployment configurations. Deployments define the blueprint for running application instances, including replica counts, rolling update strategies, and resource allocations.

Creating the Deployment

Invoke OpenShift to automatically scaffold deployment resources through simple acclimatization:

```
oc new-app myapp
```

Upon creation, OpenShift provides status updates and configures the deployment using the default configurations, which can be further refined to tailor application requirements.

Service Exposure and Routing

OpenShift services manage networking concerns, ensuring efficient pod communication and defining external service access routes.

Creating a Service

Expose application endpoints by defining a service:

64

```
oc expose dc/myapp --port=8080
```

Defining Routes

To provide external access, create exposed HTTP/S routes:

```
oc expose svc/myapp
```

Check exposed URL access through the console or by verifying routes:

```
oc get routes
```

Resource and Scaling Considerations

Once operational, evaluate the application's deployment robustness under varying loads. OpenShift inherently supports auto-scaling configurations responding to metrics such as CPU load and memory usage, formulated within the Horizontal Pod Autoscaler (HPA).

Configuring Autoscalers

Configure autoscalers to adjust replica counts in response to CPU utilization:

```
oc autoscale deployment/myapp --min=1 --max=10 --cpu-percent=80
```

Establish a monitoring approach using Prometheus and Grafana offered in Operator solutions, to observe scaling events.

Application Lifecycle Management

OpenShift excels in facilitating application lifecycle management through seamless rollout controls and declarative states for deployment configurations.

Managing Rollouts

Conduct rolling updates, scale-in operations, or rollbacks as necessary:

```
oc rollout status deployment/myapp
oc rollout undo deployment/myapp
```

Ensure proper version control within deployment manifests, aligning with releases and updates:

```
oc set image deployment/myapp myapp=myapp:newtag
```

Logging and Monitoring with OpenShift

Efficient deployment extends beyond operability into observability. OpenShift supports integrated logging solutions with Elasticsearch, Fluentd, and Kibana (EFK) stacks, capturing critical runtime insights.

Logging Fundamentals

Inspect live logs to review pod activity and handle triage in failure events:

```
oc logs -f dc/myapp
```

Maintain comprehensive access to historical log entries through Elasticsearch integration and visual analysis using Kibana dashboards.

Monitoring Strategies

Employ Prometheus for instance monitoring, offering real-time alerts and resource utilization metrics. Configure application-specific alerts tailoring to custom detection scenarios and scaling triggers.

Security and Compliance

Throughout deployment, OpenShift institutes robust security paradigms enforcing isolation and least privilege principles.

Securing Applications

Enforce compliance and security measures through network policies:

```
apiVersion: networking.k8s.io/v1
kind: NetworkPolicy
metadata:
  name: allow-http
  namespace: my-first-project
spec:
  podSelector:
    matchLabels:
      role: web
  ingress:
  - from:
    - podSelector:
        matchLabels:
          role: frontend
    ports:
    - protocol: TCP
      port: 80
```

Implement Security Context Constraints (SCCs), detailing permissions for running pods and containerized applications:

66

```
oc adm policy add-scc-to-user restricted system:serviceaccount:my-first-project:default
```

Best Practices in Deployment

Deploying applications in OpenShift should embrace best practices to maximize platform utility and foster efficient, reliable, and secure deployment outputs:

- **Adopt Declarative Configurations:** Embrace Infrastructure as Code (IaC) principles using YAML manifests and version-controlled repositories.

- **Optimize Build Strategies:** Select build strategies congruent with application architectures; leverage binary builds or pre-built image pulls as dictated by CI/CD progress.

- **Continuously Monitor Performance:** Strengthen observability using dashboards and metrics aligning with SLAs and SLOs to adhere to service reliability standards.

- **Iteratively Refine Security Models:** Frequently revisit established security models, accommodating vulnerabilities with iterative constraints and policies.

Deploying a simple application through OpenShift exemplifies its prowess in managing workloads, scaling applications, and fostering resilient operational landscapes. The platform provides comprehensive solutions across the deployment lifecycle, ensuring adherence to modern development paradigms and forming the bedrock of scalable application ecosystems. With methodical implementation of OpenShift capabilities, deployment efforts yield robust applications ready to address real-world challenges efficiently.

2.6 Using Source-to-Image (S2I) Build Process

The Source-to-Image (S2I) build process is an innovative, powerful method specific to OpenShift that automates the transformation of application source code into ready-to-run Docker-formatted container images. S2I stands out by simplifying and consolidating the development pipeline, thus optimizing the build-deploy iteration cycle. This section will explore the various facets of the S2I process in OpenShift, uncovering its integration, customization, and inherent advantages for application deployment workflows. By the conclusion of this discussion, you will possess the knowledge required to effectively harness S2I within your development environments.

At its core, Source-to-Image focuses on two primary components: source code repositories and builder images. The builder images encapsulate the necessary runtime environment and requisite libraries specific to an application or framework.

Core Elements of S2I

- **Source Code Repository:** Hosts the application's source code and relevant build configuration files. Typically integrated with Git, but alternative storage strategies can align with custom S2I workflows.

- **Builder Image:** Predefined container images that include essential build tools and languages for generating deployment-ready images. Languages such as Java, Python, Node.js, PHP, Ruby, and Go commonly feature supported builder images.

S2I Workflow Process

1. **Clone the Source Code:** S2I fetches the application's source code from a specified repository.

2. **Build Process Initiation:** Using a designated builder image, S2I executes the build process, compiling sources into runnable binaries or configurations within the container.

3. **Image Assembly:** The resulting artifacts, configurations, and runtime dependencies are assembled into a new image extending the builder image foundation.

4. **Deployment Automation:** OpenShift deploys the newly constructed container image to orchestrated environments autonomously.

To harness S2I within an OpenShift project, developers must facilitate integration between source control repositories and builder images effectively. This highlights the system's simplicity compared to traditional Docker build processes.

Using the OpenShift CLI

Commence integration by invoking pertinent 'oc' commands to define builds programmatically:

1. **Define the New Build:**

   Create a new build configuration specifying the repository URL and corresponding builder image:

   ```
   oc new-app centos/python-38-centos7~https://github.com/user/my-python-
   app
   ```

   This command directs OpenShift to initiate builds based on the specified Python builder image and repository, automatically assembling a deployment configuration.

2. **Monitor Build Process:**

   Observe real-time build processes and logs via:

   ```
   oc logs -f bc/my-python-app
   ```

3. **Deployment Confirmation:**

   Validate deployment operationality upon build completion:

   ```
   oc get pods --watch
   ```

Using the OpenShift Web Console

Alternatively, integrate S2I through the web console, offering graphical interaction within project scoping:

1. **Initiate New Application:**

   Harness the **Add to Project** menu, selecting **Import from Git**:

   - Provide repository URLs and designate suitable builder images from predefined options.

2. **Configure Build Parameters:**

   Amend build environment variables, resources, and trigger policies as necessitated.

3. **Commence and Monitor Builds:**

   Execute build processes directly from the interface, observing detailed visuals for each staged component.

Customizing builder images enables tailored environments catering to specific dependencies or frameworks critical to application building.

Creating Custom Builder Images

Establishing custom builder images involves composing a Dockerfile encapsulating required build tools, libraries, and execution models within personalized image constructs.

```
FROM centos/python-38-centos7

# Add build scripts
ADD .s2i/bin/ /usr/libexec/s2i/

# Install additional dependencies
RUN yum install -y epel-release && \
    yum install -y custom-dependency

# Set labels used in OpenShift to describe the builder image
LABEL io.openshift.s2i.scripts-url=image:///usr/libexec/s2i
LABEL io.k8s.description="Custom Python S2I Builder" \
    io.k8s.display-name="Custom Python 3.8 S2I"

# Set working directory for application source
WORKDIR /opt/app-root/src
```

Defining Build Scripts

Include custom build scripts furnishing logic for pre, post, and runtime operations. Define scripts within the '.s2i/bin/' directory:

- assemble: Script orchestrating the source code build process, performing builds and dependency installations.

- run: Launch script executing the application entry points during runtime.

- save-artifacts: Captures build artifacts preserving state across successive builds.

Ensure executable permissions are set for all build scripts:

```
chmod +x .s2i/bin/*
```

The S2I process provides multitudinal advantages within OpenShift deployments, drawing developers towards streamlined, automated solutions.

Optimization of Build Workflow

S2I minimizes build process complexity through encapsulated, battle-tested builder images. Reducing rebuild redundancies and enhancing build speeds furnish superior development agility.

Enhanced Security and Compliance

By leveraging defined builder images, developers secure consistent build environments and reinforce company-compliant practices. S2I's simplification eschews complex scripts liable to embedding security antipatterns.

Improved Resource Efficiency

S2I builds utilize controlled resource allocation, balancing resource utilization and minimizing wastage, contributing toward optimized cluster operations.

Ease of Caching and Reuse

S2I benefits from caching artifacts, enhancing iterative development speed. Common dependencies are standardized, facilitating reuse across parallel builds.

The S2I methodology represents an evolved approach within containerized applications, underpinning modern CI/CD pipelines through consistency, efficiency, and ease of use. As containerized infrastructures shift towards declarative paradigms, S2I's potential for future expansions, including complex dependency graphs and non-linear build sequences, continues to emerge.

By assimilating Source-to-Image capabilities, application developers vividly streamline their pathways from conception to deployment. OpenShift's S2I fortifies rapid iterative build cycles, guiding developers toward modern distributed service deployments with assuredness and efficiency. As development frameworks evolve, grounding applications in S2I promotes stability and innovation while elevating collaboration within growing developer ecosystems.

2.7 Configuring OpenShift for Development

Configuring OpenShift for development encompasses a wide spectrum of practices designed to tailor the environment for optimal productivity and efficiency from a developer's perspective. This section explores how to configure OpenShift environments to streamline application development workflows, from managing environments and setting up continuous integration to security practices and resource allocations. Configuring the environment appropriately ensures that developers can focus on writing and testing code without worrying about the underlying infrastructure constraints.

A robust and well-integrated development environment is foundational. To achieve this, ensure all developer tools are seamlessly connected to OpenShift.

Tool Integration

- **OpenShift CLI (oc):** Ensure your local environment is equipped with the oc command-line tool for easy interaction with the OpenShift cluster. This tool is paramount for managing resources and automating tasks.

- **IDE Plugins:** Use plugins like Red Hat OpenShift Extension for Visual Studio Code or OpenShift Connector for Eclipse to integrate your IDE directly with OpenShift, providing build, deploy, and debug capabilities directly in the IDE.

- **Version Control Systems (VCS):** Connect repositories in platforms like GitHub, GitLab, or Bitbucket. Automate deployments from VCS commits using Git hooks and OpenShift pipelines.

```
# Example to authenticate and connect OpenShift CLI
oc login https://api.openshift-cluster.local:6443 --token=<your-token-here>
oc project my-dev-project
```

The philosophy of CI/CD is critical for modern development practices, automating integration, testing, and deployment.

Implementing Jenkins Pipelines

OpenShift seamlessly integrates with Jenkins, enabling automation of build and deployment processes:

1. **Deploy Jenkins:**

Use OpenShift's Jenkins template to instantiate an ephemeral Jenkins server:

```
oc new-app jenkins-ephemeral
```

2. **Configure Jenkins Pipelines:**

Define pipeline scripts in Jenkinsfiles to handle build, test, and deployment stages:

```
pipeline {
  agent any
  stages {
    stage('Build') {
      steps {
        script {
          ocBuild(buildConfig: 'myapp-build', showBuildLogs: 'true')
        }
      }
    }
    stage('Deploy') {
      steps {
        script {
          ocDeploy(deploymentConfig: 'myapp-deployment')
        }
      }
    }
  }
}
```

3. **Triggering and Monitoring:**

Enable automatic build triggers upon source control changes, using webhooks, and monitor pipeline executions through Jenkins dashboards.

Alternative CI/CD Tools

Integrate other CI/CD tools such as GitLab CI, Travis CI, or CircleCI by configuring webhooks and automation scripts within OpenShift.

Customize your development environment settings to optimize for coding, building, and testing.

Development Namespace Setup

Create a dedicated namespace to isolate development resources:

```
oc new-project my-dev-env --description="Development Environment"
```

Ensure quotas and policies align with development needs while preserving resource allocation efficiency.

Resource Allocation

Define and apply resource quotas to simulate production workloads while keeping development resource consumption controlled:

```
apiVersion: v1
kind: ResourceQuota
metadata:
  name: dev-quota
  namespace: my-dev-env
spec:
  hard:
    requests.cpu: "10"
    requests.memory: "20Gi"
    limits.cpu: "15"
    limits.memory: "40Gi"
```

Apply this configuration using:

```
oc apply -f dev-quota.yaml
```

Security is a paramount concern in development, requiring careful configuration to protect resources and code integrity.

User Access Control

Implement Role-Based Access Control (RBAC) to manage permissions effectively:

```
oc adm policy add-role-to-user edit devuser --namespace=my-dev-env
```

This aligns user rights with development roles while maintaining security principles.

Secure Configurations

Inject secure environment variables and manage secrets through OpenShift:

74

```
oc create secret generic my-secret --from-literal=key1=value1
oc set env dc/myapp --from=secret/my-secret
```

Use strategic environment variable injection to configure applications securely and dynamically.

Effortless transition from development to test, and finally deployment environments enhances the development lifecycle's efficiency.

Environment Promotion Models

Employ stage-based configurations to smoothly transition code through dev, test, and prod environments. Implement processes to automate the promotion of builds between namespaces:

```
# Tagging and promoting a tested image to production
oc tag myapp:latest myprod/myprod-app:latest
```

Application Debugging

Enable intuitive debugging using port-forwarding and logs exploration:

```
oc port-forward svc/myservice 8080:80
oc logs -f deployment/myapp
```

Implement efficient debugging from within integrated IDEs to resolve issues rapidly and deploy fixed builds expediently.

Enable comprehensive monitoring practices and log management systems to maintain an exemplary development environment.

Integrated Logging Solutions

Stream logs to central repositories using OpenShift Fluentd, Elasticsearch, and Kibana:

```
# Access logs for monitoring
oc logs -f dc/myapp
```

Visualize logs with Kibana dashboards, aggregating logs for deeper insights and historical analysis.

Application Performance Monitoring (APM)

Employ Prometheus and Grafana for fine-grained metrics collection:

- Setup instrumented application metrics.

- Use Grafana dashboards for real-time visualization of application performance.

Adhering to established best practices ensures the development environment remains agile, secure, and optimized for continuous productivity.

- **Consistent Development Standards:** Standardize environment setups with shared YAML configuration files, promoting uniformity across teams.

- **Resource Efficiency:** Regularly review and adjust quotas, scaling policies, and resource limits according to development throughput demands.

- **Automation and Scripting:** Leverage automation scripts for daily tasks, reducing manual intervention and improving repeatability.

- **Cross-Environment Testing:** Embrace automated tests ensuring code integrity in conditions replicating production states.

Configuring OpenShift effectively for development not only aids in achieving rapid application delivery but also fosters an environment conducive to innovation and collaboration. Comprehensive configuration strategies ensure that the infrastructure underpinning development activities becomes a robust, reliable backbone complementing the development lifecycle. Through OpenShift's extensive suite of tools and customizability, developers attain sharp focus on building quality code, harnessing an ecosystem poised for high agility and maximum impact.

Chapter 3

Understanding OpenShift Architecture

This chapter delves into the structural components that constitute OpenShift's architecture, providing a comprehensive understanding of its setup and functionalities. Core elements such as the OpenShift Master, Nodes, and ETCD form the backbone of this architecture, each playing distinct roles that ensure system stability and scalability. The chapter explains how networking configurations support seamless communication within the cluster, while authentication and authorization mechanisms, including Role-Based Access Control (RBAC), maintain security. Additionally, insights into resource management and scheduling offer guidance on optimizing workload distribution, providing a solid foundation for managing an OpenShift environment effectively.

3.1   Core Elements of OpenShift Architecture

OpenShift, as a comprehensive container platform, provides a robust foundation for developing, deploying, and managing containerized applications. The architecture of OpenShift is composed of several core elements that ensure its effective operation, scalability, and resilience. These elements include the OpenShift Master, Nodes, and a suite of critical services that interplay to deliver a seamless platform experience. This section elucidates the foundational components of OpenShift's architecture, charting a clear map of how these elements interact to support enterprise-grade applications.

OpenShift can be perceived as an orchestration layer on top of Kubernetes with added functionalities and tools that make it more adaptable and efficient for managing complex systems. Understanding the architecture of OpenShift involves dissecting multiple layers of its components, including both the infrastructure level and the services level.

The OpenShift Master: The OpenShift Master serves as the control plane of the cluster, responsible for managing the overall state of the cluster. It comprises several integral components:

- **API Server:** The central access point for all REST commands used to control the cluster. It acts as a gatekeeper for all authenticate users trying to interact with any Kubernetes resource.

- **Controller Manager:** Maintains the desired state of any number of objects in the OpenShift environment. It registers for events and goes about moving the current state of the system toward the desired state.

- **Scheduler:** Analyzes the resource requests and the current state of the cluster to determine the best nodes to host new pods, thereby ensuring optimal distribution of workload across all nodes.

These components jointly support the orchestration and management of workloads, ensuring applications are efficiently deployed, managed, and scaled within the cluster. The Master communicates with all node agents in the cluster, providing them with commands and data, such as pod configurations.

Nodes: Nodes in the OpenShift architecture are critical components that provide the execution environment for containers. A node is a server, and it hosts applications in pods. Key responsibilities of a node include:

- **Kubelet:** This is the primary node agent, which ensures that containers are running in a pod as expected. It takes the pod specifications provided by the API server and manages their lifecycle.

- **Kube-Proxy:** A network proxy that runs on each node, handling network routing for the traffic destined for pods. It helps manage pod networking, ensuring reliable communication within the cluster.

- **CRI-O or Docker:** These container runtimes work under the Container Runtime Interface (CRI) in OpenShift, managing the container lifecycle from initialization to termination.

Nodes function collectively to ensure application workloads are handled, supporting dynamic scaling and robust resilience against node failures.

```
{
  "kind": "Node",
  "apiVersion": "v1",
  "metadata": {
    "name": "node-01",
    "labels": {
      "kubernetes.io/hostname": "node-01"
    }
  },
  "status": {
    "conditions": [
      {
        "type": "Ready",
        "status": "True",
        "lastHeartbeatTime": "2023-10-01T12:34:56Z"
      }
    ],
    "nodeInfo": {
      "machineID": "1234567890abcdef",
      "systemUUID": "123e4567-e89b-12d3-a456-426614174000"
    }
  }
}
```

The JSON sample above represents the status of a node within an Open-Shift cluster. It provides metadata about the node's identity and current condition, offering insights into its readiness and system specifics.

ETCD: At the heart of OpenShift's data storage capabilities lies ETCD, a consistent and highly-available key-value store. All stateful data regarding the cluster's operations, including node status, pod information, and configuration data, is stored in ETCD. The master components interact heavily with ETCD to retrieve the necessary data for orchestrating the cluster functions.

```
etcdctl snapshot save snapshot.db
```

This command exemplifies how to create a snapshot of the ETCD database, vital for disaster recovery scenarios. Ensuring regular backups of ETCD is critical for maintaining the cluster's operational integrity.

Service Account Tokens and Authentication: Every process in OpenShift runs within the context of a service account, and authentication tokens are used to validate identity and grant access to resources. These tokens are automatically generated, managed by the OpenShift API server, and it's crucial for secure communication among the master components and nodes.

```
{
  "apiVersion": "authentication.k8s.io/v1",
  "kind": "TokenRequest",
  "spec": {
    "audiences": [
      "kubernetes.default.svc"
    ],
    "expirationSeconds": 600
  }
}
```

The JSON format here displays a typical service account token request. Such tokens are essential for maintaining secure and authenticated actions within the OpenShift ecosystem.

Networking and Service Discovery: OpenShift employs a meticulously designed networking model. This ensures seamless communication both within the cluster and to the external world. Networking and service discovery in OpenShift are powered by several fundamental concepts:

80

- **SDN:** OpenShift utilizes Software-Defined Networking (SDN) to handle internal communication between nodes and pods. SDN abstracts the network complexity, allowing for easy scalability of workloads.

- **Route Objects:** These are used to expose a service (a set of pods) to outside networks, providing an external URL through which the service can be accessed.

- **DNS Service:** OpenShift's built-in DNS supports service discovery by automatically creating DNS entries for new services, enabling other pods in the cluster to find and communicate with them using simple hostnames.

Service discovery is facilitated through the automatic registration of services and endpoints, managed by the API server, making it easier for developers to integrate and access services.

```
oc expose svc/mypod-service --name=mypod-route
```

This command demonstrates the creation of a route for a service, allowing external HTTP access to the application running within OpenShift.

Persistent Storage: Applications on OpenShift may require persistent storage to keep data even after pods are shut down. OpenShift integrates with a range of storage solutions through a dynamic storage provisioning framework. It allows developers to define persistent volume claims, which can be fulfilled using either block or file storage.

```
apiVersion: v1
kind: PersistentVolumeClaim
metadata:
  name: my-pvc
spec:
  accessModes:
    - ReadWriteOnce
  resources:
    requests:
      storage: 1Gi
```

In this YAML configuration, a persistent volume claim requests 1Gi of storage using the ReadWriteOnce access mode. Persistent storage plays a crucial role in the stateful application deployment paradigm that OpenShift supports.

Understanding the interplay of these components is fundamental to mastering OpenShift. These elements, interconnected and reliant on each other, provide a powerful infrastructure that supports the lifecycle of modern containerized applications. As enterprises harness the potential of OpenShift for their cloud-native innovations, comprehending these architectural components becomes pivotal for effective management and optimization of resources within the platform.

3.2 OpenShift Master Components

The OpenShift master is the brain of the OpenShift architecture, tasked with maintaining the desired state of the cluster. Its components are responsible for orchestrating the relationships and interactions among numerous elements and facilitating an ecosystem that dynamically adapts to the demands of hosted applications. Understanding the intricacies of these components is crucial for any system administrator or developer striving to optimize an OpenShift cluster's performance and reliability.

API Server: At the core of the OpenShift master node sits the API server, which plays a pivotal role in processing API requests. It acts as an interface for all management activities within an OpenShift cluster.

- **Functionality:** The API server presents a RESTful interface, which receives requests from clients and other control plane components, validates them, and then updates the state of the cluster by communicating with ETCD.

- **Security:** The API server employs verbosity for logging, authentication mechanisms, and encryption strategies to ensure secure and traceable operations. TLS certificates are used to encrypt communications between clients and the API server.

An exemplary command that interacts with the API server to list all pods can be shown as:

```
kubectl get pods --all-namespaces
```

The output from this command, viable through the API server, displays all running pods, their associated namespaces, and corresponding states.

```
NAMESPACE      NAME                   READY  STATUS   RESTARTS  AGE
default        myapp-1234567890-abcde 1/1    Running  0         35m
kube-system    kube-dns-849f57cf-8tlgj 3/3   Running  1         11d
```

Controller Manager: The controller manager supports the cluster's control loop operations, which keeps the cluster's state aligned with the desired configurations. It is responsible for monitoring the ETCD datastore to apply the necessary changes across the cluster.

- **Role:** Each controller is a separate process responsible for managing its own resource type (e.g., replica sets, endpoints). The controller manager aggregates these controllers into a single executable.

- **Mechanism:** Implementing controller patterns involves reconciling the actual state with the desired state, perpetually adjusting and scaling deployments to match specified pod counts or configurations.

For instance, consider a deployment scaling operation managed by the replication controller:

```
kubectl scale deployment myapp --replicas=10
```

Scheduler: The scheduler is tasked with the binding of unscheduled pods to nodes. It operates by prioritizing nodes based on resource requests and availability, efficient utilization, and policy constraints.

- **Scheduling Algorithms:** OpenShift's scheduler applies complex algorithms, examining criteria such as node resource capacity, affinity rules, tolerations, and constraints.

- **Decision Making:** The scheduler decides the placement of pods, balancing loads while adhering to predetermined constraints set by users or applications.

A scheduling policy can be examined through affinity rules, an example YAML of which is shown below:

83

```
apiVersion: v1
kind: Pod
metadata:
  name: nginx-with-affinity
spec:
  affinity:
    podAffinity:
      requiredDuringSchedulingIgnoredDuringExecution:
      - topologyKey: "kubernetes.io/hostname"
        labelSelector:
          matchExpressions:
          - key: app
            operator: In
            values:
            - myapp
```

In this example, pods will be scheduled based on node labels, ensuring colocation with other pods that share similar labels, thereby optimizing access patterns or data locality requirements.

Cluster Autoscaler: The cluster autoscaler is an additional component that interacts with the master to dynamically adjust node counts. It enhances efficiency by ensuring resource supply aligns with demand, adding nodes when resources are insufficient and removing them when underutilized.

- **Autoscaling Actions:** Autoscaler observes pod occurrences such as pending pods due to resource insufficiencies, attempting to acquire metrics and thresholds to make informed scaling decisions.

- **Integration:** The autoscaler integrates tightly with cloud providers and infrastructures allowing seamless node provisioning and removal.

Autoscaling configuration often involves defining resource metrics that trigger scaling actions. A hypothetical command for scaling might include:

```
kubectl autoscale deployment myapp --cpu-percent=80 --min=3 --max=10
```

Role-Based Access Control (RBAC): RBAC secures and orchestrates permissions, enforcing policy-driven access to cluster resources.

- **RBAC Roles:** Define sets of permissions for operations such

84

as 'get', 'list', or 'create' on specified resources such as 'pods' or 'deployments'.

- **RBAC Bindings:** Links roles to users or service accounts, determining which permissions are granted to which entities.

Illustrative configuration of RBAC policy might look like:

```
apiVersion: rbac.authorization.k8s.io/v1
kind: Role
metadata:
  namespace: default
  name: myapp-role
rules:
- apiGroups: [""]
  resources: ["pods"]
  verbs: ["get", "list", "watch"]
```

OpenShift Project and Resource Quotas: Projects in OpenShift act as namespaces with additional access controls. They provide scoped environments to segregate and manage resources efficiently, using quotas to limit resource consumption.

- **Project Isolation:** Ensure separation of logs, events, and accounts, supporting multi-tenancy.

- **Resource Quotas:** Enforce bounds on resources like memory, CPU, and storage to prevent overconsumption in a shared environment.

A snippet configuring a resource quota:

```
apiVersion: v1
kind: ResourceQuota
metadata:
  name: compute-resources
  namespace: myproject
spec:
  hard:
    requests.cpu: "4"
    requests.memory: 10Gi
    limits.cpu: "8"
    limits.memory: 20Gi
```

As each aspect of the OpenShift master components has been outlined, it should be evident how integral these roles and interactions are to the effective functioning and scaling of an OpenShift cluster. These architectures are engineered to provide fail-safe operations, balancing automated processes alongside manual intervention opportunities, making OpenShift a resilient platform for contemporary application orchestration. Each component is tuned to provide a level of abstraction for simplification while ensuring the essential complexities are retained to handle advanced requirements that modern enterprises demand. With these elements collaboratively in place, OpenShift presents a confluence of flexibility and power, serving diverse user needs across varied operational landscapes.

3.3   Node Operations in OpenShift

Nodes in OpenShift are indispensable actors within the cluster architecture, providing the essential computational resources to run containerized workloads. Each node in an OpenShift cluster is a lifeline that hosts one or more pods responsible for executing application containers. Understanding node operations involves delving into the mechanisms that manage these nodes and the services that ensure their optimal function. This section extensively covers the functionalities of nodes within the OpenShift environment, focusing on the services and orchestration of containers to maintain robust operations.

Node Components: A node in OpenShift is essentially a machine, either physical or virtual, upon which Kubernetes runs. It houses several critical components:

- **Kubelet:** The node agent that communicates with the OpenShift master. It ensures containers are running as specified by the pods' configuration files. The kubelet is the heart of each node, tasked with local container management tasks.

- **Kube-Proxy:** This component manages networking and receives directives from the OpenShift master to forward network traffic internally and to external clients. It maintains network rules on nodes.

- **CRI-O or Docker:** These container runtimes adhere to the Container Runtime Interface (CRI) guidelines, facilitating the execution of containers on a node.

Each node not only serves its operative requirements but also acts as a nimble component in the broader OpenShift cluster fabric. This adaptability allows OpenShift nodes to efficiently contribute to the cluster's collective resource pool.

Pods and Container Management: In OpenShift, the foundational processing unit is the pod. A pod represents one or more containers grouped together based on shared resources. Each pod receives an IP address, maintaining connectivity within the cluster and beyond. Node operations center around maintaining these containers through management tasks, such as:

- **Pod Lifecycle Management:** The lifecycle management involves the creation, monitoring, and deletion of pods. The kubelet on each node observes pods' statuses and restarts them as necessary through created health checks.

- **Image Handling:** Nodes access container images from registries, pulling them locally to start pods. This leverages container storage solutions to handle image management operations efficiently.

A typical OpenShift pod configuration might resemble the following YAML configuration file:

```
apiVersion: v1
kind: Pod
metadata:
  name: myapp
  namespace: default
spec:
  containers:
  - name: mycontainer
    image: myregistry/myapp:latest
    ports:
    - containerPort: 8080
```

Resource Management on Nodes: Nodes in the OpenShift environment are engineered to handle resource allocation with precision. This involves the orchestration of CPU, memory, and storage, which are the lifeblood of containerized applications:

- **Resource Allocation:** Nodes use resource specifications to allocate CPU and memory capacities for each pod. This allocation is critical for maintaining application performance and ensures fairness across workloads.

- **Resource Monitoring and Reporting:** Nodes continuously monitor resources and provide feedback to the OpenShift master. The metrics collected include CPU, memory utilization, and the performance of individual containers.

Commands to query node resource usage can be enacted as follows:

```
kubectl top node
```

Possible outputs from the command might look like:

```
NAME        CPU(cores)  CPU%   MEMORY(bytes)  MEMORY%
node-01     200m        10%    2000Mi         50%
node-02     150m        7.5%   1800Mi         45%
```

Node Maintenance: Node maintenance in OpenShift requires strategies for draining nodes, cordoning nodes, and patch management. These actions ensure that nodes remain performant and operational over time:

- **Draining Nodes:** Moving off workloads from a node to another ensures minimal disruption during maintenance. The 'kubectl drain' command is typically used for such operations.

- **Cordoning Nodes:** Cordoning a node marks it unschedulable to new pods while allowing existing ones to continue running. This is executed using the 'kubectl cordon' command.

- **Patch Management:** Keeping the nodes updated with the latest patches is essential, and can be automated through integration with configuration management tools.

An illustration of commencing a drain operation is shown below:

```
kubectl drain node-01 --ignore-daemonsets
```

Upon successful completion of a drain operation, workloads will migrate to other nodes, while daemonsets continue to operate.

Node Security: Security on nodes is paramount, especially when executing untrusted or sensitive workloads. OpenShift implements several mechanisms to secure the operations on nodes:

- **Pod Security Policies (PSP):** These define permissions to control pod creation and lifecycle, preventing unauthorized access patterns.

- **Seccomp and SELinux:** Harden nodes by confining actions that running containers perform, reducing attack surfaces, and isolating applications.

- **Network Policies:** Control and restrict traffic between different pods and external sources, enhancing the overall security posture of nodes.

An example of a network policy configuration that restricts traffic can be depicted as:

```
apiVersion: networking.k8s.io/v1
kind: NetworkPolicy
metadata:
  name: deny-all
  namespace: default
spec:
  podSelector: {}
  policyTypes:
  - Ingress
  - Egress
```

Dynamic Scaling and Autoscaling: Nodes support scaling capabilities that include horizontal pod autoscaling, enabling an OpenShift environment to dynamically respond to load changes. By carefully configuring autoscalers, nodes can elastically adjust the number of running pods to match the conditions:

- **Horizontal Pod Autoscaler (HPA):** Based on CPU or memory metrics, it automatically scales the number of pod replicas.

- **Cluster Autoscaler:** Modifies the number of nodes in the cluster in response to workload demands, ensuring adequate resources are provisioned.

89

An example command defining an HPA configuration:

```
kubectl autoscale deployment myapp --cpu-percent=80 --min=1 --max=10
```

Managing node operations in OpenShift involves a comprehensive understanding of container orchestration, efficient resource usage, robust security practices, and elastic scalability. These operations collectively ensure that OpenShift nodes not only serve application workloads efficiently but also adapt to dynamic environmental changes and infrastructural fluctuations. Each node embodies an indispensable facet of OpenShift's robust orchestration architecture, contributing to a streamlined, resilient, and secure cluster ecosystem.

3.4 ETCD: The Distributed Key-Value Store

ETCD is a pivotal component within OpenShift's architecture, providing a reliable and consistent data store for all cluster data. Developed initially as a distributed key-value store by CoreOS, ETCD is integral to the operation of Kubernetes and, by extension, OpenShift. Understanding ETCD's role and operation is fundamental for mastering OpenShift's architecture, as it influences the performance, availability, and reliability of the entire cluster.

Fundamentals of ETCD: ETCD serves as a distributed, consistent, and fault-tolerant key-value store. It records the cluster's state, ranging from configuration data to runtime information. The core principles underpinning ETCD operations include:

- **Consistency:** Using the RAFT consensus algorithm, ETCD ensures that any read operation returns the most recent write for a given key, providing strong consistency.

- **High Availability:** ETCD employs a distributed nature, achieving high availability by replicating data across multiple nodes to prevent data loss due to node failures.

- **Simple Interface:** ETCD offers an easy-to-use HTTP/JSON API for adding, updating, and retrieving keys and their values.

This core design empowers ETCD to act as a robust system for persisting configuration data critical to the operation of an OpenShift cluster.

ETCD Architecture and Clustering: ETCD clusters are designed with multiple nodes to achieve durability and high availability. An ETCD cluster operates using the RAFT consensus protocol, which ensures consistency and fault tolerance.

- **Leader and Followers:** In a typical ETCD cluster, one node acts as the leader, handling all client requests, while the other nodes act as followers that replicate the leader's data.

- **Quorum:** ETCD requires a majority (quorum) of nodes to reach a consensus to serve requests, ensuring continued operation even when some nodes fail.

An exemplary cluster might consist of three or five nodes to provide fault tolerance, as demonstrated by the RAFT algorithm, which maintains data integrity across nodes.

```
etcd --name infra0 --initial-advertise-peer-urls http://infra0:2380 \
  --listen-peer-urls http://infra0:2380 \
  --listen-client-urls http://0.0.0.0:2379 \
  --advertise-client-urls http://infra0:2379 \
  --initial-cluster-token etcd-cluster-1 \
  --initial-cluster infra0=http://infra0:2380,infra1=http://infra1:2380,infra2=http://
        infra2:2380 \
  --initial-cluster-state new
```

In this example, an ETCD node is set to join a new cluster, providing URLs for peer and client interactions and specifying the initial cluster state.

Data Model and Operations: ETCD stores data in a hierarchical key space, functioning similarly to a file system. Keys can represent directories, and leaf nodes represent the actual data entries. Common operations are straightforward:

- **Put:** Insert or update a key-value pair into the ETCD store.

- **Delete:** Remove keys and their values, modifying the key space.

- **Get:** Retrieve the value associated with a key.

- **Watch:** Monitor changes to a specific key or prefix, receiving notifications upon modifications.

An example of key-value operations with ETCD is given below:

```
etcdctl put /myapp/config/application "v1.0"
etcdctl get /myapp/config/application
```

Output from the 'get' operation results in:

```
/myapp/config/application
v1.0
```

Securing ETCD: Due to the critical nature of the data stored within ETCD, securing the cluster against unauthorized access and potential malicious actions is vital:

- **TLS Encryption:** Ensure all communications within ETCD clients and peers are encrypted by deploying TLS certificates.

- **Authentication and Authorization:** ETCD version 3 supports authentication mechanisms, enforcing user credentials, role-based permissions, and access control lists (ACLs).

Creating a user and assigning roles in ETCD v3 may be carried out in sequence as follows:

```
etcdctl user add myuser
etcdctl role add myrole
etcdctl role grant-permission myrole readwrite /myapp/*
etcdctl user grant-role myuser myrole
```

This role-based access control ensures that only authorized users can manipulate the designated key space, fortifying ETCD's security posture.

Backups and Disaster Recovery: A core practice for maintaining the system's integrity is ensuring ETCD's data is backed up regularly. Failures or data losses can often be mitigated by employing prudent disaster recovery strategies:

- **Snapshot Mechanism:** Periodically create snapshots of the key-value store to facilitate restoration during catastrophic events.

- **Cluster Recovery:** Provision from backups to revive clusters either by restoring entire instances or through configuration file synchronization.

An operational backup using the 'etcdctl' command is shown below:

```
etcdctl snapshot save snapshot.db
```

Subsequently, restoring a cluster from this snapshot involves:

```
etcdctl snapshot restore snapshot.db \
  --name infra0 \
  --initial-cluster infra0=http://127.0.0.1:2380 \
  --initial-cluster-token etcd-cluster-1 \
  --initial-advertise-peer-urls http://127.0.0.1:2380
```

Performance Optimization: ETCD performance is crucial for an efficient OpenShift environment. Optimization strategies include:

- **Efficient Configuration:** Configure ETCD cluster nodes factoring in hardware capabilities and bandwidth, optimizing each node's performance.

- **Compaction:** Carry out periodic compactions to free disk space and optimize data storage.

- **Lease Management:** Manage leases efficiently to control resource locks and timeouts.

ETCD's success hinges on its robust design and operational efficiency. A masterful implementation and maintenance of ETCD within OpenShift ensure that the broader cluster benefits from resilient storage configuration, ensuring all configurations, states, and requests are effectively preserved. These properties confer the robustness required for maintaining modern distributed applications, making ETCD an invaluable component within OpenShift's architecture.

3.5 Networking in OpenShift Architecture

Networking in OpenShift is fundamental to ensuring seamless communication among the components in a cluster, both internally and with the external world. It comprises a robust model that facilitates efficient routing, service discovery, and network policy management. Understanding this networking model is pivotal to harnessing the full capabilities of OpenShift's platform. This section explores the architecture, defining components, and configuration that ensure effective networking in OpenShift.

OpenShift Network Model: OpenShift employs a highly extensible and efficient Software-Defined Networking (SDN) model, supporting dynamic and scalable network configurations essential for modern application deployments. This model supports several key operations:

- **Pod-to-Pod Communication:** Within the cluster, each pod is assigned a unique IP address and can communicate directly with any other pod without NAT (Network Address Translation).

- **Service Discovery and Load Balancing:** OpenShift automatically assigns each service its own IP address and balances the traffic between instances of a service running in different pods.

- **Network Segmentation:** Supports multitenancy by providing network isolation through the use of projects/namespaces, essential for environments where multiple teams share the same cluster.

OpenShift SDN Architecture: The architecture of OpenShift SDN involves network plugins that realize the various connectivity models. These plugins determine the policies and technical paths used to manage network traffic. Common network plugins are:

- **OVNKubernetes:** Utilizes the Open Virtual Networking abstraction to provide an advanced networking layer with robust policies and routing capabilities.

94

- **Calico:** Provides scalable cloud-native networking and network security, often employed for policies that span beyond traditional SDN boundaries.

These plugins work to ensure both optimal performance and compliance with organization-specific policies for data traffic.

Services and Routes: Services in OpenShift define a logical set of pods and the policy by which to access them. They facilitate discovery, seamless scaling, and load balancing:

- **Service Types:** Includes ClusterIP, NodePort, and LoadBalancer, each type offering different levels of accessibility for services.

- **ClusterIP:** The default type, exposing the service on an internal IP in the cluster, making it accessible only within. For example, configuring a simple service might resemble:

```
apiVersion: v1
kind: Service
metadata:
  name: myapp-service
spec:
  selector:
    app: myapp
  ports:
    - protocol: TCP
      port: 80
      targetPort: 9376
```

- **Routes:** OpenShift Routes expose services externally, encapsulating a routing layer. A route directs incoming traffic to a service using a specified hostname.

```
oc expose svc/myapp-service --hostname=myapp.example.com
```

Configuring the OpenShift Network: Network configurations are pivotal during and post-initial setup. OpenShift's networking is designed to be fully automated, but there are numerous configuration options and customizations available:

- **Ingress Controllers:** These manage HTTP and HTTPS requests to the OpenShift cluster, providing capabilities like SSL termination, path-based routing, and request rewriting.

```
apiVersion: operator.openshift.io/v1
kind: IngressController
metadata:
  name: default
  namespace: openshift-ingress-operator
spec:
  routeAdmission:
    namespaceSelector:
      matchExpressions:
      - key: "sharding.example.com/type"
        operator: In
        values: ["public"]
    endpointPublishingStrategy:
      type: LoadBalancerService
```

- **Network Policies:** These are employed to control the flow of traffic to the pods, adhering to security and compliance protocols.

```
apiVersion: networking.k8s.io/v1
kind: NetworkPolicy
metadata:
  name: allow-same-namespace
spec:
  podSelector: {}
  policyTypes:
  - Ingress
  ingress:
  - from:
    - podSelector: {}
```

Network policies define how groups of pods interact with each other and network endpoints, ensuring traffic is both secured and properly routed.

Multitenancy and Security: OpenShift's networking is built around the premise of efficient multitasking and secure deployment environments, providing usability enhancements such as:

- **Project Isolation:** Projects allow users to create isolated spaces for application development, along with dedicated resources and policies.

- **Enhanced Security Features:** These include securing communication channels with mutual TLS encryption and susceptibility prevention with limitations on pods' ingress and egress traffic controls.

96

An essential consideration in configuring multitenant environments is enabling precise traffic segmentation while simplifying operational overhead using these built-in OpenShift functionalities.

DNS and Service Discovery: OpenShift incorporates a DNS service for name resolution within the cluster. This service enables name-based service discovery, allowing pods and other components to access services by their DNS names, simplifying application configurations.

- **Pod DNS:** Pods can simply refer to services by names such as myapp-service.myproject.svc.cluster.local.

- **Automatically Managed DNS Entries:** Each service is automatically assigned a DNS name, and updates to services result in dynamic DNS updates.

The mapping of service endpoints with DNS not only eases orchestration within dynamic environments but also supports legacy service integrations without restructuring underlying architectures.

Advancing Network Performance: It is crucial to optimize the network configuration for both performance and scalability, ensuring OpenShift's production efficacy:

- **Optimized Routing Paths:** Employ network configurations that align with data locality, reducing latency by minimizing unnecessary routing stages.

- **Monitoring and Logging:** Leverage integrated solutions such as Prometheus for monitoring and Kibana for logging to manage networking metrics, identify bottlenecks, and streamline troubleshooting.

By optimizing these facets, OpenShift's networking environment can efficiently manage higher traffic loads while ensuring minimal latency and resource optimization throughout the cluster.

Integrating each piece of networking elements in OpenShift demands a detailed understanding of connectivity mechanisms, the seamless coordination of microservices, and ensuring the adaptability and security critical in modern deployments. Networking forms the backbone of

OpenShift's ability to rapidly deliver features and applications, making it indispensable for developers and administrators aiming to maximize their cloud-native deployment capabilities.

3.6 OpenShift Authentication and Authorization

Security is a critical concern in any cloud infrastructure, and in Open-Shift, authentication and authorization form the backbone of its security architecture. They work collaboratively to ensure users and services access only the data and resources they are permitted to on an OpenShift cluster. This section provides an in-depth exploration of how OpenShift handles this through various mechanisms like OAuth, Role-Based Access Control (RBAC), and related security policies.

Authentication in OpenShift: Authentication is the process of verifying the identity of a user or service account attempting to access the OpenShift cluster. OpenShift supports several authentication methods, allowing it to integrate seamlessly into existing IT infrastructure.

- **OAuth 2.0:** OpenShift relies heavily on OAuth 2.0 to provide token-based authentication. It acts as an OAuth2 provider that issues tokens used to authenticate client requests.

- **Integration with Identity Providers (IdP):** OpenShift can integrate with various identity providers like LDAP, OpenID Connect, GitHub, and Google, allowing organizations to leverage existing authentication systems.

The setup of an OAuth provider in OpenShift might look as follows:

```
apiVersion: config.openshift.io/v1
kind: OAuth
metadata:
  name: cluster
spec:
  identityProviders:
  - name: my_ldap
    mappingMethod: claim
    type: LDAP
    ldap:
      url: ldaps://ldap.example.com:636/ou=accounts,dc=example,dc=com
```

```
binddN: cn=admin,dc=example,dc=com
bindPassword:
  name: ldap-bind-password
attributes:
  id: [dn]
  email: [mail]
  name: [cn]
  preferredUsername: [uid]
```

Authentication Process Flow: Upon any OpenShift login attempt, the following process generally unfolds:

1. Request Initiation: A user or client application requests access via the OpenShift Console or API.

2. Redirect to Identity Provider: OpenShift redirects the request to the configured IdP for authentication.

3. Authentication Verification: The IdP authenticates the user and redirects them back with authorization credentials.

4. Token Issuance: Upon successful authentication, OpenShift issues an access token. This token is used for subsequent API calls.

Authorization in OpenShift: Authorization in OpenShift governs what authenticated users have permission to do. This is primarily managed through Role-Based Access Control (RBAC).

- **Roles:** Define a set of permissions. These include 'ClusterRoles' for cluster-wide resources and 'Roles' for namespace-scoped resources.

- **Role Bindings:** Associate users or groups with defined roles, effectively granting those users the permissions encapsulated in the roles.

A simple 'Role' configuration example might look like this:

```
apiVersion: rbac.authorization.k8s.io/v1
kind: Role
metadata:
  namespace: default
  name: pod-viewer
rules:
- apiGroups: [""]
  resources: ["pods"]
  verbs: ["get", "list", "watch"]
```

Followed by a 'RoleBinding' to assign this role:

```
apiVersion: rbac.authorization.k8s.io/v1
kind: RoleBinding
metadata:
  name: view-pods
  namespace: default
subjects:
- kind: User
  name: jane.doe
  apiGroup: rbac.authorization.k8s.io
roleRef:
  kind: Role
  name: pod-viewer
  apiGroup: rbac.authorization.k8s.io
```

Security Contexts and Policies: To further refine access and operation permissions, OpenShift incorporates Security Contexts and Policies:

- **Security Context Constraints (SCCs):** These define what actions pods are allowed to perform, such as running privileged containers or certain capabilities.

- **Pod Security Policies (PSPs):** Specifies security requirements for pods, ensuring that they operate within defined parameters.

Configuring an SCC in OpenShift could be established as:

```
apiVersion: security.openshift.io/v1
kind: SecurityContextConstraints
metadata:
  name: restrict
allowPrivilegedContainer: false
defaultAddCapabilities: []
requiredDropCapabilities:
- MKNOD
allowedCapabilities:
- NET_ADMIN
readOnlyRootFilesystem: true
```

SCCs manage pod-level permissions, enhancing security posture by restricting unnecessary permissions.

Managing Users and Groups: User accounts in OpenShift can be internal accounts or synchronized via an external directory service. OpenShift allows administrators to create and manage users through management scripts or commands:

```
oc create user john.smith --full-name="John Smith"
```

Administrators can further organize users into groups to streamline permission assignments, where the group serves as a container to aggregate users under common permissions.

Audit and Logging: Another layer of security within OpenShift's authentication and authorization framework is Logging and Auditing:

- **Audit Logs:** Capture all authenticated requests, allowing administrators to track access and resource operations across the cluster.

- **Integration with Log Management Tools:** The logs can be forwarded to various centralized log management solutions like Elasticsearch or Fluentd for retention and analysis.

Collectively, these mechanisms ensure that OpenShift's authentication and authorization are both robust and adaptable to specific enterprise needs, supporting organizational security mandates and regulatory compliances. Through these practices and configurations, OpenShift maintains a secure, efficient environment for the rapid development and deployment of applications, providing peace of mind in a fast-evolving cloud landscape.

3.7 Scheduling and Resource Management

The scheduling and resource management mechanisms in OpenShift are pivotal for optimizing workload distribution across nodes, ensuring resource utilization aligns with available capacities, and thereby maintaining desired application performance levels. This section delves into how OpenShift orchestrates workloads, manages resources like CPU and memory, and facilitates efficient scheduling of pods across the cluster, using Kubernetes-native capabilities tailored to OpenShift's architecture.

Fundamentals of Scheduling in OpenShift: Scheduling in Open-Shift involves assigning workloads to nodes within the cluster based on available resources, defined policies, and other constraints. The scheduler's objective is to maintain balance, optimize resource utilization, and ensure high availability:

- **Scheduling Algorithms:** Leverages a set of algorithms evaluating node suitability for a pod based on predicates such as node filters, applicable affinities/anti-affinities, and resource requests.

- **Predicates and Priorities:** Predicates determine if a pod is eligible to run on a node, while priorities rank the nodes that meet predicate conditions, selecting the optimal fit.

An example of setting pod affinities in OpenShift might be configured as follows:

```
apiVersion: v1
kind: Pod
metadata:
  name: mypod
spec:
  affinity:
    nodeAffinity:
      requiredDuringSchedulingIgnoredDuringExecution:
        nodeSelectorTerms:
        - matchExpressions:
          - key: disktype
            operator: In
            values:
            - ssd
```

Resource Requests and Limits: Defining resource requests and limits is essential for each container in a pod. These definitions ensure that workloads have adequate resources for expected performance yet do not overextend.

- **Requests:** Specifies the minimum resources required for a pod to be scheduled onto a node.

- **Limits:** Caps the maximum resources a container can consume, preventing single workloads from monopolizing shared resources.

102

A typical resource specification within a container might look like:

```
apiVersion: v1
kind: Pod
metadata:
  name: resource-demo
spec:
  containers:
  - name: example-container
    image: nginx
    resources:
      requests:
        memory: "64Mi"
        cpu: "250m"
      limits:
        memory: "128Mi"
        cpu: "500m"
```

Quality of Service Classes: OpenShift categorizes pods into different Quality of Service (QoS) classes based on how their resources requests and limits are configured, influencing scheduling priorities and eviction decisions.

- **Guaranteed:** Pods where resource limits equal requests for all containers are ensured resource availability.

- **Burstable:** Pods where at least one container's resource request is less than its limit, permitting flexibility in resource usage.

- **BestEffort:** Pods without any resource requests or limits set, subject to eviction under resource pressure.

Horizontal Pod Autoscaler (HPA): A core feature within OpenShift is the Horizontal Pod Autoscaler, which automatically scales the number of pod replicas based on observed CPU utilization or other select metrics.

- **Automatic Scaling:** HPA continually monitors pods and scales the number of replicas to match demand, using the metrics collected from the Metrics Server.

- **Configuration:** HPA can be configured to respond to different metrics, with CPU utilization a common default choice.

A command to set up HPA might look like:

103

```
kubectl autoscale deployment myapp --cpu-percent=70 --min=1 --max=5
```

Cluster Autoscaler: Complementing the HPA is the Cluster Autoscaler, which dynamically adjusts the cluster size by adding or removing nodes in response to the scheduling needs.

- **Node Scaling:** Adjusts the number of nodes as workloads fluctuate, whereas HPA adjusts the number of running instances.

- **Resource Efficiency:** Prevents resource waste in underutilized clusters while ensuring capacity to accommodate a surge in demand.

Resource Quotas and Limits: Resource quotas in OpenShift provide administrative control over the consumption of compute resources across namespaces, enforcing overall cluster limits.

- **Namespace Quotas:** Define limits for the number of resources, such as pods and services, or consumption, like CPU or memory.

- **Limit Ranges:** Specify upper and lower bounds within resource requests and limits for specific container resources.

A resource quota example could be specified as follows:
```
apiVersion: v1
kind: ResourceQuota
metadata:
  name: compute-resources
  namespace: default
spec:
  hard:
    requests.cpu: "10"
    requests.memory: 20Gi
    limits.cpu: "20"
    limits.memory: 40Gi
```

Node Allocator and Future Strategies: OpenShift allocates resources across all nodes using strategies aimed at balancing loads. Moving forward, machine learning and predictive scaling could enhance node assignments based on past usage patterns and workload behaviors.

104

- **Enhanced Prediction Algorithms:** Use historical data to predict resource needs, proactively scaling nodes.

- **Utilization-Monitoring Tools:** Employ tools such as Prometheus, Grafana, and Kiali for real-time monitoring and performance optimization.

Effective resource management and scheduling are critical to OpenShift's functionality, ensuring that workloads are efficiently distributed and resources are utilized to avoid performance bottlenecks. As the landscape of cloud-native applications continues to evolve, OpenShift's ability to adapt and scale will rely on sophisticated resource allocation strategies, providing robustness, flexibility, and scalability for enterprise and cloud applications alike.

Chapter 4

Deploying Applications on OpenShift

This chapter offers a detailed guide on deploying applications within the OpenShift environment, highlighting the various deployment strategies available, such as rolling updates and blue-green deployments. By integrating Jenkins for CI/CD pipelines, users can automate the build and deployment process, ensuring seamless upgrades and rollbacks. The chapter also covers essential configurations, including environment variables and persistent storage management, to maintain application stability and performance. Leveraging OpenShift templates and Operators, developers can streamline application lifecycle management, driving efficiency and consistency in deployments across diverse environments.

4.1 Understanding Deployment Strategies in OpenShift

OpenShift, as a Kubernetes-based platform, provides several ways to manage application deployments effectively. In order to ensure application availability, consistent updates, and minimal downtime, it is imperative to be familiar with the different deployment strategies OpenShift supports. These strategies include rolling, recreate, and blue-green deployments, each with unique characteristics and use cases.

In this section, we delve into these deployment strategies, offering detailed descriptions, scenarios of applicable usage, and pertinent examples to illustrate practical implementation in an OpenShift environment. As each deployment strategy offers unique advantages depending on the needs of the application, having a comprehensive understanding of these techniques is crucial for any developer or DevOps engineer utilizing OpenShift.

The choice of an appropriate deployment strategy influences factors like application downtime, resource utilization, and user experience. As such, selecting the right strategy necessitates careful consideration of these elements in the context of both the application's requirements and the environment in which it operates.

Rolling Strategy

The *rolling deployment strategy* is designed to update applications incrementally to avoid downtime. Unlike a full replacement of an application, rolling updates gradually replace instances of the older version with instances of the newer version. This method ensures that there is always a portion of the application running.

Rolling deployments are beneficial when you want to minimize service disruptions. However, a critical requirement for successful rolling deployments is that your application must be compatible with the older version running concurrently. This condition necessitates version compatibility and a strategic approach to database schema updates and backlog handling for stateful applications.

```
apiVersion: apps.openshift.io/v1
kind: DeploymentConfig
metadata:
```

```
  name: myapp
spec:
  strategy:
    type: Rolling
  replicas: 3
  template:
    metadata:
      labels:
        app: myapp
    spec:
      containers:
        - name: myapp
          image: myapp:latest
  triggers:
    - type: ConfigChange
    - type: ImageChange
```

In this example, a deployment configuration using the rolling strategy is shown. Here, OpenShift replaces the pods of the older version with the new version in a planned manner. By maintaining a configurable number of replicas during the transition, it guarantees availability.

To monitor the progress and ensure rolling updates execute smoothly, OpenShift provides various controls and status indicators through the web console and command-line interface, allowing real-time visibility over the deployment process.

Recreate Strategy

In contrast to the rolling strategy, the *recreate deployment strategy* stops all running instances of the application before any new instances are started. This brings about significant downtime but ensures the cleanest state transition from the old application version to the new one.

The recreate strategy is suitable when backward compatibility cannot be guaranteed between application versions or when the application requires substantial changes that do not support running multiple versions simultaneously.

```
apiVersion: apps.openshift.io/v1
kind: DeploymentConfig
metadata:
  name: myapp
spec:
  strategy:
    type: Recreate
  replicas: 3
  template:
    metadata:
```

```
    labels:
        app: myapp
    spec:
        containers:
        - name: myapp
            image: myapp:v2
triggers:
    - type: ConfigChange
    - type: ImageChange
```

Here, the 'Recreate' strategy is specified in a deployment configuration file. The process proceeds by terminating any existing pod before a new one from the updated version is instantiated. This scenario is more straightforward and is often utilized when consistency and a clean state are prioritized over availability.

Blue-Green Deployment Strategy

The *blue-green deployment strategy* involves maintaining two identical environments, referred to as blue and green. At any given time, one environment is live, receiving all user traffic, while the other is idle. When a new version is ready, it is deployed to the idle environment. Upon verification and confirmation, the traffic is switched to the now-updated idle environment.

Blue-green deployments are advantageous due to their rapid rollback capability. If the new version contains issues, the older, stable version can instantly be reactivated by routing traffic back to the original environment. This strategy supports zero-downtime deployments and simplifies the verification of new versions under production conditions before going live.

```
# Example OpenShift commands for switching routes
$ oc expose service myapp-green --name=myapp
$ oc delete route myapp-blue
```

In terms of routing, OpenShift provides powerful controls to manage such deployments. By manipulating routes, an administrator can seamlessly direct traffic between the blue and green environments. The shown commands illustrate how traffic can be redirected within OpenShift by modifying the associated services and routes.

In blue-green deployments, care must be taken to manage data consistency between the environments to ensure no data loss occurs upon switching.

Comparison and Considerations

Careful consideration is required when choosing a deployment strategy. Factors such as application architecture, downtime tolerance, team expertise, and infrastructure capability all influence this decision.

Rolling updates offer reduced downtime but require compatibility between successive versions. Recreate scenarios provide a clean switch but at the cost of brief or significant downtime, suitable for complete overhaul scenarios. Meanwhile, blue-green deployments facilitate near-zero downtime and immediate rollback capabilities, albeit at the cost of additional resource allocation.

Each strategy requires a tailored approach to monitoring and error handling. Rolling and blue-green strategies, for instance, necessitate robust health checks and rollbacks to enable automated recovery. Tools such as Prometheus for monitoring and Grafana for visualization can be integrated to provide insights into ongoing deployments, ensuring any anomalies can be immediately rectified.

The success of any deployment strategy also relies on the orchestrating platform's ability — in this case, OpenShift — to provide flexible, reliable, and responsive controls over the deployment process. Understanding the platform's capacity and leveraging its capabilities fully is a crucial aspect of efficient deployment management.

Understanding the deployment strategies within OpenShift and their implications can significantly aid in achieving highly available, reliable, and quickly recoverable deployments. The balance between minimizing downtime, ensuring consistency, and efficiently utilizing resources must be managed through informed decision-making.

4.2   Building and Deploying Applications with Jenkins

Jenkins, an open-source automation server, plays a pivotal role in Continuous Integration and Continuous Deployment (CI/CD) pipelines. By integrating Jenkins with OpenShift, organizations can automate application build, test, and deployment processes, enhancing software delivery efficiency and reliability. This section focuses on how Jenkins can be seamlessly integrated with OpenShift to facilitate automated building and deployment of applications, including setting up pipeline projects, configuring webhooks, utilizing Jenkinsfiles, and managing credentials securely.

When Jenkins becomes a key component in the build and deploy pipeline, developers benefit from automated workflows that minimize manual oversight and reduce the potential for human errors, enabling rapid iteration and reliable delivery of software updates.

Integrating Jenkins with OpenShift involves configuring a Jenkins instance to communicate with the OpenShift API, enabling the execution of jobs that build, test, and deploy applications into an OpenShift cluster.

A typical integration process begins by creating a Jenkins instance on OpenShift. This can be achieved using the provided Jenkins image streams made available by the OpenShift software catalog. The following OpenShift command deploys a Jenkins instance:

```
$ oc new-app jenkins-ephemeral
```

The 'jenkins-ephemeral' template deploys Jenkins with in-memory storage for job states and configurations, suitable for development and testing purposes. For production use, a persistent Jenkins deployment may be desirable.

The Jenkins pipeline in OpenShift is defined using a 'Jenkinsfile', which specifies the build, test, and deployment actions as code for a particular project. The following is an example 'Jenkinsfile' that builds and deploys an application:

```
pipeline {
    agent any
    stages {
        stage('Build') {
            steps {
                script {
                    echo 'Building the project...'
                    sh 'mvn clean package'
                }
            }
        }
        stage('Test') {
            steps {
                script {
                    echo 'Running tests...'
                    sh 'mvn test'
```

```
            }
          }
        }
        stage('Deploy to OpenShift') {
            steps {
                script {
                    echo 'Deploying to OpenShift...'
                    openshift.withCluster() {
                        openshift.withProject('myproject') {
                            def dc = openshift.selector('dc', 'myapp')
                            dc.rollout().status()
                        }
                    }
                }
            }
        }
    }
    post {
        always {
            echo 'Pipeline execution completed.'
        }
    }
}
```

This 'Jenkinsfile' outlines a simple three-stage pipeline: build, test, and deploy. The 'openshift' plugin for Jenkins is leveraged to directly interface with the OpenShift API for deployment actions. Here, OpenShift projects and deployment configurations (DCs) are targeted to execute rollouts.

Webhooks are integral to triggering Jenkins jobs automatically. By configuring webhooks in the OpenShift environment, Jenkins can receive notifications of code changes pushed to a source code repository, thereby initiating a build process.

Typically, this involves setting up webhook integration within both the version control system (e.g., GitHub, GitLab) and OpenShift, ensuring Jenkins is notified when a commit to the codebase occurs:

```
# Add this webhook URL to GitHub repository settings:
https://jenkins.example.com/github-webhook/
```

Once configured, every time code is pushed to the repository, GitHub will notify Jenkins via the webhook endpoint, triggering the associated build job. This seamless integration is a quintessential feature of an efficient CI/CD pipeline, enabling instantaneous feedback on code changes.

Managing credentials securely is paramount when dealing with deployments that access sensitive information, such as container registries or external databases. Jenkins provides mechanisms to handle credentials securely using the Jenkins Credentials Plugin.

Storing credentials securely ensures that sensitive information, such as tokens and keys, are not exposed in plain text within Jenkins scripts or console outputs. The stored credentials can be accessed within a Jenkins pipeline as follows:

```
pipeline {
    agent any
    environment {
        DOCKER_CREDENTIALS = credentials('docker-creds')
    }
    stages {
        stage('Build Image') {
            steps {
                script {
                    sh 'docker login -u $DOCKER_CREDENTIALS_USR -p
                        $DOCKER_CREDENTIALS_PSW'
                    sh 'docker build -t myimage:latest .'
                }
            }
        }
    }
}
```

In this script, the 'credentials' method fetches the username and password for 'docker-creds', which are then utilized to authenticate Docker actions securely. Proper handling of credentials is one of the several secure practices required to maintain a robust CI/CD ecosystem.

Jenkins provides numerous advanced features that can be integrated into an OpenShift build pipeline, ranging from parallel execution of tasks to input directives that require manual intervention under certain conditions.

For instance, a pipeline might involve parallel tasks to expedite execution, especially useful in scenarios involving independent test suites or multi-platform builds:

```
pipeline {
    agent any
    stages {
        stage('Parallel Tasks') {
            parallel {
                stage('Unit Tests') {
                    steps {
                        sh 'mvn test -DskipIntegrationTests=true'
                    }
```

```
            }
        stage('Integration Tests') {
            steps {
                sh 'mvn verify -DskipUnitTests=true'
            }
        }
    }
  }
 }
}
```

This snippet exemplifies how two test stages can run concurrently, optimizing the pipeline efficiency and reducing total execution time. Integrating such features allows pipelines to be flexible and scalable, accommodating complex software lifecycle requirements.

When managing multiple application environments, deploying specific versions based on tags and branches becomes essential. Jenkins' integration offers automation of these deployments through parameterized builds and environment variables that specify the desired configuration.

Here is a way to use branch name or tags in your pipeline:

```
pipeline {
    agent any
    environment {
        BRANCH_NAME = sh(script: "git rev-parse --abbrev-ref HEAD",
            returnStdout: true).trim()
    }
    stages {
        stage('Build and Tag') {
            steps {
                script {
                    sh "docker build -t myapp:${BRANCH_NAME} ."
                    sh "docker push mycompany/myapp:${BRANCH_NAME}"
                }
            }
        }
    }
}
```

This uses the current branch or tag as part of the Docker image tag, allowing for precise deployment configurations that align with the codebase's state. Implementing such strategies ensures that deployment environments are tightly coupled to the source of origin, fostering reliable and reproducible deployments.

Leveraging Jenkins within OpenShift enables robust automation of application lifecycle processes, enhancing efficiency, consistency, and security. By understanding the detailed configurations and SMART usage of pipelines, organizations can realize continuous delivery goals aligned with modern development practices, undoubtedly improving the deployment cadence and maintaining highest levels of software quality assurance.

4.3 Managing Deployments with OpenShift Web Console

The OpenShift Web Console provides a graphical user interface (GUI) that facilitates the management of application deployments, providing users the ability to perform sophisticated tasks without requiring deep command-line expertise. The console provides an intuitive platform for administrators, developers, and operators alike, supporting activities such as configuring deployment strategies, monitoring application performance, managing resources, and troubleshooting issues.

Utilizing the OpenShift Web Console, users can gain insights into the overall health of the system and easily navigate through application settings, logs, and events. This section explores the various functionalities offered by the web console for managing deployments effectively within an OpenShift environment.

The OpenShift Web Console is a comprehensive dashboard accessible through a web browser that permits users to manage OpenShift clusters and address day-to-day operational challenges. Upon logging into the console, users access a high-level view of all projects, applications, and resources managed within the cluster.

The console encapsulates vital information regarding resource utilization, application health, and configuration details, thus enabling efficient management and decision-making processes. Each application or service deployed within OpenShift is represented as a manageable object, often termed a resource, which may be a pod, service, route, build configuration, or deployment configuration.

Deployment configurations (DCs) are core to managing how applications are deployed within OpenShift. They define how updates are rolled out, replicas are handled, and strategies are applied. Through

116

the web console, deployment configurations can be easily altered by selecting a project and navigating to the applicable DC.

Within the DC, users can:

- Adjust the number of replicas: Scale the application by modifying the replica count, which directly affects resource allocation and availability.

- Change environment variables: Configure parameters that the application uses to operate, enhancing flexibility across different environments.

- Modify deployment strategies: Select from rolling, recreate, or other supported strategies based on application compatibility and downtime tolerance.

The web console simplifies these changes through a point-and-click interface, offering a convenient alternative to deploying configurations via the command line. This accessibility is particularly advantageous for those less familiar with terminal commands or those requiring visualization of deployment changes.

```
# OpenShift Web Console View
Navigate to: Applications -> Deployments -> [Select Deployment]
- Adjust "Replicas" slider for scaling
- "Environment" tab to edit variables
- "Actions" menu to update strategy
```

OpenShift offers comprehensive monitoring capabilities through the web console, presenting real-time data on deployments' performance and resource utilization. These insights include CPU and memory usage, network I/O, and pod status, which aid in identifying bottlenecks and optimizing resource distribution.

The web console integrates tools for visualizing these metrics over time, showcasing trends and enabling proactive measures to address potential concerns. Users can access logs and metrics through specific deployment views, leveraging the console's integration with monitoring tools like Prometheus and Grafana for detailed dashboards.

Additionally, automated alerts can be configured to notify administrators of anomalies such as resource constraint breaches or unresponsive applications, enhancing the reactive capacity of operations teams toward unforeseen issues.

The need to perform rollbacks arises when a deployment results in failures or suboptimal performance. OpenShift's web console expedites this process by allowing users to revert deployments to a previous stable version with minimal effort.

To initiate a rollback:

1. Navigate to the Deployment section in the console.

2. Select the respective application deployment.

3. Choose from the list of previously successful deployment revisions.

4. Execute the rollback by confirming the action.

This rollback mechanism is implemented through the creation of new deployment configurations based on the selected previous version, ensuring that the application state is restored instantly without impacting ongoing operations.

```
# Rollback Procedure in OpenShift Web Console
Navigate to: Applications -> Deployments -> [Select Deployment]
- "Revisions" tab to review past deployment versions
- Select desired version to "Rollback" to
- Confirm action under "Actions" menu
```

Managing application accessibility and networking aspects are integral to deploying applications within a cloud-native environment like OpenShift. The web console provides interfaces for handling the routing layers, services, and network policies that dictate connectivity.

Services and routes, which abstract communication inside and outside the OpenShift cluster, can be managed via the console. Users can create new routes, update existing ones, and set hostname paths, providing seamless L7 routing powered by ingress controllers.

Network policies further allow controlling ingress and egress traffic based on specified conditions, enhancing security through fine-grained access controls.

To manage routes and network policies:

1. Navigate to the Networking section in the web console.

2. Adjust service and route settings, including load balancing configurations.

3. Define restrictive network policies to regulate traffic flow securely.

```
# OpenShift Web Console for Networking
Navigate to: Networking -> Services/Routes -> [Select Route]
- "Create Route" to expose services
- Modify Ingress rules under "Network Policies"
```

Effective management of cluster and application access rights is crucial in maintaining security and operational integrity. OpenShift's Role-Based Access Control (RBAC) is extensively managed through the web console, allowing administrators to assign permissions based on user roles and project requirements.

Actions available through the web console enable administrators to:

- Create and modify role bindings: Ensure that users only have access to necessary resources pertinent to their role.

- Assign or revoke permissions: Instantly apply changes to user access, responding dynamically to changes in team composition or job requirements.

- View audit logs: Track actions performed within the cluster, supporting compliance and forensic investigations.

These operations ensure that governance policies are adhered to, leveraging the web console to maintain oversight on user actions and permissions.

```
# OpenShift RBAC via Web Console
Navigate to: Administration -> Roles -> [Select Role]
- Create/Edit role bindings within project scope
- Assign Users/Groups to roles on "Access Control" page
```

An essential component of managing deployments is diagnosing and resolving issues that occur within the cluster. The OpenShift web console provides centralized access to logs, events, and error messages, facilitating effective troubleshooting methods.

Developers and operators can use the console to:

- Access pod logs: Obtain detailed output from containers to identify runtime issues.

- Review cluster events: Monitor warnings or failures, correlating events to troubleshoot root causes.

- Execute shell commands directly within pods: Identify configuration issues or perform hot-fixes.

```
# Logging and Events via OpenShift Web Console
Navigate to: Applications -> Pods -> [Select Pod]
- "Logs" tab for real-time container output
- "Terminal" tab for direct shell access
- "Events" section for historical logging events
```

In a multi-tenant environment, the web console simplifies the management of isolated projects and environments that different teams may manage within the same OpenShift cluster. It provides a hierarchical organization of projects, allowing streamlined navigation and segregation of resources.

In such environments, the console empowers different tenant teams to independently manage their resources while administrators maintain oversight through centralized dashboards without jeopardizing the underlying infrastructure's stability.

Given OpenShift's inherent support for continuous updates and shared infrastructure, the web console becomes an indispensable tool that bridges user interaction and system administration seamlessly, fostering both productivity and system reliability through an intuitive interface.

4.4 Configuring Environment Variables and Secrets

In containerized applications, managing configuration data and protecting sensitive information is pivotal for building secure and adaptable applications. OpenShift offers comprehensive mechanisms to handle environment variables and secrets, facilitating this management with extensive flexibility and security. This section delves into the approaches to configure these parameters effectively, the best practices for managing sensitive data, and the technical intricacies underpinning these processes.

Leveraging environment variables ensures that applications can be easily adapted without altering their operational code, supporting better scalability and maintenance. Simultaneously, using secrets to manage confidential configuration data, such as API keys or database passwords, ensures that sensitive information is handled with the utmost security. Understanding these components and their implementation within OpenShift is crucial for developers and operators seeking to maintain best practices in application deployment.

Environment variables are used to configure dynamically application parameters and operational settings, typically set externally rather than hardcoded within applications. This capability supports twelve-factor apps principles, allowing developers to deploy flexible and scalable applications across multiple environments without modifying codebases.

OpenShift supports setting environment variables at multiple levels, allowing precise control over environment configurations throughout the deployment lifecycle. These variables can be applied at build configurations, pods, and containers via the OpenShift Web Console or configuration files. Below is an example of setting an environment variable using a Deployment Configuration (DC):

```
apiVersion: apps.openshift.io/v1
kind: DeploymentConfig
metadata:
  name: myapp
spec:
  template:
    spec:
      containers:
      - name: myapp-container
        image: myapp:latest
        env:
        - name: APP_ENV
          value: "production"
        - name: APP_DEBUG
          value: "false"
```

This example demonstrates applying two environment variables

121

APP_ENV and APP_DEBUG to the container myapp-container within a deployment configuration. These variables can control behaviors like enabling debug modes or defining operational parameters depending on the deployment stage.

In applications running within OpenShift, environment variables are accessed like any other operating system environment variable. For instance, in a Node.js application, accessing the environment variable is as simple as:

```
const environment = process.env.APP_ENV;
console.log('Current Environment: ${environment}');
```

Developers can strategically deploy code that dynamically adapts behaviors based on the environment, ensuring alignment across development, testing, and production orchestrations.

Configuration Maps (ConfigMaps) in OpenShift provide a method to pass non-sensitive configuration data into pods. ConfigMaps decouple environment-specific configuration from container images, enabling its easy management during operations.

```
apiVersion: v1
kind: ConfigMap
metadata:
  name: myapp-config
data:
  database_url: "localhost:5432/mydb"
  log_level: "warn"
```

Once a ConfigMap is defined, it can be mounted into a pod or referenced as environment variables to dynamically inject configuration data:

```
apiVersion: apps.openshift.io/v1
kind: DeploymentConfig
metadata:
  name: myapp
spec:
  template:
    spec:
      containers:
      - name: myapp-container
        image: myapp:latest
        envFrom:
        - configMapRef:
            name: myapp-config
```

This linkage transparently feeds configuration properties from the myapp-config ConfigMap into the application container, offering flexibility in swapping ConfigMaps to cater to diverse environmental situations.

Handling sensitive data, such as passwords, tokens, and keys, securely is essential for safeguarding crucial application interactions. OpenShift secrets are built to manage this information securely, supporting base64 encoding to protect data while retaining ease of use.

```
apiVersion: v1
kind: Secret
metadata:
  name: db-credentials
type: Opaque
data:
  username: bXlVc2Vy
  password: bXlQYXNzdzByZA==
```

In this YAML configuration, a Secret named db-credentials stores base64 encoded username and password. Opaque types indicate arbitrary user-defined data and are widely used for application secrets.

To decode and utilize the information contained within secrets, applications must directly incorporate these references within their configurations:

```
apiVersion: apps.openshift.io/v1
kind: DeploymentConfig
metadata:
  name: myapp
spec:
  template:
    spec:
      containers:
      - name: myapp-container
        image: myapp:latest
        env:
        - name: DB_USERNAME
          valueFrom:
            secretKeyRef:
              name: db-credentials
              key: username
        - name: DB_PASSWORD
          valueFrom:
            secretKeyRef:
              name: db-credentials
              key: password
```

This example binds secret data directly to environment variables within a container, enabling secure and unobtrusive utilization of sensitive information during application execution.

Adhering to best practices is vital for managing environment variables and secrets effectively within OpenShift. These practices serve to bolster security, maintainability, and operational integrity across containerized applications.

- **Segregate Data Between ConfigMaps and Secrets**: Separate non-sensitive configuration (ConfigMaps) from sensitive data (Secrets) to ensure that sensitive information is only accessible to authorized personnel and processes.

- **Utilize Fine-Grained Access Controls**: Employ Role-based Access Control (RBAC) to restrict access to secrets. Limiting permissions reduces the risk of unauthorized data exposure.

- **Avoid Hardcoding Sensitive Data**: Never hardcode sensitive information within application logic or deployment configurations. Use OpenShift Secrets to manage this data with a dedicated secret management protocol.

- **Regularly Rotate Secrets**: Implement a routine schedule for key rotation to minimize risk exposure and ascertain that credentials are promptly updated across all relevant applications.

- **Monitor and Audit Access to Secrets**: Log access attempts and modifications to secrets as part of regular security audits to detect any irregular activity and enhance compliance.

- **Decode Environment Variables Sparingly**: Only decode secrets within the application code when necessary, ensuring usage is kept minimal and aligned with operational requirements.

Implementing such practices assures that environment variables and secrets are managed effectively, promoting secure and efficient application operations within OpenShift's container orchestration environment.

For organizations with advanced security requirements, OpenShift can integrate with external secrets management tools such as HashiCorp

Vault, CyberArk, or AWS Secrets Manager. These solutions provide additional layers of security and automation around secrets management processes.

Utilizing external vaults enables features such as dynamic secrets, automatic secret expiration, and centralized auditing:

```
apiVersion: v1
kind: Secret
metadata:
  name: external-db-credentials
annotations:
  vault.hashicorp.com/role: "openShift-role"
  vault.hashicorp.com/agent-inject: "true"
  vault.hashicorp.com/agent-inject-secret-db-username: "database/creds/db-username"
type: Opaque
```

In this configuration, annotations define how secrets should be retrieved from the external Vault system, specifying credentials paths and roles. This method ensures that sensitive data handling is both securely and seamlessly executed in accordance with external management solutions standards.

In practice, OpenShift's approach to managing environment variables and secrets empowers developers to create scalable, secure applications. Integrating configuration management directly into the development lifecycle offers operational transparency and flexibility, essential elements for thriving in modern software ecosystems. Employing OpenShift's functionalities in tandem with best industry practices allows organizations to maintain security postures while unlocking the extensive potential of agile, reliable deployments.

4.5   Working with Persistent Storage

In containerized environments like OpenShift, persistent storage is critical for applications that require statefulness across pod restarts, as ephemeral storage typically cannot persist data. This necessitates the use of persistent storage to maintain application data consistency and availability across lifecycle stages. OpenShift's integration of Kubernetes' persistent storage concepts significantly enhances its flexibility when managing storage requirements for diverse applications.

This section provides an in-depth exploration of persistent storage in OpenShift. Key concepts include Persistent Volumes (PVs), Persistent Volume Claims (PVCs), dynamic provisioning, access modes, and storage classes, each playing a vital role in the interface between applications and storage providers. Successfully implementing these storage configurations requires an understanding of their implications and best practices.

- A Persistent Volume (PV) is a cluster-wide resource representing a piece of storage in the cluster. It is created by an administrator or via dynamic provisioning and exists independently of any individual pod.

- Persistent Volume Claims (PVC), on the other hand, are requests for storage by a user. PVCs allow users to specify the desired storage attributes, such as size and access modes, enabling OpenShift to bind the claim to an appropriate PV automatically.

The relationship between PVs and PVCs abstracts physical storage management, allowing separation between storage consumers and providers:

```
apiVersion: v1
kind: PersistentVolume
metadata:
  name: my-pv
spec:
  capacity:
    storage: 10Gi
  accessModes:
   - ReadWriteOnce
  persistentVolumeReclaimPolicy: Retain
  nfs:
    path: /exported/path
    server: nfs-server.example.com
```

In this YAML definition, a PV named 'my-pv' with a capacity of 10Gi is created. It uses Network File System (NFS) as a storage backend. The 'accessModes' indicates that the volume supports 'ReadWriteOnce', meaning it can be mounted as read-write by a single node.

```
apiVersion: v1
kind: PersistentVolumeClaim
metadata:
  name: my-pvc
spec:
```

```
accessModes:
  - ReadWriteOnce
resources:
  requests:
    storage: 5Gi
```

The PV shown here will satisfy the PVC named 'my-pvc' because it matches the storage request and access mode criteria. This flexibility allows users to request storage without having to manage the details of the underlying storage resource.

Dynamic provisioning in OpenShift automates the creation of Persistent Volumes based on demand when a Persistent Volume Claim is created. This negates the need for pre-provisioning the storage and is achieved through storage classes.

A storage class provides a way for administrators to describe the "class" of storage they offer. It defines provisioners, parameters, and a reclaim policy. Here's an example of a storage class:

```
apiVersion: storage.k8s.io/v1
kind: StorageClass
metadata:
  name: fast
provisioner: kubernetes.io/aws-ebs
parameters:
  type: io1
  iopsPerGB: "10"
  fsType: ext4
reclaimPolicy: Delete
```

This StorageClass named 'fast' provisions AWS EBS volumes with a specific type and IOPS setting, indicating its suitability for high-performance I/O requirements. The 'reclaimPolicy: Delete' ensures the PV is automatically deleted when its PVC is deleted, freeing up resources.

Whenever a PVC referencing a StorageClass is created, OpenShift automatically triggers the creation of an appropriate PV, simplifying the storage allocation process:

```
apiVersion: v1
kind: PersistentVolumeClaim
metadata:
  name: my-dynamic-pvc
spec:
  storageClassName: fast
  accessModes:
    - ReadWriteOnce
```

```
resources:
  requests:
    storage: 10Gi
```

This YAML example showcases how a dynamic PVC requests a 'fast' storage class, triggering PV creation that meets these requirements.

Understanding access modes is essential when working with persistent volumes. These determine the potential ways a volume can be used by a pod:

- **ReadWriteOnce (RWO)**: The volume can be mounted as read-write by a single node.

- **ReadOnlyMany (ROX)**: The volume can be mounted read-only by many nodes.

- **ReadWriteMany (RWX)**: The volume can be mounted as read-write by many nodes.

Choosing the appropriate access mode depends on the application's nature and its expected storage interaction. For example, databases often use 'ReadWriteOnce' for data consistency, while shared file systems might use 'ReadWriteMany'.

Reclaim policies determine what happens to a PV when its PVC is deleted:

- **Retain**: The manual reclaim process is required. Data remains in the volume because it's not automatically cleaned. Administrators must handle future reuse or deletion.

- **Delete**: The volume's data and its associated storage resources are deleted along with the PVC.

- **Recycle**: The volume's data is scrubbed (e.g., rm -rf /thevolume/*) before being available again.

Choosing the appropriate reclaim policy ensures storage resources are correctly managed across the application lifecycle, balancing data retention with resource efficiency.

Once a PVC is bound to a PV, pods can utilize this storage. Mounting a volume in a pod involves defining it within the pod specification:

```
apiVersion: v1
kind: Pod
metadata:
  name: myapp-pod
spec:
  containers:
  - name: myapp-container
    image: myapp:latest
    volumeMounts:
    - mountPath: "/data"
      name: myapp-storage
  volumes:
  - name: myapp-storage
    persistentVolumeClaim:
      claimName: my-pvc
```

In this configuration, 'myapp-container' mounts the persistent volume claim at '/data' within the pod, enabling data persistence across restarts and facilitating data retention for stateful applications. This linkage ensures applications have seamless read/write access as prescribed by the access mode.

Beyond basic configurations, OpenShift supports advanced storage management techniques, enhancing data resilience, availability, and performance. These include:

- **Backup and Restore Strategies**: Automating snapshotting and backup processes ensures data integrity and availability, even in the face of system failures. Tools like Velero enable scheduling and management of backups directly within Kubernetes ecosystems.

- **Multipathing and High Availability Storage Setups**: For critical applications, utilizing high availability storage solutions with multipathing ensures redundancy and optimized throughput.

- **Scalability Considerations**: Plan storage infrastructure to accommodate growth by leveraging dynamically scalable storage backends and monitoring solutions to preemptively address storage constraints.

- **Compliance and Encryption**: Ensure persistent data meets industry regulatory requirements by adopting encryption mechanisms, both at rest and in transit, following organizational and legal data protection policies.

- **Monitoring and Observability**: Implement storage monitoring practices using tools like Prometheus and Grafana to observe storage performance and health metrics, enabling proactive maintenance and troubleshooting.

Staying vigilant about these considerations ensures that persistent storage implementations align with application needs and organizational standards, driving efficient and effective data management within OpenShift.

Effective utilization and management of persistent storage provide a backbone for running stateful applications within OpenShift, expanding its capabilities for handling complex workloads with diverse data persistence requirements. By adhering to established best practices, developers and operators can extract the full benefits of OpenShift's robust storage offerings, underpinning reliable, scalable deployments with strong data resilience and integrity.

4.6 Creating and Managing OpenShift Templates

OpenShift templates are powerful tools that permit the definition and reuse of application objects as configurable, parameter-driven blueprints. They streamline the process of deploying applications by encapsulating best practices and standard configurations into reusable files, thereby increasing efficiency and reducing potential errors during deployment processes. This section delves into the nuances of creating and managing OpenShift templates, describing their structure, functionalities, and benefits, alongside practical guidelines for implementing them effectively.

By leveraging OpenShift templates, developers can define application structures once and instantiate them multiple times with different parameters, ensuring consistency across environments and smoothing development workflows. These templates facilitate not only the deployment of complex applications but also standardize development practices across teams.

An OpenShift template is typically defined as a JSON or YAML file that describes a set of objects within the OpenShift ecosystem. Each template file consists of several key elements: metadata, parameters, objects, and labels.

- **Metadata**: Descriptive information about the template, including name, namespace, and annotations.

- **Parameters**: Dynamic variables that can be substituted into objects, allowing customization without altering the template structure.

- **Objects**: The set of OpenShift or Kubernetes resources (such as Pods, Services, DeploymentConfigs) that constitute the application.

- **Labels**: Identifiers used for organizing, selecting, and managing groups of resources.

A basic example of an OpenShift template that describes a simple application deployment is illustrated below:

```yaml
apiVersion: v1
kind: Template
metadata:
  name: myapp-template
  labels:
    app: myapp
parameters:
- name: APP_NAME
  description: The name of the application
  required: true
- name: IMAGE_STREAM
  description: The image stream tag for the application
  required: true
objects:
- kind: DeploymentConfig
  apiVersion: apps.openshift.io/v1
  metadata:
    name: ${APP_NAME}
  spec:
    replicas: 3
    template:
      metadata:
```

```
      labels:
        app: ${APP_NAME}
    spec:
      containers:
      - name: ${APP_NAME}
        image: ${IMAGE_STREAM}
- kind: Service
  apiVersion: v1
  metadata:
    name: ${APP_NAME}
  spec:
    ports:
    - port: 8080
```

This template illustrates core concepts: metadata labels for identification, parameters for dynamic input substitution (APP_NAME, IMAGE_STREAM), and objects (DeploymentConfig, Service) that define the actual application components deployed.

The true power of templates lies in parameterization that grants flexibility and reusability across different environments. Parameters within a template can have default values and validations. Defining parameters succinctly ensures that users have clear guidelines for necessary environment inputs while deploying applications.

Parameters can be further configured to suit interactive needs:

```
parameters:
- name: MEMORY_LIMIT
  description: Maximum amount of memory the container can use
  value: "512Mi"
- name: ENVIRONMENT
  value: "production"
  generate: "expression"
  from: "[a-zA-Z]+"
```

The above declaration of parameters showcases default values (MEMORY_LIMIT), direct input (ENVIRONMENT), and uses a regular expression generator for creating values dynamically.

Once a template is defined, it can be instantiated to deploy new instances of the described configuration. Users generally initiate templates through the OpenShift Web Console or the CLI using the oc process command, followed by oc create.

```
$ oc process -f myapp-template.yaml \
-p APP_NAME=myapp \
-p IMAGE_STREAM=myapp:latest | oc create -f -
```

The oc process command substitutes parameter values within the template, subsequently submitting it via oc create to instantiate the resources described.

The deployment initiated via templates can be managed through OpenShift's robust suite of management tools. The web console and CLI provide functions to scale resources, update configurations, and monitor performance, thereby ensuring operational stability and responsiveness.

Employing OpenShift templates within an application lifecycle introduces several advantages that assist in standardizing and accelerating deployment processes:

- **Consistency**: Templates ensure uniform configurations, minimizing configuration drift across deployments and environments.

- **Reusability and Scalability**: Once developed, templates become scalable assets reusable across multiple instances, saving time and resources.

- **Ease of Use**: Reduces reliance on manual scripting or repetitive configurations, granting users a user-friendly interaction experience.

- **Customizable**: Parametrization enables easy tailoring to specific needs, accommodating varied deployment environments and workflows.

For effective template deployment, adhering to best practices is recommended:

- **Namespace Management**: Avoid hardcoding namespaces within templates unless necessary to ensure flexibility in resource allocation across projects.

- **Strict Parameter Validation**: Employ robust parameter constraints to prevent erroneous deployments due to invalid input values.

- **Modular Design**: Keep template files modular and maintainable; avoid excessive complexity within a single template.

- **Source Control**: Store template files within version-controlled repositories to track changes, maintaining historical and auditable records.

- **Documentation and Annotation**: Thoroughly document templates to describe their purpose and function clearly, improving accessibility for new users.

By adhering to these guidelines, organizations maximize the utility of templates, fostering a culture of best practices and replicable success.

Extending OpenShift templates to manage complex microservice architectures further typifies their utility. For such architectures, a single template file can coordinate multi-resource components, including databases, caching layers, and backend microservices, encapsulating the entire stack's operational blueprint.

Multi-resource templates simplify orchestration, where managing dependencies and facilitating communication between services is paramount. Here's an example of how a complex setup might be defined:

```
apiVersion: v1
kind: Template
metadata:
  name: complex-app-template
parameters:
- name: FRONTEND_IMAGE
  description: Frontend service image stream
- name: BACKEND_IMAGE
  description: Backend service image stream
objects:
- kind: DeploymentConfig
  metadata:
    name: frontend
  spec:
    replicas: 2
    template:
      spec:
        containers:
        - name: frontend
          image: ${FRONTEND_IMAGE}
- kind: DeploymentConfig
  metadata:
    name: backend
  spec:
```

```
    replicas: 2
    template:
      spec:
        containers:
        - name: backend
            image: ${BACKEND_IMAGE}
- kind: Service
  metadata:
    name: backend
  spec:
    ports:
    - port: 8080
```

This template creates both a frontend and backend deployment, which simplifies coordination and reduces deployment overhead when deploying an application stack.

As OpenShift evolves, integrating templates with Kubernetes Operators and Cloud-native services offers a pathway to sophisticated application management strategies. An operator-aware template paradigm involves embedding lifecycle logic directly within the template parameters, allowing seamless configuration and upgrade paths for managed services.

Moreover, templates' alignment with infrastructure-as-code practices anchors them as pivotal components in CI/CD pipelines, interfacing with systems like Jenkins, Tekton, or GitOps workflows to automate deployment, scaling, and monitoring. By leveraging automation frameworks, teams can ensure rapid, consistent deployment cycles with feedback loops that elevate code quality and reduce time-to-market pressures.

OpenShift templates encapsulate a powerful methodology for deploying and maintaining complex applications at scale. By translating deployment settings into versioned, parameter-driven files, templates foster robust DevOps practices that leverage automation and consistency for delivering high-quality, dependable software solutions. Navigating the nuances of creating and optimizing templates grants teams the ability to harness the full potential of OpenShift, driving transformational benefits across the application lifecycle.

4.7 Managing Application Lifecycle with Operators

Operators in OpenShift are a paradigm that extend Kubernetes' functionality, providing a means to manage complex applications effectively throughout their lifecycle using custom controllers. Operators encapsulate application-specific domain knowledge and operational practices into an executable model, significantly reducing the complexity and manual intervention typically associated with application management. This section explores the role of Operators in OpenShift, how they automate and simplify application lifecycle management, and practical considerations for developing and deploying custom Operators.

Operators leverage Kubernetes' declarative nature but extend it with capabilities such as provisioning, scaling, managing configuration updates, handling failure recovery, and providing seamless upgrades. This enriches the Kubernetes ecosystem, enabling administrators and developers to adopt more sophisticated patterns for managing applications at scale.

Understanding Operators and Their Role

Operators are essentially Kubernetes controllers that manage complex applications or services. They watch for changes in custom resources—specialized objects defined by the developer—and act to reconcile those with the current state of the cluster, automating routine and complex tasks.

An Operator manages its application by continually observing the state defined in its custom resources and performing the prescribed actions necessary to transition the current state towards the specified desired state, effectively encoding the expertise of a human operator into code.

Operators can manage all aspects of application lifecycle, including:

- Provisioning: Initial deployment of application resources and dependencies.

- Scaling: Adjusting resource allocations to meet current demand conditions.

136

- Configuration Management: Automating configuration updates while ensuring application integrity.

- Fault Detection and Recovery: Identifying problems and performing automated recovery measures.

- Updates and Upgrades: Managing seamless application updates without downtime.

Core Components and Architecture of Operators

The architecture of an Operator includes several core components, each playing a critical role in its operation:

- Custom Resource Definitions (CRDs): Extend Kubernetes API to define new resource types. They represent the desired state for custom applications.

- Controllers: Services that watch for changes in CRDs and take corrective actions based on the current state versus desired state differences.

- Reconciliation Loops: Processes by which differences between the observed state and the desired state are resolved.

A sample CRD might look as follows:

```
apiVersion: apiextensions.k8s.io/v1
kind: CustomResourceDefinition
metadata:
  name: myapps.example.com
spec:
  group: example.com
  versions:
    - name: v1
      served: true
      storage: true
  names:
    kind: MyApp
    plural: myapps
  scope: Namespaced
```

This 'CustomResourceDefinition' enables a new resource type 'MyApp', which is then managed by an Operator tailored to handle the specific needs and operations of this resource.

Developing Operators

Developing a custom Operator involves writing the logic required to manage an application's lifecycle. Various frameworks and software development kits (SDKs) have been created to aid in Operator development, making the process more efficient. Notable options include the Operator SDK, Helm-based Operators, and Ansible-based Operators.

- Operator SDK: This toolkit simplifies the process of building reliable Operators using Kubernetes and controller-runtime libraries. It offers a standard scaffold for rapid development and testing.

- Helm Operators: For users comfortable with Helm charts, Helm-based Operators leverage charts to manage applications with Operator-like automation capabilities.

- Ansible Operators: They use Ansible tasks and roles to define application logic, allowing those familiar with Ansible to implement automation effortlessly.

Below is an example of a simple reconciliation loop using the Operator SDK:

```
func (r *MyAppReconciler) Reconcile(req ctrl.Request) (ctrl.Result, error) {
    ctx := context.Background()
    logger := r.Log.WithValues("myapp", req.NamespacedName)

    var myapp myappv1.MyApp
    if err := r.Get(ctx, req.NamespacedName, &myapp); err != nil {
        logger.Error(err, "unable to fetch MyApp")
        return ctrl.Result{}, client.IgnoreNotFound(err)
    }

    if condition := checkSomeCondition(&myapp); condition {
        logger.Info("Condition met, taking action")
        // Perform application-specific actions
    }

    return ctrl.Result{}, nil
}
```

This code provides a basic reconciliation loop that checks a condition in the 'MyApp' resource and takes actions accordingly, demonstrating the core function of an Operator controller.

Deploying Operators in OpenShift

Deployment of an Operator involves several steps, each ensuring it is correctly integrated and harmonized with the OpenShift environment:

- Define CRDs: Install CRDs that describe the custom objects your Operator will manage.

- Package the Operator: Build the Operator into a container image ready for deployment.

- Deploy the Operator: Use OpenShift's Operator Lifecycle Manager (OLM) to manage the installation, upgrade, and configuration of Operators.

- Create Custom Resources: Once the Operator is in place, create instances of the custom resources that it manages to drive the application lifecycle.

For instance, with the OLM, Operators come with capabilities like dependency resolution between services, multi-tenancy, and cluster monitoring integration.

The OperatorHub and Ecosystem Benefits

OperatorHub is a centralized repository in OpenShift, offering a wide selection of pre-built Operators from the community and commercial ecosystem. It provides ready-made automation flows for common applications — databases, monitoring tools, message brokers, and more — that can be leveraged with minimal configuration, streamlining processes significantly.

Benefits of leveraging Operators from the OperatorHub include:

- Reduced Maintenance: Operators encapsulate complex operational logic, reducing manual intervention.

- Automatic Updates: Operators ensure that application instances remain up-to-date with minimal downtime.

- Ecosystem Standardization: Adoption of community and vendor-supported Operators ensures adherence to industry standards and best practices.

User interactions through the OperatorHub in the OpenShift web console involve selecting desired Operators and following guided installation and configuration processes, making adoption straightforward and user-friendly.

Best Practices for Operator-Based Lifecycle Management

To fully harness the potential of Operators in managing applications, adhering to best practices is essential:

- Immutable Infrastructure Philosophy: Operators should be designed to ensure infrastructure is immutable, facilitating efficient rollbacks and minimal intervention for state corrections.

- Comprehensive Documentation: Crystal-clear documentation combined with detailed examples increases Operator usability and fosters community engagement.

- Proper Error Handling: Ensure the Operator implements robust error detection and recovery mechanisms to address unexpected events gracefully.

- Testing and Simulation: Rigorously test Operators under various scenarios and stress conditions. Simulation tools can provide insight into Operator behavior during testing.

- Community Contribution: Engaging with the Kubernetes and OpenShift communities for feedback and feature requests can enrich the Operator's capabilities and reliability.

- Regular Updates and Security Audits: Maintain Operator versions in alignment with Kubernetes upgrades, including conducting periodic security reviews to address vulnerabilities.

By embracing these concepts, organizations deploy Operators that robustly manage applications, improving lifecycle management and operational efficiency.

Operators represent a transformative shift within OpenShift and Kubernetes environments by embedding operational knowledge into code, thus streamlining complex application management tasks. The continuous evolution of Operator capabilities fosters an environment conducive to agile development practices, ensuring that applications are robustly managed from initial deployment through updates, scaling, and eventual decommissioning. By empowering teams with the ability to automate intricate application behaviors, Operators ease administrative burdens, enabling focus on innovation and delivering higher value across application lifecycles.

Chapter 5

Managing and Monitoring Applications in OpenShift

This chapter examines the tools and practices essential for effective management and monitoring of applications within OpenShift. Focus is placed on configuring application setups with the use of ConfigMaps and Secrets, allowing for seamless updates and rollbacks. OpenShift's built-in monitoring and logging tools, including the EFK stack, are discussed for their roles in performance monitoring and issue diagnosis. By implementing automated health checks and alerts, administrators can proactively maintain application health. The chapter also emphasizes leveraging metrics to guide performance optimizations and ensure applications run efficiently in the OpenShift ecosystem.

5.1 Managing Application Configurations

In the context of OpenShift, managing application configurations involves utilizing tools and techniques that ensure applications are correctly set up and adaptable to changing requirements. This involves a meticulous approach to configuration management, utilizing ConfigMaps and Secrets, to effectively handle sensitive data and non-confidential application settings.

ConfigMaps are Kubernetes objects that can store configuration data in key-value pairs. They provide a mechanism to separate configuration details from application code, allowing for a streamlined deployment process where configurations can be modified without necessitating changes to the container image. This design allows for an easier adaptation of the same application across different environments, such as development, testing, and production.

To create a ConfigMap in OpenShift, one can utilize the command-line interface (CLI), YAML configuration files, or directly through the OpenShift web console. Here, let us explore the representation and creation of a ConfigMap both via YAML and using the OpenShift CLI.

```
# OpenShift CLI command to create a ConfigMap
oc create configmap my-app-config --from-literal=key1=value1 --from-literal=key2=
    value2
```

In this example, a ConfigMap named 'my-app-config' is created with two key-value pairs. This method is effective for quick configurations. However, for more complex or numerous configurations, YAML files offer a more organized approach:

```
apiVersion: v1
kind: ConfigMap
metadata:
  name: my-app-config
data:
  key1: value1
  key2: value2
```

To apply this configuration using a YAML file, save the file as 'configmap.yaml' and apply it using the CLI:

```
# Apply the ConfigMap configuration
```

```
oc apply -f configmap.yaml
```

The data stored in ConfigMaps can then be accessed by the application in various ways, such as environment variables or mounted volumes, depending on the application's requirements and architecture.

For sensitive configuration data such as passwords, API keys, or security certificates, Secrets are used instead of ConfigMaps. Secrets encrypt the stored data, adding a layer of security in the management of sensitive information.

Creating a Secret is similar to a ConfigMap, with the primary distinction being the handling and encoding of the data:

```
# Create a secret with encoded values
oc create secret generic my-secret --from-literal=username=admin --from-literal=
    password=secretpassword
```

To ensure sensitive data is encoded, OpenShift processes these keys and values, wherein the values are stored as base64 encoded strings. For YAML configurations, a similar approach is taken:

```
apiVersion: v1
kind: Secret
metadata:
  name: my-secret
type: Opaque
data:
  username: YWRtaW4= # base64 encoded 'admin'
  password: c2VjcmV0cGFzc3dvcmQ= # base64 encoded 'secretpassword'
```

In practical application deployment scenarios, both ConfigMaps and Secrets are accessed in pods through environment variables or as mounted files. The choice between these methods typically depends on the application design or developer preference.

```
apiVersion: apps/v1
kind: Deployment
metadata:
  name: my-deployment
spec:
  replicas: 1
  template:
    spec:
      containers:
      - name: my-container
        image: my-app-image
        env:
        - name: CONFIG_KEY1
```

145

```
valueFrom:
   configMapKeyRef:
      name: my-app-config
      key: key1
```

In this deployment configuration snippet, the key-value pair from the ConfigMap is accessed as an environment variable within the container, which the application can easily read using standard methods for accessing environment variables.

For accessing Secret data in a secure manner, a similar configuration setup is required:

```
apiVersion: apps/v1
kind: Deployment
metadata:
  name: my-deployment
spec:
  replicas: 1
  template:
    spec:
      containers:
      - name: my-container
        image: my-app-image
        env:
        - name: USERNAME
          valueFrom:
            secretKeyRef:
              name: my-secret
              key: username
        - name: PASSWORD
          valueFrom:
            secretKeyRef:
              name: my-secret
              key: password
```

Furthermore, with OpenShift's web console, developers can create, modify, and view ConfigMaps and Secrets with ease, providing a user-friendly interface for managing these configurations without relying solely on CLI commands or YAML files. This accessibility simplifies operations, especially for teams unfamiliar with command-line interaction.

Strategically using ConfigMaps and Secrets streamlines the deployment process and enhances security by segregating sensitive information from application logic. This separation aligns well with modern DevOps practices that foster infrastructure as code (IaC) principles and microservices architectures, where modularity and flexibility are paramount.

When managing application configurations in an enterprise setting, it is critical to establish robust access controls and audit trails. OpenShift provides Role-Based Access Control (RBAC) to help govern who can view or modify ConfigMaps and Secrets, ensuring that only authorized users have the necessary permissions. Configuring these access policies prevents unauthorized access and modification, aligning with industry best practices for security and compliance.

Additionally, organizations often implement configuration change management policies that involve peer review and automated checks before changes are applied to production environments. These policies reduce deployment risks and improve system reliability. Automated CI/CD pipelines can incorporate stages that verify ConfigMaps and Secrets against predefined templates or standards, ensuring configurations meet the organization's security and performance thresholds.

The implications of misconfigurations can be severe, potentially leading to application failures or data breaches. Consequently, it is advisable to conduct periodic reviews and audits of configuration settings. Audits help identify unused or obsolete configurations that could be leveraged inadvertently, simplifying maintenance and enhancing security posture.

The versatility offered by OpenShift's ConfigMaps and Secrets fosters a seamless flow of configuration data across diverse development environments and aligns with the continuous delivery models practiced by modern development and operations teams. This flexibility supports rapid innovation without compromising on manageability or security, fostering an agile development environment that can dynamically adapt to evolving business needs.

5.2 Handling Application Updates and Rollbacks

The process of handling application updates and rollbacks in OpenShift is integral to maintaining an agile and resilient application infrastructure. The goal is to implement changes efficiently while minimizing downtime and mitigating the risk of issues that might arise during updates. OpenShift, built on Kubernetes, provides robust mechanisms for updating applications and supports automated rollback features if updates do not proceed as planned.

OpenShift embraces the concept of rolling updates, which is a powerful feature allowing the updating of applications with zero-downtime deployment capabilities. By gradually replacing instances of an older version of an application with a newer version, rolling updates ensure uninterrupted service availability to end-users.

To perform a rolling update on an OpenShift deployment, you can use the oc command-line interface (CLI), or manage updates through the OpenShift web console. Below is an example of how a rolling update might be configured and initiated using the CLI for a deployment defined by a DeploymentConfig:

```
# Trigger a rolling update by updating the image
oc set image deployment/my-deployment my-container=my-app-image:latest
```

This command updates the container image for my-container within the my-deployment deployment to the specified image version my-app-image:latest. OpenShift automatically handles the creation and termination of pods to achieve the desired state without disrupting service.

The behavior of rolling updates, such as maximum surge and maximum unavailable pods during the update, can be fine-tuned using strategy settings. These configurations allow operators to define the pace and constraints of the update process:

```
apiVersion: apps/v1
kind: Deployment
metadata:
  name: my-deployment
spec:
  strategy:
    type: RollingUpdate
    rollingUpdate:
      maxUnavailable: 1
      maxSurge: 1
```

In this YAML snippet, the RollingUpdate strategy is specified, allowing one additional pod to be provisioned (maxSurge: 1) while up to one pod can be temporarily unavailable (maxUnavailable: 1) during the update process. The balance between these two values helps manage resources and service availability, ensuring a smooth transition.

OpenShift supports further customization by allowing developers to define pre- and post-deployment hooks. These hooks execute custom logic before or after an application's deployment and help in verifying conditions or cleaning up resources. Below is a simple example of using lifecycle hooks in a deployment:

```
apiVersion: apps/v1
kind: Deployment
metadata:
  name: my-deployment
spec:
  template:
    spec:
      containers:
      - name: my-container
        image: my-app-image:latest
        lifecycle:
          preStop:
            exec:
              command: ["sh", "-c", "echo Pre-stop hook triggered"]
```

The preStop hook is an example of a lifecycle event that performs specific actions just before the container is terminated, in this case, logging a message.

Despite careful planning, deployment issues can arise, such as compatibility errors, misconfigurations, or unforeseen application behavior. OpenShift's rollback feature provides a straightforward way to revert to a previous application version when issues are detected.

To execute a rollback on a DeploymentConfig, the oc CLI command restores a previous replication controller, effectively rolling back the application to its earlier state:

```
# Perform a rollback to the previous revision
oc rollout undo deployment/my-deployment
```

This command resuscitates the previous iteration of the project, restoring the application to its pre-update state. Rollbacks in OpenShift can be performed multiple times, allowing incremental undo actions across several update cycles if necessary.

Another critical aspect in handling updates and rollbacks is maintaining detailed versioning and extensive logging. Ensuring that a detailed log of every update is maintained provides an audit trail for troubleshooting and analysis. OpenShift comes with built-in support for logging and version control, which can be further enhanced using external integrations.

Integration with external Continuous Integration/Continuous Deployment (CI/CD) pipelines ensures that updates are pre-tested in a staging environment, reducing the likelihood of production issues. Popular CI/CD systems such as Jenkins, GitLab CI, and others can integrate with OpenShift to automate tests, notifying development teams about potential issues before they impact end-users.

Automated testing can, for example, perform unit, integration, and end-to-end tests on a proposed application update. A typical pipeline would include stages that build the latest application version, run automated tests, and if successful, trigger a deployment in a testing environment before moving to production.

```
# Trigger a Jenkins pipeline job from CLI for OpenShift deployment
oc start-build my-pipeline
```

This integration enables rapid feedback loops, allowing teams to address issues swiftly. It helps maintain operational stability by ensuring that only thoroughly vetted updates are pushed to production.

For more sophisticated scenarios, incorporating canary deployments into the update strategy provides an extra level of assurance. A canary deployment rolls out changes to a small subset of users or instances before wide-scale deployment, effectively capturing performance metrics and user feedback.

The architecture of OpenShift makes it compatible with diverse frameworks and systems, enabling canary releases by deploying a secondary environment for the canary audience and progressively shifting users to observe its effect:

```
apiVersion: apps/v1
kind: Deployment
metadata:
  name: my-deployment
spec:
  replicas: 3
  selector:
    matchLabels:
      app: my-app
  template:
    metadata:
      labels:
        app: my-app
    spec:
      containers:
```

```
    - name: my-container
      image: my-app-image:v1.1 # New canary version
---
apiVersion: route.openshift.io/v1
kind: Route
metadata:
  name: my-route
spec:
  to:
    kind: Service
    name: my-app # Main service points to deployment with older image
  alternateBackends:
  - kind: Service
    name: my-app-canary
    weight: 10 # Diverts 10\% of traffic to the canary version
```

In this setup, a small percentage of incoming traffic is routed to the service running the new version (my-app-canary), allowing the team to observe behavior and performance, mitigating risks before scaling the update throughout the entire infrastructure.

Efficient monitoring and thorough post-release analysis for updates enhance success probabilities and minimize rollback scenarios. Metrics collection and real-time monitoring with tools like Prometheus and Grafana further ensure that every aspect of the deployment and its impact is visible to operations teams for immediate intervention if required.

Ensuring application reliability during updates requires not only robust processes and tooling but also a culture geared towards agile iterative improvements and a proactive identification of issues. By leveraging OpenShift's capabilities, alongside an organized workflow and processes, applications can remain both dynamic and reliable, maximizing availability and efficiency within the chaotic and demanding environments of modern software operations.

5.3 Monitoring Applications with OpenShift's Built-in Tools

Monitoring is an essential aspect of managing applications in OpenShift, providing insights into system performance, resource utilization, error tracking, and service health. OpenShift's built-in monitoring tools offer comprehensive capabilities for observability and diagnosis through metrics collection and visualization.

OpenShift integrates seamlessly with Prometheus for monitoring and alerting, providing a flexible and scalable approach to capturing real-time metrics from a variety of sources. By employing a push-based model, applications and nodes export metrics to Prometheus, which queries and stores them efficiently. The ecosystem supports a range of collection strategies that target containerized applications, nodes, and infrastructure metrics.

Setting up Prometheus in OpenShift is straightforward as it comes pre-integrated into the platform. The deployment includes Prometheus, Alertmanager, Grafana, and other essential components for a complete monitoring suite. Customizing and scaling these components can be managed by editing the Cluster Monitoring Configuration YAML. For example:

```
apiVersion: v1
kind: ConfigMap
metadata:
  name: cluster-monitoring-config
  namespace: openshift-monitoring
data:
  config.yaml: |
    prometheusK8s:
      retention: 15d
      volumeClaimTemplate:
        spec:
          resources:
            requests:
              storage: 100Gi
```

This configuration enhances Prometheus by extending data retention to 15 days and increasing storage allocations to 100GiB, accommodating environments with extensive metric data.

For visualization, Grafana is the standard tool used in the OpenShift monitoring stack. OpenShift dashboards provide instant visibility into cluster metrics, deployed applications, networking, compute workloads, and storage status. Custom Grafana dashboards can be created or imported to suit specific application needs, depicting complex scenarios or performance trends.

Grafana's data exploration functions allow developers to create queries over collected data and further support multiple data source integrations. By visualizing collected metrics, trends and potential issues are identified proactively, aiding in performance tuning, resource optimization, and incident response.

Integrating applications with Prometheus involves exposing metrics through an application endpoint, usually in a format compatible with Prometheus. Utilizing client libraries, applications can expose custom metrics alongside default system metrics, enhancing observability. Here's an example of a Python application using the Prometheus client library:

```python
from prometheus_client import start_http_server, Summary
import random
import time

# Create a metric to track time spent and requests made.
REQUEST_TIME = Summary('request_processing_seconds', 'Time spent processing
    request')

# Decorate function with metric.
@REQUEST_TIME.time()
def process_request(t):
    """A dummy function that takes some time."""
    time.sleep(t)

if __name__ == '__main__':
    # Start up the server to expose the metrics.
    start_http_server(8000)
    # Generate some requests.
    while True:
        process_request(random.random())
```

Here, the Python application exposes a Prometheus metric request_processing_seconds that tracks the time taken to process requests. By running a metrics HTTP server, this application makes metrics available to Prometheus for scraping and analysis.

The Alertmanager component plays a crucial role in the monitoring ecosystem, pairing with Prometheus to deliver alerts based on predefined rules. Alerts can be configured to trigger notifications through various channels, such as email, Slack, or PagerDuty, enabling rapid response to critical incidents.

To configure alerts, users define alert rules using Prometheus Query Language (PromQL). A sample alert rule might be:

```yaml
groups:
- name: example.rules
  rules:
  - alert: HighMemoryUsage
    expr: node_memory_MemAvailable_bytes / node_memory_MemTotal_bytes *
```

```
        100 < 10
  for: 5m
  labels:
     severity: warning
  annotations:
     summary: "Node Memory is almost full (< 10% left)"
```

This alert triggers when available memory drops below 10% for more than five minutes, warning administrators of potential memory exhaustion issues, and allowing preemptive scaling or resource reallocation.

OpenShift's native logging is another pivotal tool in monitoring applications. Integrated with the EFK (Elasticsearch, Fluentd, Kibana) stack, OpenShift centralizes logs from nodes, services, and applications, enhancing visibility and facilitating rich search and analysis capabilities.

The Fluentd component acts as a data collector, gathering logs from applications running on the cluster. Using configuration files, log routing rules and filters are crafted to customize the format, destination, and enrichment of logs before storing them.

```
<source>
  @type tail
  path /var/log/myapp.log
  pos_file /var/log/td-agent/myapp.pos
  tag myapp.log
  format /^(?<timestamp>[^\s]+) (?<severity>[^\s]+) (?<message>.*)$/
</source>

<match myapp.log>
  @type elasticsearch
  host elasticsearch
  port 9200
  logstash_format true
</match>
```

In this Fluentd configuration, an application log file is read, tagged, and sent to Elasticsearch. The output can be visualized and queried in Kibana, aiding operations teams to filter through massive volumes of logs efficiently using powerful queries.

The insights derived from comprehensive metrics and log analysis inform team decisions on infrastructure scaling, application performance optimization, and fault resolution, bolstering the reliability and robustness of services.

Given the pace and complexity of modern applications, it is essential to establish a culture of adaptive monitoring. Teams should continually revisit and calibrate their metrics and alert rules, adapting to changes in application architecture and load patterns. This iterative improvement process ensures visibility keeps pace with innovative developments, securing operational excellence.

Furthermore, monitoring in OpenShift is not just limited to these default tools. OpenShift's extensibility allows integration with additional third-party monitoring solutions such as DataDog, New Relic, or Splunk for environments with specific requirements or existing monitoring standards. These integrations provide a holistic view of applications, facilitating seamless observability across hybrid cloud environments.

The application of OpenShift's built-in monitoring tools is intrinsic to achieving a robust and responsive system capable of proactively managing modern, dynamic workloads. By embracing these tools and thoughtfully configuring them, organizations enhance operational awareness and responsiveness, underpinning the reliability and scalability of the services upon which business continuity, customer satisfaction, and operational success depend.

5.4 Implementing Logging with EFK Stack

In modern cloud-native environments like OpenShift, efficient logging systems are essential for tracking application behavior, system interactions, and diagnosing issues. The EFK Stack—consisting of Elasticsearch, Fluentd, and Kibana—is a widely adopted solution for centralized logging in Kubernetes-based environments like OpenShift. This stack facilitates the collection, aggregation, analysis, and visualization of log data in a streamlined manner.

Elasticsearch

Elasticsearch is a highly scalable open-source search and analytics engine used for storing, searching, and analyzing large volumes of data in real-time. It forms the backbone of the EFK stack, providing robust capabilities to store logs and make them easily accessible through fast search capabilities.

Elasticsearch organizes data into indices and offers full-text search capabilities. By automatically indexing logs as they are ingested, users can retrieve data using a sophisticated query language, enabling powerful searching and filtering based on a variety of criteria.

To effectively set up Elasticsearch in an OpenShift environment, one can utilize templates and operators provided by OpenShift. Operators simplify the deployment and management of Elasticsearch clusters by encapsulating the configurations in Custom Resource Definitions (CRDs).

Here is an example configuration for deploying Elasticsearch using OpenShift's Cluster Logging Operator:

```
apiVersion: "logging.openshift.io/v1"
kind: "Elasticsearch"
metadata:
  name: "elasticsearch"
  namespace: "openshift-logging"
spec:
  managementState: "Managed"
  nodeSpec:
    resources:
      requests:
        memory: 4Gi
        cpu: 2
  redundancyPolicy: "SingleRedundancy"
```

This configuration creates an Elasticsearch cluster managed by the Cluster Logging Operator, ensuring that the instance scales with resource demands. The replication and instance count can be adjusted to enhance redundancy and scalability.

Fluentd

Fluentd is a versatile log collector and processor that aggregates logs from various sources and routes them to different storage systems. In the EFK stack, Fluentd is responsible for collecting logs from OpenShift nodes and forwarding them to Elasticsearch for retention and searchability.

Fluentd tailors the format, filters the logs, and applies additional processing rules as required before delivering the logs to Elasticsearch. This processing capability empowers you to transform logs into JSON, enrich them with tags, or exclude unnecessary data.

Configuration of Fluentd involves specifying the source of the logs (e.g., container logs within the OpenShift cluster), defining filters, and setting the destination.

Here's a simple example of a Fluentd configuration file:

```
<source>
  @type tail
  path /var/log/containers/*.log
  pos_file /var/log/td-agent/tmp/gcp-log.pos
  tag kubernetes.*
  format json
  read_from_head true
</source>

<filter kubernetes.**>
  @type kubernetes_metadata
</filter>

<match kubernetes.**>
  @type elasticsearch
  host elasticsearch
  port 9200
  logstash_format true
  logstash_prefix myapp-logs
  reload_connections false
  data_type "json"
</match>
```

In this configuration, Fluentd tails all log files present in a directory, applies the Kubernetes metadata plugin to enrich logs with useful pod and namespace information, then routes them to Elasticsearch.

Kibana

Kibana provides a powerful web-based interface for visualizing the log data stored in Elasticsearch. With Kibana, users can create dashboards, generate visual reports, and interactively explore logs to extract actionable insights.

To make effective use of Kibana, it's important to define indices that categorize logs into relevant collections. Users can leverage a range of visualization types, such as line charts, bar charts, and heat maps, to represent the data, yielding a comprehensive view of system behavior and facilitating event correlation.

Setting up Kibana requires connecting to the Elasticsearch deployment to access the stored logs:

157

```
apiVersion: "logging.openshift.io/v1"
kind: "Kibana"
metadata:
  name: "kibana"
  namespace: "openshift-logging"
spec:
  managementState: "Managed"
```

This Kubernetes custom resource definition manages Kibana's lifecycle within the OpenShift cluster, ensuring consistent availability alongside the Elasticsearch cluster.

Implementing the EFK Stack in OpenShift

To deploy the entire EFK stack within OpenShift, consider using the OpenShift Logging Operator which simplifies setup. Below is a concise workflow detailing key steps:

- Install the OpenShift Logging Operator: Use the OperatorHub in OpenShift to locate and install the OpenShift Logging Operator, ensuring that you have the appropriate permissions.

- Deploy Elasticsearch: Create an instance of the Elasticsearch cluster tailored to your log data retention and processing needs.

- Configure and Deploy Fluentd: Set Fluentd to capture logs from all OpenShift sources, process, and route them to Elasticsearch.

- Deploy Kibana: Set up Kibana to connect to Elasticsearch. Customize your visualizations and dashboards to suit specific operational requirements.

Advanced Logging Use Cases

The EFK stack offers a versatile suite for addressing advanced logging challenges, improving operational outcomes. Here are some compelling use cases:

- Log Correlation: By centralizing logs from multiple sources across an OpenShift cluster, operators can correlate logs, identify patterns, and quickly diagnose issues without manually sifting through disparate log files.

- Security and Audit Compliance: EFK enables persistent log storage, facilitating compliance with regulations that mandate log retention for security audits. Kibana can automate reports to demonstrate adherence to these policies.

- Real-time Monitoring and Alerts: Transform Kibana visualizations into monitoring alerts. For instance, through integrations with third-party alerting tools, anomalous events within log data can trigger real-time alerts.

- Performance Analysis: Logs processed through Fluentd are frequently enriched with HTTP status codes, response times, and configuration settings, offering a powerful dataset for identifying performance bottlenecks and optimizing response efficiency.

Incorporating the EFK Stack into an OpenShift environment significantly enhances logging capabilities, providing the necessary transparency into application and infrastructure operations. By tailoring each component of the stack through strategic configuration and integration, organizations gain a comprehensive window into runtime behavior, improving their ability to respond to issues and maintain high-performance standards. These observability enhancements facilitate more informed decision-making, influence architecture optimization, and underscore the strategic value OpenShift brings to the domain of Enterprise DevOps.

5.5 Utilizing Metrics for Performance Monitoring

Performance monitoring through metrics is an essential practice for ensuring the reliability, efficiency, and optimization of applications deployed in OpenShift. By capturing quantitative data about the system's operation, developers and administrators can understand resource usage, detect anomalies, and make data-driven decisions to enhance application performance. OpenShift's metrics ecosystem, built upon the capabilities of Prometheus and advanced visualization tools like Grafana, provides a robust framework for this purpose.

- **Metrics in OpenShift**: OpenShift leverages Prometheus to collect and store metrics from the platform and application workloads. These metrics comprise extensive quantitative data representing CPU usage, memory consumption, network traffic, disk I/O, and application-specific KPIs (Key Performance Indicators). Prometheus, a time-series database, scrapes metrics at specified intervals, storing them for historical analysis and real-time monitoring.

- **Monitoring System Metrics**: System metrics are fundamental indicators of the health and performance of the underlying infrastructure. They reveal how each component—such as the nodes, pods, networking, and storage—is functioning and interacting. Analyzing these metrics helps administrators optimize resource allocation and resolve bottlenecks.

  To collect system metrics, OpenShift deploys Prometheus-node-exporter Daemons on each node, which exposes hardware and OS metrics. The metrics include:

  - **CPU Usage**: Captures utilization stats for each core, illustrating workload distribution and processor efficiency.
  - **Memory Metrics**: Provides insights into memory allocation, usage, buffers, cached, and free memory data. Detailed exploration of heap and non-heap usage guides optimization strategies.
  - **Disk and I/O Metrics**: Reflects usage patterns of disk storage, read/write speeds, and volume utilization, aiding capacity planning and identifying I/O bottlenecks.

Example Prometheus query for CPU utilization:

```
sum(rate(container_cpu_usage_seconds_total{namespace="default", pod_name=~"
    my-app.*"}[5m])) by (pod_name)
```

This query calculates the average CPU usage over the past 5 minutes across all pods matching the pattern "my-app.*" in the default namespace.

- **Monitoring Application Metrics**: Beyond infrastructure metrics, application-level metrics allow developers to gain fine-grained insights into application behavior and performance. OpenShift applications can leverage Prometheus client libraries to expose custom metrics, aligning with their specific performance and operational needs.

Implementing custom metrics entails:

– **Instrumenting Code**: Integrate Prometheus client libraries into application code to record metrics at critical points. These might include response times, request counts, error rates, or cache hits.

– **Exposing Metrics**: Host a /metrics endpoint within the application from which Prometheus scrapes the metrics.

Below is an example of a Java application using the Prometheus client library for metrics exposure:

```
import io.prometheus.client.Counter;
import io.prometheus.client.exporter.HTTPServer;
import io.prometheus.client.hotspot.DefaultExports;

public class MyApp {
    static final Counter requests = Counter.build().name("requests_total").help("Total
        requests.").register();

    public static void main(String[] args) throws Exception {
        DefaultExports.initialize();
        HTTPServer server = new HTTPServer(1234);

        // Simulate handling requests
        while (true) {
            // Process request logic
            requests.inc(); // Increment requests counter
            Thread.sleep(2000); // Simulate processing time
        }
    }
}
```

This Java snippet shows a web server that increments a requests_total counter every time a request is processed, making the metric available to Prometheus.

• **Analyzing Metrics with Grafana**: Grafana, integrated with OpenShift, serves as the visualization layer for Prometheus metrics. It empowers users to create complex dashboards that provide in-depth insights into the monitored metrics. Grafana supports powerful querying capabilities over time-series data, embodies flexibility with variable support, and enhances operational oversight with alerting functionalities.

Creating an insightful Grafana dashboard involves:

- **Defining Queries**: Use PromQL to define queries that target specific metrics of interest. Each panel in Grafana represents a query result visualized as a chart, gauge, or table.

- **Visualizing Data**: Choose appropriate visualization types (e.g., line charts, histograms) that contextually represent the queried metrics, revealing patterns, anomalies, and correlations.

- **Setting Alerts**: Establish threshold-based alerts that trigger when metric values exceed defined limits. These can be connected to notification systems, ensuring actionable responses during anomalies.

Example Grafana panel query to create a visualization of HTTP request throughput:

```
rate(http_requests_total{handler="/api"}[1m])
```

This query calculates the per-second rate of incoming HTTP requests to the /api endpoint over the last minute, providing instant insights into request loads and helping gauge server capacity.

- **Leveraging Metrics for Performance Optimization**: Performance optimization rooted in metrics-driven insights can significantly improve application reliability, user experience, and resource efficiency. Key optimization areas include:

  - **Capacity Planning**: Analyze historical trends in workload volume, resource utilization, and application performance metrics to make informed decisions about scaling, infrastructure investments, and provisioning.

  - **Bottleneck Identification**: Use metrics to pinpoint areas of congestion, excessive load, or resource contention. For instance, atypical CPU spike logs coupled with escalated request count could urge further investigation into application scalability.

162

- **Anomaly Detection**: Implement automatic anomaly detection algorithms that leverage metrics to recognize deviations from normal performance patterns, assisting in preemptive issue mitigation.

Prometheus offers recording rules or uses machine learning-driven anomaly detection libraries to streamline detecting and responding to abnormal patterns.

- **Best Practices for Metrics Management**: Implementing successful metrics-based monitoring involves adopting best practices that ensure accurate, actionable insights:

  - **Metric Selection**: Ensure metrics collected reflect core business operations and technical requirements. Avoid redundancy that can obfuscate analysis.

  - **Aggregation**: Use Prometheus's label sets to aggregate metrics data. This reduces the dataset's dimensionality while preserving meaningful insights.

  - **Monitoring Strategy**: Establish continuous monitoring strategies incorporating metrics, alerts, and logs. This end-to-end visibility fosters an informed operational posture capable of proactive incident management.

  - **Documentation**: Regularly document metrics definitions, alert conditions, and dashboards to maintain organizational knowledge, empower teams, and alleviate response times during incidents.

Through disciplined adoption of these practices, metrics monitoring in OpenShift becomes a powerful enabler, extending beyond simple observability. Organizations can proactively steer through intricate environments, scale efficiently, sidestep critical failures, and optimize user satisfaction, ultimately advancing towards operational excellence in the fast-evolving landscape of cloud-native applications.

5.6 Automating Health Checks and Alerts

In the dynamic and complex environment of OpenShift, automating health checks and alerts is paramount for maintaining application reliability and performance. Health checks ensure application components function correctly, while alerts provide timely notifications of status changes or anomalies. Together, they enable proactive management and rapid response to potential issues, enhancing system resilience.

Health Checks in OpenShift

Health checks in OpenShift, realized through liveness and readiness probes, determine the health and availability of applications running in containers. These checks are automated, lightweight processes that communicate with containers to assess their operational state, guiding remedial actions like restarts or rescheduling.

Liveness Probes

A liveness probe assesses whether a container is active or has encountered a state from which it cannot recover (such as a deadlock). If a liveness probe fails, OpenShift restarts the container, assuming the issue is transient and can be resolved by resetting the application state.

Three types of liveness probes are commonly used:

- **HTTP GET Probe**: Sends an HTTP GET request to the specified path on the container. The probe is considered successful if it receives a response within the designated range of HTTP success status codes.

```
apiVersion: v1
kind: Pod
metadata:
  name: example-pod
spec:
  containers:
  - name: example-container
    image: example-image
    livenessProbe:
      httpGet:
        path: /health
        port: 80
```

```
initialDelaySeconds: 5
periodSeconds: 10
```

- **TCP Socket Probe**: Attempts to open a TCP connection to the specified host and port. If the connection is successful, the container is deemed alive.

```
livenessProbe:
  tcpSocket:
    port: 8080
  initialDelaySeconds: 15
  periodSeconds: 20
```

- **Exec Probe**: Executes a specified command inside the container. If the command returns a zero exit code, the container is considered healthy.

```
livenessProbe:
  exec:
    command:
    - cat
    - /tmp/healthy
  initialDelaySeconds: 20
  periodSeconds: 30
```

Readiness Probes

A readiness probe determines if the container is prepared to start accepting traffic. Unlike liveness probes, a failure in a readiness probe does not result in a container restart. Instead, OpenShift stops sending traffic to the pod, which remains within the pool of available resources.

The configurations for readiness probes are analogous to liveness probes. They play a crucial role in maintaining service quality during startup or maintenance, ensuring only healthy and fully initialized components receive traffic:

```
readinessProbe:
  httpGet:
    path: /ready
    port: 80
  initialDelaySeconds: 5
  periodSeconds: 10
```

Integrating Health Checks

Well-designed health checks are pivotal to maintaining high availability and service reliability. However, care must be taken to configure appropriate parameters—such as delay intervals, timeout durations, and failure thresholds—to avoid unnecessary container instability.

To achieve intelligent and resilient deployment strategies, enable health checks that:

- Reflect actual application health by checking critical components and dependencies.

- Are lightweight and non-blocking to prevent additional system load.

- Increase probe granularity and frequency after observed deviations to quickly identify problematic conditions.

Alerting in OpenShift

Automated alerts are central to operational intelligence, allowing teams to identify, diagnose, and rectify issues promptly. Alerts are typically generated based on predefined thresholds, deviations in metrics, or failure of health checks.

Prometheus and Alertmanager

Using Prometheus in OpenShift, alerting rules can be defined with PromQL expressions that capture abnormal states or performance patterns. Alertmanager manages these alerts, handling deduplication, grouping, and routing to designated stakeholders through defined notification channels.

Example alerting rule for memory utilization:

```
groups:
- name: memory-alert.rules
  rules:
  - alert: HighMemoryUsage
    expr: node_memory_MemAvailable_bytes / node_memory_MemTotal_bytes <
        0.1
    for: 1m
    labels:
      severity: critical
    annotations:
      summary: "High Memory Usage Detected!"
      description: "Node's available memory has dropped below 10% for over a minute."
```

Configuring Alertmanager

Alertmanager's configuration determines how and where alerts are sent. This includes routing alerts, configuring silence periods, and defining notification endpoints (e.g., email, Slack, or PagerDuty):

```
route:
  receiver: 'team-x-notifications'
  group_wait: 30s
  group_interval: 5m
  repeat_interval: 3h
receivers:
  - name: 'team-x-notifications'
    email_configs:
    - to: 'team-x@example.com'
      from: 'alertmanager@example.com'
      smarthost: 'smtp.example.com:587'
      auth_username: 'alertmanager'
      auth_identity: 'alertmanager@example.com'
      auth_password: 'password'
```

By configuring alerts mindfully, operations teams receive relevant and actionable information, minimizing noise and focusing attention on significant events.

Enhancing Alert Effectiveness

For alerts to be effective, they must be aligned with the operational impact and informed by historical data on system behavior. Techniques to enhance alerting reliability include:

- **Contextual Alerts**: Provide contextual information in alert messages to allow quick triage and resolution. Integrations with issue-tracking tools can automatically create tickets with pertinent incident data.

- **Multi-channel Notifications**: Ensure alerts reach the right people quickly through diverse channels. Use role-specific routing, such as different notifications for developers, on-call engineers, and management.

- **Alert Fatigue Management**: Implement threshold-based and rate-limited alerts to minimize excessive or redundant notifications.

- **Adaptive Alerting**: Incorporate machine learning techniques to dynamically adjust alerting thresholds based on observed patterns and anomalies, reducing false positives and improving sensitivity.

Orchestrating Health Checks and Alerts

In OpenShift, orchestrating health checks and alerts requires a thorough understanding of the application architecture and the dependencies involved. Adopting advanced practices further refines operational outcomes:

- **Test Health Checks in Development**: Validate liveness and readiness probes in development and testing environments, ensuring that configured conditions accurately represent application health without triggering unwarranted proactivity in production.

- **Align Alerting with SLOs**: Synchronize alerting rules with Service Level Objectives (SLOs) and business criticality. This alignment guarantees that essential metrics and performance indicators directly reflect service commitments and desired outcomes.

- **Continuous Improvement**: Initiate regular reviews of health checks and alerting configurations based on operational feedback, post-mortem analyses, and evolving infrastructure needs. This iterative enhancement enables systems to adapt as complexity grows.

By leveraging automated health checks and alerts, organizations maintain robust control over application operations and lifecycle management within OpenShift. This autonomy equips teams to deliver heightened service quality, sustain operational integrity, and drive technological advancement in today's competitive and fast-paced environment.

Chapter 6

Scaling Applications with OpenShift

This chapter explores the strategies and tools available for scaling applications in OpenShift, emphasizing both manual and automated approaches. By implementing Horizontal Pod Autoscaler, users can dynamically scale applications based on predefined metrics such as CPU and memory usage. The chapter delves into best practices for scaling stateful applications, ensuring data integrity and performance are preserved during scaling operations. It also covers load balancing and traffic management techniques to efficiently distribute traffic across application instances. Additionally, troubleshooting techniques address common scaling issues, equipping users with skills to maintain optimal application performance and resource utilization.

6.1 Fundamentals of Scaling in Open-Shift

In the landscape of modern software development, scaling is a cornerstone of maintaining efficient and reliable application performance. OpenShift, a robust container orchestration platform powered by Kubernetes, facilitates seamless scaling for applications through two primary methodologies: horizontal scaling and vertical scaling. Understanding these concepts is critical in leveraging OpenShift to its full potential. This section explores these fundamental scaling techniques within OpenShift, providing insights into their mechanisms, benefits, potential challenges, and implementation nuances.

Horizontal scaling in OpenShift involves the adjustment of the number of application instances, known as pods, running within a cluster. This approach is often employed when service demand fluctuates, requiring the system to handle varying workloads effectively. Horizontal scaling can be manual or automatic, with OpenShift providing advanced features such as the Horizontal Pod Autoscaler (HPA) for automated scaling based on observable metrics.

To scale an application horizontally, consider a scenario where an application currently runs three replicas, each encapsulated within its pod. Increasing the replica count to five can be achieved using the following OpenShift Command Line Interface (CLI) command wrapped in the lstlisting environment for clarity:

```
oc scale --replicas=5 deployment/my-app
```

In this command, my-app refers to the application deployment name, and the number of replicas specifies the desired state. The OpenShift scheduler identifies available nodes in the cluster and distributes the new instances accordingly, ensuring optimal resource utilization and load balancing.

Furthermore, OpenShift's Horizontal Pod Autoscaler (HPA) component enables automatic horizontal scaling based on specified resource consumption metrics, typically CPU usage. To enable the HPA for an application, the following YAML configuration can be applied:

```
apiVersion: autoscaling/v1
```

```
kind: HorizontalPodAutoscaler
metadata:
  name: my-app-hpa
spec:
  scaleTargetRef:
    apiVersion: apps/v1
    kind: Deployment
    name: my-app
  minReplicas: 2
  maxReplicas: 10
  targetCPUUtilizationPercentage: 70
```

This configuration specifies a minimum and maximum number of replicas while targeting a specific CPU utilization percentage. The HPA controller continually monitors the specified resource metrics and automatically scales the number of pods as needed, constrained by the defined limits.

Vertical scaling, on the other hand, deals with changing the resource allocation for existing pods. This strategy is typically employed when performance bottlenecks are identified in resource-starved pods. Vertical scaling involves adjusting the CPU and memory limits for workloads.

OpenShift allows setting resource requests and limits within the pod definition. Consider the following example configuration that defines both the requested and maximum resources for each pod instance:

```
apiVersion: apps/v1
kind: Deployment
metadata:
  name: my-app
spec:
  template:
    spec:
      containers:
      - name: my-app-container
        image: my-app-image:v1
        resources:
          requests:
            memory: "512Mi"
            cpu: "500m"
          limits:
            memory: "1024Mi"
            cpu: "1"
```

The requests field indicates the guaranteed resources available to the pod, while the limits field sets the upper threshold. By reconfiguring these parameters based on application profiling and monitoring data,

OpenShift users can optimize the performance of their applications.

Understanding the trade-offs between horizontal and vertical scaling is essential for making informed decisions in OpenShift. Horizontal scaling is advantageous for applications that can operate across multiple instances without state sharing, such as stateless microservices. This method allows applications to handle massive traffic bursts efficiently. However, it necessitates load balancing mechanisms to distribute traffic among instances evenly.

Vertical scaling is more suited for monolithic applications or those with shared state where scaling horizontally might require complex state management or synchronization. The downside is the limited scalability bounded by the maximum resource capacity of a single node and potential cost implications of procuring resource-dense nodes.

OpenShift's robust API and CLI not only facilitate the scaling processes but also provide feedback mechanisms for troubleshooting and optimization. The output from scaling commands can be observed in a

```
deployment.apps/my-app scaled
```

Effective scaling in OpenShift also demands a robust understanding of the underlying architecture, including the configuration of nodes, the resource quota system, and monitoring tools available. OpenShift integrates seamlessly with Prometheus and Grafana, enabling detailed monitoring and visualization of application performance metrics which are crucial when developing scaling strategies.

Integrating scaling strategies with OpenShift's security and networking features further enhances application resilience. Network policies must be dynamically adjusted to ensure that new or removed instances comply with established security practices. Similarly, deploying network solutions such as OpenShift Service Mesh can abstract complexity and provide detailed traffic insights and controls.

Incorporating these scaling techniques into the continuous deployment (CD) pipeline maximizes OpenShift's automation capabilities. Advanced deployment strategies such as Blue-Green and Canary can be augmented with scaling strategies to ensure the new application version is not only functional but also optimized for scalability.

Scaling in OpenShift involves a complex interplay of strategies aimed at maintaining performance and resource efficiency. By leveraging the detailed configurations provided by both horizontal and vertical scaling mechanisms facilitated by OpenShift, developers and operators can ensure their applications remain resilient in the face of evolving user demands and technological advancements. Understanding these foundational principles of scaling is pivotal to unlocking the full potential of OpenShift's capabilities in production environments.

6.2   Manual Scaling of Applications

In OpenShift, scaling an application manually is a fundamental practice that enables system administrators to adjust resource allocations according to specific needs and application requirements. Manual scaling is a critical process, especially in scenarios where dynamic scaling algorithms may not be suitable due to unique application characteristics or specific operational requirements. It provides granular control over resource distribution, allowing operators to directly influence performance and efficiency by tailoring application deployment to predicted loads or strategic resource management goals.

This section delves into the methodologies for manual scaling within OpenShift, leveraging both the OpenShift Web Console and the Command Line Interface (CLI). Understanding manual scaling is vital, as it not only offers immediate control over application resources but also provides a foundational understanding that enhances the application of automated scaling techniques.

Manual scaling is commonly executed by adjusting the number of replicas within a deployment, thereby distributing application workloads across a series of pods. This can be accomplished using the OpenShift CLI, which provides a straightforward interface for scaling operations.

Consider the scenario where a deployment requires an increase in the number of running pods from three to six. The operation can be executed using the following command:

```
oc scale --replicas=6 deployment/my-application
```

In this command, the flag –replicas specifies the desired number of application instances, and my-application refers to the name of the deployment that requires scaling. Once executed, OpenShift's control plane interacts with the Kubernetes API to adjust the number of pods to meet the specified count, subject to resource availability and configuration constraints within the cluster.

The oc command-line tool is versatile, allowing administrators to monitor the status of scaling operations and obtain real-time insights into pod deployment. To verify the current state of the deployment and to confirm the successful scaling operation, use the following command:

```
oc get deployment my-application
```

The output from this command will detail the number of deployed replicas, their current status, and available resources, facilitating instant feedback and confirmation of the scaling process.

NAME	READY	UP-TO-DATE	AVAILABLE	AGE
my-application	6	6	6	23m

While the CLI serves as a powerful tool for operators familiar with text-based interfaces, the OpenShift Web Console offers an alternative, user-friendly platform for manually scaling applications. Through the console, operators can manage scaling operations via intuitive graphical interfaces, which are invaluable in environments where visual confirmation and ease of access are prioritized.

To scale an application using the Web Console, navigate to the Workloads section, select Deployments, and choose the deployment in question. Within the deployment's overview page, operators can adjust the replica count through an editable field or a slider component. After confirming the desired number of replicas, the Web Console quickly implements the changes within the OpenShift cluster infrastructure.

Understanding the circumstances and implications of manual scaling is essential. Manual scaling decisions can be driven by predictable traffic patterns, system maintenance activities, or infrastructural changes. For instance, anticipating a considerable increase in user traffic due to a scheduled marketing event or product launch may necessitate manually increasing the application replicas proactively to handle anticipated demand.

However, manual scaling demands a comprehensive understanding of the application's architecture, particularly concerning resource consumption patterns and overall system performance. Lack of adequate foresight can result in resource exhaustion or underutilization, leading to unanticipated operational challenges, from performance degradation to increased costs.

Resource management emerges as a critical consideration in manual scaling. Every instance of a scaled application consumes a certain amount of CPU and memory, which cumulatively impacts the cluster's overall resource pool. Ensuring the cluster's capacity can absorb these changes without sacrificing performance for other services is crucial. OpenShift operators often set quotas and limits to ensure resource availability across various projects and prevent any single application from monopolizing resources.

For instance, in a scenario where multiple applications coexist within a cluster, a well-defined resource quota can safeguard against over-provisioning scenarios. The following configuration, applied at the project level, exemplifies how resource management can be enforced:

```
apiVersion: v1
kind: ResourceQuota
metadata:
  name: compute-resources
spec:
  hard:
    requests.cpu: "2"
    requests.memory: 4Gi
    limits.cpu: "4"
    limits.memory: 8Gi
```

In this YAML snippet, compute-resources defines a resource quota that limits the total amount of CPU and memory resources available to applications within a specific project. By adhering to these quotas, manual scaling operations can be conducted without impinging on the cluster's stability and performance benchmarks.

Moreover, manual scaling also plays a pivotal role in development and testing environments. Here, developers may manually scale applications to test performance and behavior under various loads or to simulate production-grade traffic conditions. This approach enables developers to fine-tune application performance and make informed decisions based on empirical data collected from controlled environments.

Scaling operations should be corroborated with rigorous monitoring and logging to ensure the system behaves as expected under different load conditions. OpenShift integrates with monitoring tools such as

Prometheus and Grafana, allowing teams to visualize resource usage patterns and proactively identify scaling opportunities or anomalies.

By implementing dashboards that reflect key performance indicators (KPIs), such as request latencies, error rates, and resource utilization metrics, teams have a comprehensive visual understanding that facilitates intelligent manual scaling decisions.

Ultimately, manual scaling within OpenShift offers a level of autonomy and precision critical to many operational strategies. While automation holds transformative potential in scalability practices, manual scaling remains integral, particularly when dealing with unique operational requirements or environments where predictable scaling patterns endure. Balancing the strategic deployment of manual interventions with the benefits of automated scaling paves the path toward operational excellence in managing applications within OpenShift's ecosystem.

6.3   Implementing Auto-Scaling Policies

Auto-scaling in OpenShift provides the flexibility and efficiency required to dynamically allocate resources, ensuring applications can handle varying loads efficiently. The automation of scaling activities minimizes manual intervention and optimizes resource usage, which is particularly beneficial in production environments with unpredictable traffic patterns. Implementing auto-scaling policies effectively requires an understanding of the underlying mechanisms, thoughtful configuration, and continuous monitoring to ensure they operate as intended.

Central to auto-scaling in OpenShift is the Horizontal Pod Autoscaler (HPA), an integral Kubernetes component that automatically adjusts the number of pod replicas in a deployment based on observed resource metrics, such as CPU utilization or custom metrics. This section outlines the process of implementing auto-scaling policies using HPA, exploring the steps, considerations, and best practices necessary for effective deployment.

Auto-scaling policies begin with defining the criteria upon which the scaling decisions are made. The most common metric used is CPU utilization; however, OpenShift's integration with Kubernetes' extensible framework allows for the incorporation of additional metrics such as memory usage, network I/O, or any custom application-specific metric available via an API.

A typical setup for CPU-based auto-scaling can be initiated with the following YAML configuration file, which defines an HPA policy:

```yaml
apiVersion: autoscaling/v1
kind: HorizontalPodAutoscaler
metadata:
  name: sample-app-hpa
spec:
  scaleTargetRef:
    apiVersion: apps/v1
    kind: Deployment
    name: sample-app
  minReplicas: 2
  maxReplicas: 10
  targetCPUUtilizationPercentage: 70
```

This configuration specifies that the deployment named sample-app should maintain CPU utilization at approximately 70%. Should the resource monitoring detect utilization above or below this threshold, the number of replicas adjusts between the specified minimum of 2 and maximum of 10 to compensate accordingly.

Understanding each parameter is key to leveraging HPA effectively. The scaleTargetRef field indicates the target deployment and its resource version, while minReplicas and maxReplicas set boundaries to ensure that scaling remains within reasonable limits. This mitigates runaway scaling scenarios that could deplete resources or incur additional costs.

OpenShift allows for more sophisticated configurations, involving additional or alternate metrics. Custom metrics can be introduced to better suit application-specific needs. This might include scaling based not solely on CPU but also a combination of factors like memory usage or application-level metrics such as request counts per second.

To enable custom metrics, the Kubernetes Metric Server must be configured correctly, or an equivalent Prometheus Adapter must be deployed. The configuration could then be modified to include these new metrics, using something akin to the following example:

```yaml
apiVersion: autoscaling/v2beta2
kind: HorizontalPodAutoscaler
```

```
metadata:
  name: advanced-hpa
spec:
  scaleTargetRef:
    apiVersion: apps/v1
    kind: Deployment
    name: advanced-app
  minReplicas: 1
  maxReplicas: 15
  metrics:
  - type: Resource
    resource:
      name: cpu
      target:
        type: Utilization
        averageUtilization: 65
  - type: Resource
    resource:
      name: memory
      target:
        type: Utilization
        averageUtilization: 75
  - type: Pods
    pods:
      metric:
        name: requests-per-second
      target:
        type: AverageValue
        averageValue: 100
```

The metrics list describes multiple scaling inputs, targeting CPU and memory utilization, alongside a custom metric requests-per-second, requiring appropriate adapters and metrics providers.

Effectively implementing auto-scaling policies also hinges on understanding the application's scaling behavior. Certain applications, especially stateful or monolithic services, may not scale linearly. Therefore, thorough load-testing is advisable to define suitable minimum and maximum thresholds and to anticipate latency or performance changes that occur as the application scales.

Auto-scaling in OpenShift also presents challenges regarding synchronization and consistent operation, particularly under rapid changes in load. Concerns such as "thrashing," where the system oscillates too frequently between scale levels due to minor fluctuation in metrics, can degrade performance. To mitigate such issues, OpenShift allows for parameter tuning, such as cooldown periods, that enforce a delay between scaling operations, permitting the system time to stabilize.

The following YAML adjustment exemplifies incorporation of addi-

178

tional parameters to control the responsiveness of scaling:

```
behavior:
  scaleUp:
    stabilizationWindowSeconds: 300
    selectPolicy: Max
    policies:
      - type: Pods
        value: 4
        periodSeconds: 60
  scaleDown:
    stabilizationWindowSeconds: 300
    selectPolicy: Min
    policies:
      - type: Pods
        value: 2
        periodSeconds: 60
```

Here, stabilizationWindowSeconds defines a time frame during which scaling remains stable, smoothing out transient spikes in metric readings. The policies parameters manage the allowance for growth or shrink across defined periods to further refine scaling responses.

Crucial to maintaining efficient auto-scaling policies is continuous performance monitoring and analysis. OpenShift's robust ecosystem integrates with observability tools such as Prometheus and Grafana for deep insights into metric behavior and resource consumption patterns. By creating detailed dashboards and alerting mechanisms, operators can ensure auto-scaling behavior aligns with service level agreements (SLAs) and performance expectations.

Moreover, experimentation with configurations in non-production, test-heavy environments is advised. Such environments enable the validation of scaling logic and the identification of optimal parameters without risking end-user experience. Understanding application idiosyncrasies, such as initialization times and dependency checks, can help refine auto-scaling configurations for seamless transitions.

Ultimately, the successful implementation of auto-scaling policies in OpenShift involves thoughtful integration of metric-based decision making with strategic operational planning. By embracing intelligent configuration, vigilant monitoring, and thorough understanding of application dynamics, auto-scaling becomes an invaluable tool in the pursuit of operational excellence, cost efficiency, and sustained reliability in dynamic application environments.

6.4 Configuring OpenShift Horizontal Pod Autoscaler

The Horizontal Pod Autoscaler (HPA) in OpenShift is a sophisticated mechanism designed to automatically adjust the number of pods in a deployment or replication controller based on real-time metrics. By continuously monitoring application workloads, the HPA ensures that resource allocation within a Kubernetes cluster adapts dynamically to changes in demand. Configuring this tool effectively requires a deep understanding of its components, operational context, and the underlying metrics that drive scaling decisions. In this section, we will explore the intricacies involved in setting up the HPA, providing comprehensive insights and examples for leveraging its capabilities in OpenShift environments.

The HPA's function is articulated through its interaction with the Kubernetes metrics server, which continuously collects data about resource utilization, such as CPU and memory metrics, across the cluster. This server acts as the cornerstone for the HPA, providing the real-time data which informs scaling decisions.

To effectively configure the HPA, begin with the prerequisites: ensure that the metrics server is installed and operational. Without this, the HPA will lack the necessary data to function. Initial steps include deploying the metrics server and validating its operation by confirming resource data collection through commands like:

```
oc get --raw "/apis/metrics.k8s.io/v1beta1/nodes"
oc get --raw "/apis/metrics.k8s.io/v1beta1/pods"
```

These commands should return JSON listings of node and pod resource usage metrics, confirming the metrics server's functionality. Once verified, configuration of the HPA typically begins with a YAML manifest specifying the desired behaviors for the deployment.

Consider the following fundamental HPA configuration using CPU metrics:

```
apiVersion: autoscaling/v1
kind: HorizontalPodAutoscaler
metadata:
  name: basic-cpu-hpa
spec:
```

```
scaleTargetRef:
  apiVersion: apps/v1
  kind: Deployment
  name: cpu-intensive-app
minReplicas: 2
maxReplicas: 10
targetCPUUtilizationPercentage: 50
```

This straightforward configuration sets the cpu-intensive-app deployment to scale between 2 and 10 replicas, maintaining an average target CPU utilization of 50%. The HPA controller, using data from the metrics server, continuously evaluates the current CPU utilization and adjusts the number of pod replicas accordingly.

Beyond basic CPU utilization policies, OpenShift allows more refined HPA configurations, utilizing multiple metrics through its v2beta2 API version. This enables scaling logic based on a combination of CPU, memory, and even custom application-level metrics. For instance:

```
apiVersion: autoscaling/v2beta2
kind: HorizontalPodAutoscaler
metadata:
  name: comprehensive-hpa
spec:
  scaleTargetRef:
    apiVersion: apps/v1
    kind: Deployment
    name: composite-app
  minReplicas: 3
  maxReplicas: 15
  metrics:
  - type: Resource
    resource:
      name: cpu
      target:
        type: Utilization
        averageUtilization: 65
  - type: Resource
    resource:
      name: memory
      target:
        type: Utilization
        averageUtilization: 75
  - type: Pods
    pods:
      metric:
        name: transactions-per-second
      target:
        type: AverageValue
        averageValue: 200
```

This configuration introduces complexity by measuring CPU and memory utilization along with a custom metric, transactions-per-second. Such configurations necessitate a defined adapter for acquiring custom metrics, relying on services like the Prometheus Adapter, which extends the metrics server's capabilities.

Establishing a reliable metrics collection and retrieval mechanism for custom metrics is critical. Ensure that Prometheus is deployed within the cluster and configured properly to scrape necessary application metrics. Prometheus accomplishes this through a series of scrape configurations within its configuration file, directing it to collect data from a specified set of endpoints.

With Prometheus operational, leverage the Prometheus Adapter to make these metrics available to Kubernetes, effectively allowing them to drive the HPA's decisions:

```
rules:
- seriesQuery: 'http_requests_total{namespace!="",pod!=""}'
  seriesFilters: []
  resources:
    overrides:
      namespace: {resource: "namespace"}
      pod: {resource: "pod"}
  name:
    matches: "^(.*)_total"
    as: "${1}"
  metricsQuery: sum(rate(<<.Series>>[5m])) by (<<.GroupBy>>)
```

This Prometheus Adapter configuration snippet establishes a query rule for an application-level metric, aggregating HTTP request totals over a five-minute interval into a metric Kubernetes can consume.

While setting up the HPA, it is also necessary to consider operational constraints such as stabilization-window, tolerances, and policies, which can mitigate against frequent scaling actions in response to transient workload spikes. An example adjustment may look as follows:

```
behavior:
  scaleUp:
    stabilizationWindowSeconds: 300
    selectPolicy: Max
    policies:
      - type: Percent
        value: 100
        periodSeconds: 15
  scaleDown:
    stabilizationWindowSeconds: 300
    selectPolicy: Min
    policies:
```

```
        - type: Percent
          value: 50
          periodSeconds: 15
```

These configurable parameters allow for tailored scaling behavior by defining limits on replica changes, providing stability, and smoothing out metric oscillations.

An essential aspect of implementing HPA is validation through testing. Conduct load tests to evaluate the autoscaling behavior under various scenarios, measuring its responsiveness and impact on performance. Tools like Apache JMeter or Locust can simulate concurrent load and traffic patterns, offering insight into whether the current configuration meets the desired outcome.

Additionally, operators must remain cognizant of resource quotas and limits set within the cluster, as these affect the scaling potential of deployments. Properly aligned resource requests and limits ensure that autoscaled applications do not inadvertently disrupt the balance within the shared resources of the cluster.

Monitoring tools such as Grafana, integrated with Prometheus, offer visualization and alerts that enhance the oversight of HPA activities. Configure dashboards to present real-time metrics pertinent to scaling, such as replica count trends, utilization rates, and application-specific performance indicators.

Ultimately, configuring the Horizontal Pod Autoscaler in OpenShift involves a multifaceted approach, incorporating proficient metric analysis, application behavior comprehension, and judicious policy settings. By finely tuning the nuances of the HPA to align with application needs and environmental realities, administrators and developers can ensure scalable, robust applications that thrive within dynamic cloud environments.

6.5 Best Practices for Scaling Stateful Applications

Scaling stateful applications in OpenShift presents unique challenges and considerations compared to their stateless counterparts. Unlike

stateless applications, which can typically scale horizontally with rela-
tive ease due to their lack of reliance on persisted data or session adherence, stateful applications inherently require diligent management
of data consistency, storage, and network configurations. This section
explores best practices for scaling stateful applications within Open-
Shift, examining the necessary configurations, strategies, and potential
pitfalls to avoid in order to maintain data integrity, performance, and
high availability.

Stateful applications retain session information or data across different interactions, making consistency and reliability paramount during
scaling operations. OpenShift provides a mechanism known as StatefulSets, fundamental in achieving such scaling. StatefulSets manage
the deployment and scaling of a set of pods while guaranteeing the or-
dering and uniqueness necessary for stateful application components.

The following is a typical configuration for a StatefulSet, illustrating
the fundamental structure:

```
apiVersion: apps/v1
kind: StatefulSet
metadata:
  name: example-statefulset
spec:
  serviceName: "statefulset-service"
  replicas: 3
  selector:
    matchLabels:
      app: example
  template:
    metadata:
      labels:
        app: example
    spec:
      containers:
      - name: app-container
        image: example-image:v1
        ports:
        - containerPort: 80
        volumeMounts:
        - name: data-volume
          mountPath: /data
  volumeClaimTemplates:
  - metadata:
      name: data-volume
    spec:
      accessModes: [ "ReadWriteOnce" ]
      resources:
        requests:
          storage: 1Gi
```

A key aspect of the StatefulSet is the volumeClaimTemplates section, which allows each pod (or all instances in the StatefulSet) to have its own PersistentVolumeClaim (PVC), ensuring data is not shared and stays consistent across many instances. This template automatically provisions persistent storage for each pod according to the specified requirements, crucial for maintaining state across replicas.

An essential consideration for scaling stateful applications involves the choice and management of storage. OpenShift supports several types of persistent storage solutions, such as network-attached storage (NAS), block storage, and cloud-native persistent storage from providers like AWS, Google Cloud, and Azure. Selecting the appropriate storage solution depends on application requirements such as IOPS (Input/Output Operations Per Second), latency, and data management needs.

To prevent performance degradation, ensure the persistent storage employed supports the necessary performance metrics tailored to the application's needs. Using slow disk storage on a database application, for instance, could create bottlenecks that negate scaling benefits.

Network configuration is another critical element when scaling stateful applications. StatefulSets in OpenShift are often complemented with Headless Services, which enable direct access to individual pods by providing a stable network identity. This capability is essential for applications that require consistent naming and IP address management, such as databases and message brokers.

For example, to configure a Headless Service aligned with the StatefulSet, use a configuration like:

```
apiVersion: v1
kind: Service
metadata:
  name: statefulset-service
spec:
  ports:
  - port: 80
    name: http
  clusterIP: None
  selector:
    app: example
```

With clusterIP: None, this Headless Service facilitates direct connectivity to each StatefulSet pod instance, supporting seamless discovery and communication indispensable for distributed stateful applications.

Beyond infrastructure setup, scaling stateful applications demands consideration of application consistency models, such as strong, eventual, or causal consistency. Understanding these models guides decisions regarding data replication strategies, consensus algorithms (e.g., for leader election), and transaction management.

For instance, implementing a sharded database architecture might demand robust orchestration for rebalancing shards without informational inconsistencies. Automated shard management tools or customized scripts could be employed to automate this orchestration within OpenShift, optimized through control loops that continuously reconcile desired state against the actual state.

Monitoring becomes an essential tool for scaling operations. Utilize solutions like Prometheus and Grafana alongside OpenShift's integrated observability features to monitor key metrics and log data, pinpoint performance bottlenecks, and predict capacity limits. Establishing thresholds and custom alerts can preemptively signal issues, enabling proactive responses to potential disruptions.

```
# Prometheus alert rule example
- alert: HighMemoryUsage
  expr: sum(container_memory_working_set_bytes) by (pod) / sum(
      machine_memory_bytes) > 0.8
  for: 5m
  labels:
    severity: warning
  annotations:
    summary: "High memory usage detected"
    description: "Pod {{ $labels.pod }} is using more than 80\% of node memory."
```

This YAML snippet defines a Prometheus alert rule monitoring memory usage, providing an alert if a pod's consumption exceeds 80% of available node memory, facilitating immediate resolution steps.

Finally, testing plays a pivotal role in the readiness and robustness of scale-out architectures. Conduct comprehensive tests to evaluate performance under increased load, ensuring that replication logic, data consistency measures, and network configurations perform optimally and remain reliable. Employ test-driven development models, automated testing frameworks, and simulation tools to validate the application's ability to scale under increased load.

Maintaining a mature DevOps culture also aids in scaling stateful applications effectively. Practices such as continuous integration (CI), continuous delivery (CD), and infrastructure as code (IaC) ensure that changes and configurations are carefully managed, reviewed, and versioned, reducing risks during scaling events.

Scaling stateful applications in OpenShift requires a meticulous approach, addressing persistence management, network configuration, application logic, and observability. By embracing these best practices, administrators and developers can ensure that their applications maintain reliability, consistency, and availability, even as they scale to meet demanding operational goals. Through careful planning and diligent management, stateful applications can scale effectively, providing resilience and high performance within the containerized landscape of OpenShift.

6.6 Load Balancing and Traffic Management

Load balancing and traffic management are integral to the successful deployment and operation of applications within OpenShift. By efficiently distributing network traffic and managing connections, these processes ensure applications perform optimally, providing resilience and high availability. Proper configuration and management of load balancing within OpenShift can alleviate bottlenecks and reduce latency, thereby enhancing the end-user experience. This section explores various strategies and configurations available in OpenShift for load balancing and traffic management, providing insights and examples for implementing robust solutions.

OpenShift utilizes Kubernetes Services to manage load balancing. Within Kubernetes, a Service defines a logical set of pods and a policy to access them. By abstracting the underlying pods, it provides a stable endpoint, allowing external consumers and other services to reliably interact with the application instances.

The following YAML configuration establishes a basic Service for a deployment:

```
apiVersion: v1
kind: Service
metadata:
  name: example-service
spec:
  selector:
    app: example
  ports:
  - protocol: TCP
    port: 80
    targetPort: 8080
  type: ClusterIP
```

In this setup, the Service named example-service routes traffic to the set of pod replicas labeled with app: example. ClusterIP, the default type, is an internal load balancer visible to the cluster, handling internal service requests.

For accessing services outside the cluster, OpenShift deploys the Load-Balancer and NodePort service types. LoadBalancer services cooperate with external load balancers, automatically provisioning them for handling ingress traffic. Conversely, NodePort services expose an explicit port on each node, rerouting traffic through the cluster's networking layer.

Services of type LoadBalancer require support from an external load balancing solution, which may be supplied by cloud providers such as AWS, GCP, or Azure. To configure a LoadBalancer service, the configuration may look like this:

```
apiVersion: v1
kind: Service
metadata:
  name: external-service
spec:
  selector:
    app: public-app
  ports:
  - protocol: TCP
    port: 80
    targetPort: 8080
  type: LoadBalancer
```

This exposes the public-app application to external clients, with the load balancer evenly distributing requests across available pods based on network configurations.

Additionally, OpenShift Routes provide a mechanism surpassing the limitations of native Kubernetes capabilities, offering domain management and TLS termination for HTTP/S applications. Routes facilitate more control over ingress settings, establishing secure endpoints for services and enabling path-based or host-based routing rules.

Creating a Route in OpenShift involves the following configuration:

```
apiVersion: route.openshift.io/v1
kind: Route
metadata:
  name: example-route
spec:
  host: example.com
  to:
    kind: Service
    name: example-service
  tls:
    termination: edge
```

Here, example-route is bound to the domain example.com, directing traffic to the backend example-service. Edge termination is specified, directing OpenShift to manage TLS, ensuring secured communications.

For applications demanding advanced traffic management, OpenShift supports Service Mesh implementations, like Istio, offering comprehensive management over traffic flows. Service Mesh injects a proxy (sidecar) alongside each service, providing granular network control, metrics, and resilience features such as load balancing, security policies, and request retries.

With Istio, traffic management may introduce custom routing logic, implementing policies based on weights, routing headers, or other attributes:

```
apiVersion: networking.istio.io/v1beta1
kind: VirtualService
metadata:
  name: canary-release
spec:
  hosts:
  - "example.com"
  http:
  - route:
    - destination:
        host: stable-service
        subset: v1
      weight: 90
    - destination:
        host: canary-service
        subset: v2
      weight: 10
```

This VirtualService configures a canary release strategy, distributing 90% of the traffic to stable-service and the remaining 10% to canary-service. Such nuanced policies enable developers to release new software versions with minimal risk, gradually increasing traffic to the newer version as confidence in the release builds.

Security within traffic management is also paramount. Implement proper access control with network policies and secure communications with mutual TLS (mTLS) enforced via Service Mesh. Utilize Kubernetes Network Policies to create policy rules defining allowed traffic between entities:

```
apiVersion: networking.k8s.io/v1
kind: NetworkPolicy
metadata:
  name: allow-frontend
spec:
  podSelector:
    matchLabels:
      role: frontend
  ingress:
  - from:
    - podSelector:
        matchLabels:
          role: backend
    ports:
    - protocol: TCP
      port: 80
```

This NetworkPolicy rule permits ingress traffic into frontend pods exclusively from backend pods over TCP port 80, fortifying the internal network architecture against unauthorized access.

Ensure that observability tools are set up to monitor the system comprehensively. Tools like Prometheus and Grafana provide insights into the performance of services, analyzing traffic patterns and identifying any anomalies or inefficiencies. Define alerts for metrics such as response times, error rates, or HTTP status codes to act swiftly on service-level issues.

Load testing should accompany ongoing traffic management configurations, validating system performance and load balancing efficacy under simulated conditions. Use tools like JMeter or Locust to craft test scenarios, mimicking expected traffic patterns to ensure the robustness of deployments and configurations.

Lastly, establish process-oriented best practices through DevOps methodologies, emphasizing CI/CD workflows and Infrastructure-as-Code (IaC) to maintain consistency and track changes in configurations. Utilize version control to record every configuration or policy change, empowering teams to analyze historical configurations and enhance deployments iteratively.

By adhering to these best practices, OpenShift administrators and developers can implement effective load balancing and traffic management strategies that maximize application performance, improve availability, and ensure a secure and resilient containerized environment. Through continuous optimization and strategic planning, leveraging OpenShift's capabilities equips teams to effectively navigate the complexities of modern application deployments.

6.7 Troubleshooting Scaling Issues

Effective scaling in OpenShift is integral to maintaining application performance and user satisfaction. However, while scaling mechanisms such as manual scaling and autoscaling offer potent capabilities for dynamic resource management, issues can arise that impede their effectiveness. Troubleshooting scaling issues is a critical skill, requiring a deep understanding of both OpenShift and Kubernetes environments. This section delves into common scaling challenges, diagnostics, and resolutions, providing a comprehensive guide to maintaining optimal application performance.

The first step in troubleshooting scaling issues is identifying the symptoms. Scaling issues might manifest as degraded performance, increased error rates, resource exhaustion, unexpected pod terminations, or failure to scale to the desired number of replicas. Understanding these symptoms allows operators to narrow down potential root causes and apply structured diagnostics.

A frequent issue in scaling involves resource limitations, where the requested resources exceed available cluster resources. This restriction can halt pod scheduling, preventing applications from scaling appropriately. Key diagnostics for this scenario include verifying node capacity and resource requests. Use the following command to check resource usage and availability across nodes:

```
oc describe node <node-name>
```

Review the Capacity and Allocatable fields alongside the current pod resource allocations to determine if hardware resources are overcommitted. In many cases, optimizing resource requests and limits within deployments can alleviate scheduling conflicts. For instance, ensure that requests do not deplete available CPU or memory by carefully balancing demand with actual utilization data.

Consider an underlying resource definition:

```
resources:
  requests:
    memory: "512Mi"
    cpu: "200m"
  limits:
    memory: "1Gi"
    cpu: "500m"
```

Adjust these settings based on capacity and observed consumption to expand the node's ability to schedule more pods efficiently.

Another prevalent issue is misconfigured Horizontal Pod Autoscaler (HPA). The HPA relies on accurate metrics to initiate scaling actions. Misconfigurations, such as incorrectly set utilization thresholds or unresponsive metrics servers, can disrupt scaling operations. Verify HPA configuration:

```
oc get hpa <hpa-name> -o yaml
```

Inspect fields like targetCPUUtilizationPercentage and ensure metrics sources like Prometheus are operational:

```
oc get --raw "/apis/metrics.k8s.io/v1beta1/nodes"
oc get --raw "/apis/metrics.k8s.io/v1beta1/pods"
```

If metrics are unavailable, investigate metric server health, validating that endpoints are correctly configured, and address network policies blocking communication with the server.

Latency and network issues can also impact scaling operations, with network partitions or DNS resolution failures directly affecting communication between Kubernetes components and the control plane.

Analyze network policies, service configurations, and potential network bottlenecks:

```
oc get networkpolicy
```

For DNS or service discovery issues, validate core DNS health and investigate connectivity between pods and services.

```
oc exec -it <pod-name> -- nslookup <service-name>
```

Software misconfigurations, such as erroneous deployment logic or improper service labels, may lead to scaling issues by misdirecting traffic or failing to bind the correct pod instances to services. Ensure that deployment configurations accurately represent service dependencies and workloads. Review ReplicaSets and rollout statuses:

```
oc get replicaset
oc rollout status deployment <deployment-name>
```

Container readiness and liveness probes, when improperly configured, can mislead the scheduler into treating healthy pods as unserviceable, triggering redundant scaling actions or pod restarts. Validate probe configurations:

```
readinessProbe:
  httpGet:
    path: /healthz
    port: 8080
  initialDelaySeconds: 5
  periodSeconds: 10

livenessProbe:
  httpGet:
    path: /status
    port: 8080
  initialDelaySeconds: 15
  periodSeconds: 20
```

Adjust probe parameters to suit application response time and latency appropriately. Update or augment probe paths to align with actual service endpoints.

Concurrency limits imposed by application logic can lead to limitations, such as throttling requests when the application hits a processing ceiling. Review code logic and middleware configurations that may limit concurrent processing, threading support, and handling of incoming requests. Consider scaling to improve concurrency mediation.

Moreover, scaling downward improperly configured applications can lead to service disruption when critical stateful data or session details are lost. Anticipate these challenges by designing applications with statelessness in mind where feasible, persisting state outside pods (e.g., using databases, caching layers, etc.) or adopting Kubernetes StatefulSets for stateful service scaling.

For persistent scaling challenges, enable and scrutinize verbose logging across services, capturing insights into operational issues. Standard log management solutions like ELK (Elasticsearch, Logstash, Kibana) or OpenShift's integrated logging with Fluentd can aggregate logs, enabling operators to parse through rich datasets to find discrepancies or repeated error patterns.

In cases involving complex application stacking or architecture, simulation and load testing in controlled environments furnish insight into scaling impacts, aiding the configuration of more effective scaling policies. Apply load generation tools like Apache Benchmark or k6 to test realistic traffic patterns.

Should these methods not resolve issues, consider these advanced troubleshooting actions:

- Audit Kubernetes API logs for anomalies in scaling events, leveraging tools like Kubernetes audit-logs.

- Re-evaluate cluster capacity planning and node provisioning, especially for workloads with varying consumption phases.

- Cross-examine cloud provider configurations affecting Ingress Controllers or Load Balancers in hybrid models.

Ultimately, troubleshooting scaling issues in OpenShift demands a nuanced understanding of Kubernetes operations, infrastructure, and application behaviors. By iteratively analyzing and rectifying nuances that hinder scaling, operators can fortify application reliability, safeguarding performance as demand ebbs and flows. Building on these strategies ensures systems not only react but thrive under scaling demands, continually meeting operational and business objectives.

Chapter 7

Networking and Security in OpenShift

This chapter addresses the critical aspects of networking and security within the OpenShift platform, outlining its software-defined networking model and configuration of network policies to manage pod communication. It examines traffic management strategies for ingress and egress flows, ensuring secure and efficient data transfer. The integration of service mesh for managing microservices security and performance is discussed, along with implementing Role-Based Access Control (RBAC) for resource access regulation. The chapter also guides on aligning OpenShift with organizational security practices, emphasizing encryption methods to protect data both in transit and at rest.

7.1 Understanding OpenShift Networking Model

The networking model in OpenShift is a multifaceted construct that forms the backbone of communication within containerized environments. At the core of this model lies Software-Defined Networking (SDN), a pivotal technology that abstracts and manages the network infrastructure in a manner that enhances flexibility, automation, and efficiency. OpenShift's integration with SDN technologies provides a robust framework for orchestrating communication across diverse microservices and containerized workloads.

A comprehensive understanding of the OpenShift Networking Model involves familiarizing oneself with its fundamental components, architecture, and operation. This section delves into these elements, offering detailed insights into how OpenShift employs SDN for scalable, secure, and manageable network communication.

Software-Defined Networking (SDN)

Software-Defined Networking (SDN) decouples the control plane from the data plane in networking, enabling more centralized and flexible network management. In OpenShift, SDN plays a critical role in establishing virtual networks that allow for seamless interaction between containers, irrespective of their underlying physical network.

The SDN model in OpenShift can be visualized as consisting of three primary layers:

- **Network Abstraction Layer**: This layer abstracts the physical network infrastructure, creating a virtual network layer that provides consistent networking capabilities to all containers. This ensures that the containers can interact with one another without direct concerns about the underlying hardware configurations.

- **Control Layer**: In this layer, network administrators can define routing, switch operational behaviors, and set policies that guide how network traffic should flow. This centralization simplifies the process of network management, enabling administrators to apply global policies across all networked components.

- **Application Layer**: This layer interacts with the control layer to automate the management and orchestration of network resources. Applications can dynamically request network configurations and manage their networking needs programmatically, thereby increasing the agility of deployment in dynamic environments.

The Open vSwitch (OVS) is a commonly used technology within OpenShift's SDN architecture. It enables the implementation of virtual network bridges and switches, facilitating advanced network functionalities such as traffic routing, load balancing, and virtual local area network (VLAN) configurations.

```
# Display available bridges
sudo ovs-vsctl show

# Add a new bridge
sudo ovs-vsctl add-br br-int

# Add a port to bridge
sudo ovs-vsctl add-port br-int eth1

# Display bridge configuration
sudo ovs-vsctl list bridge
```

In practice, the SDN implementation in OpenShift enhances the ability to deploy microservices in a decentralized manner while maintaining centralized control over the network infrastructure.

OpenShift SDN Modes

The OpenShift SDN provides several operational modes, each catering to specific network management needs. The modes include:

- **Open vSwitch (OVS) Multitenant**: This mode provides network segregation between different projects (or tenants) within OpenShift. Each project is assigned a unique Virtual Network Identifier (VNI), ensuring that traffic remains isolated. This is particularly important in multi-tenant environments where security and privacy are key considerations.

- **OVS NetworkPolicy**: This mode supports Kubernetes Network Policies to allow or block traffic to and from specific pods. Network Policies are crucial for implementing fine-grained con-

197

trol over the network interactions within the cluster, aligning with specific security requirements.

- **OVS Subnet**: The most basic mode of operation which provides flat networking with no isolation between different namespaces. All pods can communicate with each other, regardless of their namespaces.

Selecting the appropriate SDN mode depends on the specific requirements of the deployment, such as the need for isolation, policy enforcement, or performance considerations.

```
# Configure OpenShift to use the NetworkPolicy mode
oc patch clusternetwork default --type=merge -p '{"spec": {"networkType": "
    OVNKubernetes"}}'
```

Network Policies for Communication Control

Network policies in OpenShift are akin to firewall rules in traditional networks. They enable administrators to control traffic flow between pods within the cluster. Through the definition of rules that specify 'allowed' and 'denied' communication paths, network policies enhance the security posture of the application environment.

Network policies use labels to select pods and define the permissible ingress (incoming) and egress (outgoing) traffic. The following is an example of a network policy configuration:

```
apiVersion: networking.k8s.io/v1
kind: NetworkPolicy
metadata:
  name: allow-frontend
  namespace: mynamespace
spec:
  podSelector:
    matchLabels:
      role: frontend
  ingress:
  - from:
    - podSelector:
        matchLabels:
          role: backend
  policyTypes:
  - Ingress
```

In the above policy, pods labeled as 'frontend' are allowed ingress traffic from pods labeled 'backend', effectively controlling and securing inter-pod communication.

Container Network Interface (CNI) in OpenShift

OpenShift supports Container Network Interface (CNI) plugins, which define networking configurations and options for pods. CNI is a specification that outlines how containers can communicate over a network. OpenShift employs CNI plugins to provide a modular and flexible approach to networking, offering a consistent API to implement various network functionalities, such as IP address management or port allocation.

```
# Install calico CNI plugin
kubectl apply -f https://docs.projectcalico.org/manifests/canal.yaml
```

CNI plugins allow OpenShift users to integrate alternative networking solutions—such as Flannel, Calico, or Weave—in place of the default OpenShift SDN, empowering users to design a customizable network topology that best suits their unique requirements.

Service Discovery and Load Balancing

Service discovery and load balancing are essential components of the OpenShift networking architecture that ensure applications are accessible and performant.

- **Service Discovery**: OpenShift provides DNS-based service discovery for inter-pod communication. This automatic service discovery mechanism involves assigning each service a DNS entry, which pods can use to access the service without needing to know its underlying IP address.

```
apiVersion: v1
kind: Service
metadata:
  name: my-service
spec:
  selector:
    app: MyApp
  ports:
  - protocol: TCP
    port: 80
    targetPort: 9376
```

- **Load Balancing**: OpenShift uses an internal load balancer to evenly distribute incoming network traffic across multiple pods. This ensures that no single pod becomes a performance bottleneck, thereby improving the application's scalability and reliability. Pods are added or removed from the endpoints of a service as replicas are scaled up or down through the OpenShift deployment configurations.

The above elements contribute to the efficiency of application deployment and operation within OpenShift, securing reliable service accessibility across dynamic scale-outs and scale-ins.

Summary of Critical Elements

Understanding the OpenShift networking model involves understanding its SDN foundation, the modes available for configurations, how network policies enforce security, the role of CNI plugins for flexibility, and the mechanisms of service discovery and load balancing. These components form a cohesive network architecture capable of supporting complex, distributed application environments through automated and policy-driven operations. The ability to abstract, control, and manage network resources centrally while allowing flexible deployment patterns characterizes the inherent power of OpenShift's networking model.

7.2   Configuring Network Policies

Network policies in OpenShift are fundamental to ensuring that communication between pods and services is secure and compliant with organizational requirements. These policies serve as rules or sets of rules that dictate the allowed traffic flow within an OpenShift cluster, helping to enhance the security posture by regulating which pods can interact and which cannot. As the importance of securing workloads in a shared cluster environment grows, mastering the configuration of network policies becomes an essential skill for operators and administrators.

Network policies in OpenShift are an implementation of Kubernetes network policies, designed to provide an application-centric methodology to manage communication boundaries. They enable the definition of policies that control pod-to-pod and pod-to-service communications, which are critical in a microservices architecture where numerous components communicate across various touchpoints.

By default, in OpenShift, there is an "allow all" policy, meaning all pods can communicate with each other without restrictions. When a network policy is applied, it changes this paradigm to a "deny by default" approach for any traffic not explicitly allowed by a policy. This shift ensures that pods are protected from unwarranted network traffic both from within and outside the cluster.

A network policy in OpenShift is defined using YAML configurations, which specify how groups of pods are allowed to communicate with each other and with other network endpoints. The primary components of a network policy are:

- **Namespace**: The namespace specifies the scope within which the network policy applies. Policies are bound to a specific namespace, and thus, they only affect the pods within the specified namespace.

- **Pod Selector**: The pod selector determines which pods the policy applies to. It uses labels to match one or more pods, thus making the policy applicable only to those specific pods.

- **Policy Types**: The types include both Ingress and Egress policies, allowing specification of allowed inbound and outbound traffic, respectively. If no egress rule is defined, it defaults to allow all traffic that is not denied.

- **Ingress and Egress Rules**: These rules define specific conditions for allowed traffic, either ingress to the pod or egress from the pod. Conditions can include source or destination IP block, the specific ports involved, and even protocol types.

```
apiVersion: networking.k8s.io/v1
kind: NetworkPolicy
metadata:
  name: example-network-policy
  namespace: demo
spec:
  podSelector:
    matchLabels:
      role: db
  policyTypes:
  - Ingress
  ingress:
  - from:
    - podSelector:
```

```
    matchLabels:
        role: frontend
  ports:
  - protocol: TCP
    port: 3306
```

The above YAML demonstrates a typical network policy that allows ingress traffic to all pods with the label 'role: db' from any pods with the label 'role: frontend', but only over TCP port 3306. This selectiveness in traffic allows more tightened access control, reducing the surface area for potential attacks.

The process of designing network policies involves careful planning and consideration of the application architecture, communication flows, and security requirements. An effective approach begins with identifying critical communication paths between components of an application. Security-centered questions should guide the design:

- What are the trusted sources of communication?

- Are there any services that should only communicate internally without exposure to external networks?

- Which paths need to be tightly monitored and logged for compliance or security audits?

These questions aid in drafting network policies that serve both security and operational efficiency purposes. It's recommended to start with broad policies that cover essential boundaries and iteratively refine them to incorporate more detailed rules.

To ensure seamless continuity of services while applying network policies, administrators should follow best practices such as:

- **Incremental Rollout**: Apply new network policies or changes in stages, starting with non-critical namespaces or workloads. Monitor the effects and make necessary adjustments before full-scale application.

- **Isolation Testing**: Before enforcing policies across production, test them in isolated environments that mimic production as closely as possible. This step helps in spotting unforeseen side effects that stricter policies might cause.

- **Log and Monitor**: Integration with logging and monitoring systems such as Prometheus or Grafana can provide insightful details into the behavior of network traffic under enforced policies. This visibility is crucial for detecting policy violations or unexpected traffic patterns.

- **Continuous Review**: Dynamic environments evolve rapidly; hence, network policies must be reviewed and updated regularly to respond to expanding feature sets or new security threats.

Depending on the application topology, network policies may be crafted to meet diverse requirements. Let's explore a few plausible scenarios:

- **Restrict External Access**: An organization might want a service to be accessible only within the cluster, preventing any ingress traffic from outside the cluster's internal network.

```
apiVersion: networking.k8s.io/v1
kind: NetworkPolicy
metadata:
  name: deny-external-ingress
  namespace: internal
spec:
  podSelector:
    matchLabels:
      role: internal-service
  ingress:
  - from:
    - podSelector: {}
```

In this policy, ingress traffic is only allowed from pods within the same namespace, effectively blocking external access.

- **Application Segmentation**: To enhance microservice security, applications can be segmented into logical units with controlled interactions.

```
apiVersion: networking.k8s.io/v1
kind: NetworkPolicy
metadata:
  name: multi-tier-segmentation
  namespace: production
spec:
```

```
podSelector:
  matchLabels:
    tier: backend
ingress:
- from:
  - podSelector:
      matchLabels:
        tier: frontend
  ports:
  - protocol: TCP
    port: 8080
```

This policy ensures that only traffic from the 'frontend' tier can access the 'backend' tier at a specified port, isolating backend operations.

Advanced network policies can integrate with identity and access management systems to automatically update rules based on verified identities or roles, thus achieving dynamic policy enforcement. Machine learning algorithms can analyze historical traffic patterns to suggest optimal policies or detect anomalies pointing to potential unauthorized access or breaches.

Furthermore, policies can interact with environment variables through initialization scripts at deployment to align with deployment-specific configurations, enhancing flexibility in multi-cloud or hybrid cloud setups.

By effectively configuring network policies, enterprises can safeguard sensitive data flows within OpenShift clusters, detect and mitigate risks, and align with compliance standards. As technology and threat landscapes evolve, adapting to best practices in network policy management, such as automation tools or policy-as-code frameworks, can elevate security operations from reactive to proactive, sustaining application integrity and trustworthiness in a distributed, rapidly changing environment. Understanding the depth and capabilities of network policies enhances an operator's toolkit, equipping them to manage OpenShift environments with precision and confidence.

7.3 Ingress and Egress Traffic Management

Effective management of ingress and egress traffic is critical in ensuring secure, efficient, and reliable communication within OpenShift clusters. Ingress traffic refers to data entering the cluster, typically aiming to reach services exposed to external consumers. Egress traffic, conversely, is the data leaving the cluster, often communicating with external services or infrastructures. Balancing these traffic flows while ensuring security and performance requires a comprehensive understanding of the corresponding configurations and policies within OpenShift.

Ingress traffic management in OpenShift is centered around guiding external requests to internal services in a secure and scalable manner. This is achieved using Ingress Controllers and resources defined within the cluster, which map external requests to internal services seamlessly.

Ingress Controllers are the entry points for handling incoming requests. They leverage Ingress resources, which specify routing rules to manage the traffic directed by the controllers. Common Ingress Controllers in OpenShift include HAProxy, Traefik, and NGINX, each offering distinct features appropriate for different operational needs.

```yaml
apiVersion: networking.k8s.io/v1
kind: Ingress
metadata:
  name: example-ingress
  namespace: demo
spec:
  rules:
  - host: www.example.com
    http:
      paths:
      - path: /
        pathType: Prefix
        backend:
          service:
            name: example-service
            port:
              number: 80
```

The above YAML defines an Ingress resource that routes all requests to 'www.example.com' to 'example-service'. Such backend service abstraction allows scalable management of traffic, enabling load balancing and SSL/TLS termination at the Ingress level.

Modern ingress controllers support advanced features such as sticky sessions, custom load balancing algorithms, and session affinity, which are crucial for optimizing data flow.

- Sticky Sessions: In environments catering to stateful applications, maintaining session affinity ensures requests from a client get consistently routed to the same backend instance.

- TLS Termination: By implementing TLS termination at the Ingress, encryption and decryption occur at the edge, freeing backend services from handling encryption overhead.

- Custom Rules: Custom routing rules can enhance flexibility, allowing for scenarios such as rewriting URLs, adding custom headers, or implementing advanced security policies.

Ingress traffic management involves several security considerations to protect both data and services. TLS, as previously mentioned, forms the first line of defense by encrypting traffic between clients and the server. Moreover, administrators should ensure that only validated Ingress controllers process external requests to prevent unauthorized access or interference.

In addition to utilizing network policies, application firewalls at the Ingress level help detect and filter anomalies or potential attacks, including Distributed Denial of Service (DDoS) attacks, SQL injections, and cross-site scripting (XSS). Properly configured Ingress security policies form a critical part of the cluster's defensive architecture.

Egress traffic management ensures that outbound communication from the cluster remains secure and compliant with organizational policies. This involves configuring network policies to control what external destinations pods can communicate with, and how data leaves the cluster.

As Kubernetes-based environments often operate in a "deny by default" mode for ingress policies, egress policies require explicit configuration to restrict or enable outbound connections. The management strategy typically involves managing which external IPs or endpoints pods are allowed to connect to, thereby limiting the exposure of sensitive data.

```
apiVersion: networking.k8s.io/v1
kind: NetworkPolicy
metadata:
  name: restrict-egress
  namespace: demo
spec:
  podSelector:
    matchLabels:
      role: backend
  policyTypes:
  - Egress
  egress:
  - to:
    - ipBlock:
        cidr: 192.168.5.0/24
    ports:
    - protocol: TCP
      port: 80
```

In this example, the network policy restricts egress traffic for pods with the label 'role: backend' to communicate only with the subnet '192.168.5.0/24' over TCP port 80.

Centralized egress points involve routing all cluster egress traffic through a central exit node or gateway, which can monitor, audit, and control outbound traffic. These setups enhance network security and provide unified management points for implementing policies like encryption, IP whitelisting, and more.

Tools such as virtual private networks (VPNs) and tunneling within OpenShift can help establish secure egress pathways, which are essential for transmitting sensitive or regulatory compliant data outside the cluster.

Utilizing service meshes within OpenShift further enhances egress management. Implementations like Istio provide egress gateways that uniformly manage external traffic, applying policies such as retry mechanisms, fault injection, load balancing, and mutual TLS. This adds another layer of security and stability by ensuring consistent egress behavior under varied routing circumstances and potential network failures.

Monitoring and logging are indispensable in understanding traffic behaviors and performance across ingress and egress pathways. Tools integrated with OpenShift such as Prometheus and Grafana allow for real-time collection and visualization of traffic metrics, stating data on request latency, error rates, throughput, and more.

Alongside monitoring, logging strategies leveraging tools like Fluentd or Elastic Stack (ELK) capture traffic history and anomalies, enabling root cause analysis or audits for compliance or troubleshooting.

Managing ingress and egress in OpenShift involves numerous practical scenarios crucial for efficient deployment patterns:

- Multi-Tenant Isolation: For environments hosting applications from multiple tenants, separate ingress and egress controls can prevent accidental or malicious inter-tenant traffic, enforcing isolation and privacy regulations.

```
apiVersion: networking.k8s.io/v1
kind: NetworkPolicy
metadata:
  name: tenant-isolation
  namespace: tenant-a
spec:
  podSelector:
    matchLabels: {}
  policyTypes:
  - Ingress
  - Egress
  ingress:
  - from:
    - namespaceSelector:
        matchLabels:
          purpose: internal
  egress:
  - to:
    - namespaceSelector:
        matchLabels:
          purpose: external
```

These policies ensure that traffic intended for internal consumption is routed accordingly without trespassing into another tenant's space or data.

- Geo-Location Traffic Management: Enterprises with global architectures may route ingress traffic to region-specific data centers, optimizing latency and compliance with data residency regulations.

```
apiVersion: networking.k8s.io/v1
kind: Ingress
metadata:
  name: region-routing
  namespace: global
spec:
  rules:
  - host: eu.example.com
    http:
      paths:
      - path: /
        pathType: Prefix
        backend:
          service:
            name: eu-service
            port:
              number: 80
```

This demonstrates a distribution of traffic based on the domain, ensuring that requests from Europe are handled by European data centers specifically.

- Data Residency and Sovereignty: Policies that control egress are vital in adhering to data residency laws which enforce where data can be stored or processed, commonly in sectors such as finance or healthcare.

Managing ingress and egress traffic in OpenShift demands a strategic approach that leverages advanced configurations, security measures, and monitoring practices. Ensuring that these practices align with business objectives and regulatory compliance standards, administrators can empower their OpenShift environments to operate securely, efficiently, and resiliently in a rapidly evolving digital landscape.

7.4   Service Mesh in OpenShift

The integration of service mesh technologies in OpenShift represents a significant advancement in managing communications and security among microservices. Service meshes provide a layer that transparently manages service-to-service interactions by offering capabilities such as traffic management, security, and observability. Among the various service mesh solutions, Istio is one of the most prominent implementations in OpenShift, enabling intricate control over microservice interactions without necessitating changes in application code.

A service mesh introduces an intermediary infrastructure layer within an application architecture that controls how data flows between services. It consists of a data plane and a control plane. The data plane is composed of a set of intelligent network proxies deployed alongside application instances, and the control plane manages and configures the proxies to route traffic.

The service mesh provides three core functionalities:

- **Traffic Management**: This provides powerful control over the flow of network traffic across services. It allows for sophisticated strategies such as load balancing, traffic splitting, and mirroring requests.

- **Security**: Service mesh enhances microservice security through enforcing mutual TLS, fine-grained access control, and providing insights into security metrics.

- **Observability**: It grants deep insights into system behaviors by offering detailed telemetry, monitoring, and tracing of service interactions.

Istio is a leading service mesh offering a rich set of features for microservice management, and it integrates seamlessly with OpenShift. It serves as a robust implementation to leverage the full potential of the capabilities offered by a service mesh.

Istio's architecture comprises the Envoy proxy, which forms the data plane, and the Istiod control plane. Together, they provide comprehensive management of microservice environments.

- **Envoy Proxy**: It is a high-performance proxy deployed as a sidecar to application services, intercepting all network communications.

- **Istiod**: It is the core component of Istio's control plane that manages the configuration and deployment of the Envoy proxies. It provides APIs to define traffic policies, security requirements, and observability settings.

Talents employed by Istio in OpenShift enable dynamic service discovery, load balancing, failure recovery, fault injection, and metrics collection.

```
apiVersion: install.istio.io/v1alpha1
kind: IstioOperator
metadata:
  namespace: istio-system
  name: example-istiocontrolplane
spec:
  profile: demo
  components:
    ingressGateways:
    - name: istio-ingressgateway
      enabled: true
    egressGateways:
    - name: istio-egressgateway
      enabled: true
```

In this example, the YAML file deploys an example service mesh control plane using the demo profile that includes Istio's ingress and egress gateways.

The traffic management features of Istio allow for the enforcement of policies that manage the flow of traffic to the involved microservices. These include:

- **Routing Rules**: Using virtual services and destination rules, Istio enables complex request routing scenarios, such as traffic splitting based on version or A/B testing with weights assigned to different services.

```
apiVersion: networking.istio.io/v1alpha3
kind: VirtualService
metadata:
  name: example
spec:
  hosts:
  - example
  http:
  - route:
    - destination:
        host: example-v1
        weight: 80
    - destination:
        host: example-v2
        weight: 20
```

In the YAML configuration above, Istio routes 80% of the traffic to 'example-v1' while the remaining 20% is directed to 'example-v2', facilitating sophisticated traffic control strategies.

- **Fault Injection**: It enables the introduction of faults such as delays and aborts into services, allowing developers to test how services respond under failure conditions.

- **Retry and Timeout Policies**: Istio lets you define retry attempts and timeout values to enhance the reliability of service invocations.

Istio enhances service-to-service communication security within Open-Shift through capabilities like:

- **Mutual TLS Authentication**: Istio can automatically secure service-to-service communications by issuing and managing certificates for mTLS authentication without modifying the application code.

- **Authorization Policies**: Policies can be defined based on attributes like source identity or request headers to control who can access specific services.

```
apiVersion: "security.istio.io/v1beta1"
kind: PeerAuthentication
metadata:
  name: default
  namespace: example
spec:
  mtls:
    mode: STRICT
```

The provided YAML configures mTLS in an entire namespace to enforce secure communications between services, thus strengthening the security posture.

Observability features in Istio give unparalleled insights into the state and performance of microservices. Key aspects include:

- **Telemetry**: Metrics collection on request counts, latency, and errors offer insights into service health and assist in performance tuning.

- **Distributed Tracing**: Integration with tools such as Jaeger allows detailed tracing of requests as they move across services, helping to pinpoint bottlenecks or failures.

- **Logging**: Granular logging through Envoy provides contextual log data aiding in audits or debugging.

Deploying a service mesh such as Istio in OpenShift requires adhering to several best practices to achieve its full potential:

- **Gradual Adoption**: Introduce the service mesh gradually, starting with non-critical services. Validate and refine configurations in a testing environment before production rollout.

- **Resource Considerations**: Understand the overhead introduced by running a sidecar proxy for each service instance. Sufficient resources must be allocated to meet performance and scalability needs.

- **Policy Consistency**: Maintain consistency in security and traffic policies across services to ensure predictable behavior.

- **Continuous Monitoring and Alerting**: Utilize Istio's telemetry features to continuously monitor services and set up alerts for proactive incident management.

Service mesh adoption manifests in several critical use cases:

- **Progressive Delivery**: Organizations can leverage traffic management capabilities for blue-green deployments or canary releases, thereby reducing the risk associated with new deployments.

- **Security and Compliance**: Financial institutions can enforce strict security protocols throughout service communications to meet regulatory compliance using Istio's policy configuration.

- **Operational Resilience**: By simulating real-world failures and observing behavior through Istio's fault injection, organizations can build more robust systems.

A thoughtfully deployed service mesh in OpenShift enhances microservices orchestration by providing greater control, resilience, and security. As enterprises progressively shift toward cloud-native architectures, harnessing the power of Istio within OpenShift positions organizations to navigate complex service dependencies and scaling needs effectively.

7.5 Securing OpenShift with Role-Based Access Control (RBAC)

Role-Based Access Control (RBAC) is an essential framework within OpenShift, providing a method of regulating access to resources commonly used in cloud environments. RBAC minimizes the risk of unauthorized data access and modification by associating roles, permissions, and resources with user identities. In OpenShift, RBAC serves as a foundational security feature, enforcing who can execute specific actions on various resources.

RBAC in OpenShift builds on Kubernetes' RBAC system, offering granular control over permission management. It is fundamental to comprehend the primary constructs of RBAC, which include:

- **Role**: Defines a set of permissions or rules that determine allowable actions on certain resources. Roles are confined to specific namespaces unless specified as ClusterRoles, expanding their scope to the entire cluster.

- **ClusterRole**: Similar to a Role, but applicable cluster-wide, potentially impacting resources across all namespaces.

- **RoleBinding**: Associates a Role with a set of users, groups, or service accounts, binding them to the permissions specified in that Role within a particular namespace.

- **ClusterRoleBinding**: Extends RoleBinding's concept to ClusterRoles, associating identities with cluster-wide permissions.

Role and permission mappings in OpenShift are typically expressed using YAML, offering a structured and human-readable format for access control definitions.

```
apiVersion: rbac.authorization.k8s.io/v1
kind: Role
metadata:
  namespace: project
  name: pod-reader
rules:
- apiGroups: [""]
  resources: ["pods"]
  verbs: ["get", "watch", "list"]
```

In this example, the role 'pod-reader' within the 'project' namespace allows a user or service account to list, watch, and get pods.

The implementation of effective RBAC requires a structured approach to defining roles and bindings that align with organizational needs and security practices. This typically involves the following steps:

- **Identify Resources and Actions**: Catalog the resources within the OpenShift environment and the actions users should be able to take on these resources.

- **Define Roles and Permissions**: Create Roles and Cluster-Roles representing different levels of permission granularity. For instance, a 'developer' role may have permissions to create and manage pods, services, and deployments, whereas an 'auditor' role might only have read permissions across namespaces.

- **Configure RoleBindings and ClusterRoleBindings**: Bind users or service accounts to these roles based on their functional roles in the enterprise, such as 'developer', 'admin', or 'auditor'.

- **Audit and Adjust**: Regularly audit the roles and permissions defined, adjusting them in response to changes in security policies or organizational needs.

- **Automate RBAC Configuration**: Use automation tools to deploy and manage RBAC configurations at scale, ensuring consistency and compliance across environments.

Several best practices can enhance the security effectiveness of RBAC in OpenShift:

- **Principle of Least Privilege**: Assign permissions based on the minimum access required for users to perform their job functions. Avoid granting more privileges than necessary.

- **Resource Namespacing**: Leverage namespace scoping to confine user actions to specific areas of the cluster, reducing cross-namespace data exposure.

- **Consolidated Roles**: Attempt to create consolidated roles that encapsulate typical use case scenarios, reducing redundancy and complexity in role definitions.

- **Regular Auditing**: Implement regular audits using tools that monitor and report on RBAC configurations, ensuring roles adapt to evolving operational contexts and compliance mandates.

- **Inheritance and Hierarchies**: Utilize role hierarchies where higher-level roles inherit permissions from more specific roles, streamlining administrator work in assigning role bindings.

Consider the application of such practices in scenarios such as development vs. production environments, ensuring that access differences reflect the critical nature of deployed applications.

Advanced configurations in RBAC allow additional customization that can further bolster a security posture:

- **Custom Roles and API Groups**: Define custom roles that include specific API groups, leveraging OpenShift's extensive API to fine-tune access control down to the operation level.

```
apiVersion: rbac.authorization.k8s.io/v1
kind: Role
metadata:
  namespace: custom-namespace
  name: custom-role
rules:
- apiGroups: ["apps"]
  resources: ["deployments"]
  verbs: ["create", "update", "patch"]
```

Here, the custom role permits creating, updating, and patching deployments within the 'apps' API group in the 'custom-namespace'.

- **Service Accounts for Automated Expressions**: Apply roles selectively to service accounts running automated tasks, ensuring these systems operate with just the necessary permissions.

- **Integrated Identity Management**: Integrate third-party identity providers using OpenShift's OAuth functionalities to streamline authentication processes and extend existing enterprise identity frameworks into OpenShift environments.

- **Delegation**: Enable delegation by granting ClusterRoles that permit operations such as role creation to specific trustworthy users, allowing admins to decouple centralized operations rendering flexibility.

In practical scenarios, RBAC configurations can become complex, especially within large-scale systems:

- **Multi-Tenant Clusters**: Implementing RBAC in multi-tenant OpenShift clusters can be challenging, as role definitions must align with varied tenant requirements without impacting the system's overall security.

- **Dynamic Workloads**: Many modern environments are characterized by dynamic workload deployment, where roles must adapt to periodically changing resource requirements. Automation tools deploy manifest files compatible with GitOps or CI/CD pipeline frameworks to ensure real-time alignment.

- **Compliance with Regulatory Standards**: Ensuring RBAC configurations meet compliance requirements such as PCI DSS or HIPAA involves rigorous policy definitions and audits to align operational roles with legal obligations.

The sophistication of RBAC as a framework makes it uniquely suited for managing enterprise applications within OpenShift, provided administrators leverage well-defined practices and tool integrations.

RBAC is integral to OpenShift's ability to deliver secure, resilient, and compliant environments. As enterprises aim to adopt cloud-native technologies, the strategic implementation of RBAC can encompass security and operational efficiencies. By understanding its architecture, adhering to established best practices, configuring advanced role definitions, and regularly auditing roles, organizations can significantly bolster their cluster defenses. Consequently, RBAC remains a vital aspect of comprehensive security strategies within OpenShift deployments.

7.6 Integrating OpenShift with Organizational Security Practices

Integrating OpenShift with existing organizational security practices is a crucial step in harmonizing infrastructure management and security standards within enterprises. As OpenShift encapsulates containerized applications, ensuring that its operational framework aligns with broader security policies becomes essential for comprehensive threat mitigation. This section explores the methodologies and practices for aligning OpenShift with enterprise-level security measures, focusing on identity management, compliance controls, data protection, and best governance practices.

- **Identity and Access Management Integration**

Identity and Access Management (IAM) is paramount in regulating who has access to systems and services. Seamless integration of OpenShift with corporate IAM systems streamlines authentication processes and enforces consistent access controls throughout all platforms.

- **Single Sign-On (SSO)**: Implementing SSO mechanisms within OpenShift can simplify authentication across services and applications. By integrating OpenShift with enterprise identity providers (IdP) like LDAP, Active Directory, or SAML-compliant IdPs, administrators can leverage pre-established authentication protocols, ensuring uniform identity verification.

```
apiVersion: config.openshift.io/v1
kind: OAuth
metadata:
```

```yaml
  name: cluster
spec:
  identityProviders:
  - name: my_ldap
    mappingMethod: claim
    type: LDAP
    ldap:
      url: ldaps://ldap.example.com:636/ou=People,dc=example,dc=com
      bindDN: "uid=lookup,ou=people,dc=example,dc=com"
      bindPassword:
        name: ldap-bind-password
      insecure: false
      attributes:
        id: ["uid"]
        preferredUsername: ["uid"]
        name: ["cn"]
        email: ["mail"]
```

This YAML configuration provides a template for integrating Open-Shift with an LDAP directory service to incorporate identity verification using existing credentials.

- **Federated Identity Models**: Supporting federated identity models allows OpenShift to interface securely with multiple identity domains, essential for organizations employing collaboration across disparate operational units.

- **Compliance Control Frameworks**

Integrating OpenShift within enterprises requires adherence to compliance standards such as HIPAA, GDPR, SOX, or PCI DSS, necessitating processes that protect sensitive data while demonstrating regulatory compliance.

- **Policy-Based Management**: OpenShift administrators should employ policy-based management strategies, defining compliance-sensitive configurations that automate governance based on standardized rules. Tools like Open Policy Agent (OPA) integrated with OpenShift's admission controllers can enforce runtime rules critical for compliance.

```yaml
apiVersion: v1
kind: ConfigMap
metadata:
```

```
  name: opa-config
  namespace: opa
data:
  policy.rego: |
    package kubernetes.admission

    deny[msg] {
      input.request.kind.kind == "Pod"
      not input.request.object.spec.securityContext.runAsNonRoot
      msg = "Containers must not run as root user"
    }
```

OPA rules can dynamically scrutinize deployment configurations, ensuring they adhere to defined best practices restricting root privilege usage, hence boosting compliance.

- **Data Protection and Encryption Practices**

To prevent unauthorized data access, OpenShift environments need robust encryption protocols, ensuring data security both in transit and at rest.

- **TLS Encryption**: Implement Transport Layer Security (TLS) across all service endpoints to assure encryption during data transit. Using OpenShift's built-in capabilities, administrators should enforce mTLS between microservices, ensuring encrypted, authenticated communication.

- **Secret Management**: Effective secret management practices within OpenShift include leveraging Kubernetes Secrets, encrypted using custom encryption providers or hardware security modules (HSMs), promoting robust password and token protection.

```
apiVersion: v1
kind: Secret
metadata:
  name: my-database-secret
  namespace: production
type: Opaque
data:
  username: YWRtaW4=
  password: MWYyZDFlMmU2N2Rm
```

Encoded base64 usernames and passwords maintain sensitive information's confidentiality as stored secrets, evaluated and controlled through RBAC.

- **Enhancing Threat Detection and Response**

Aligning OpenShift with organizational security frameworks includes deploying robust monitoring and incident response mechanisms for proactive threat detection.

- **Security Information and Event Management (SIEM) Integration**: Strengthening OpenShift's ability to report and act upon suspicious activities by integrating with SIEM platforms can synchronize forensic data collection and real-time alerts within established security operations centers (SOCs).

- **Intrusion Detection Systems (IDS)**: Deploying IDS solutions within the OpenShift cluster actively monitors traffic and application behavior. Insights gathered help in profiling legitimate service interactions against potential misuse, enabling rapid anomaly detection.

```
# Installing Snort IDS in OpenShift
oc new-app centos/snort --dockerfile=$DOCKERFILE

# Running Snort on an OpenShift node
snort -dev -l /var/log/snort -h 10.0.0.0/16 -c /etc/snort/snort.conf
```

Snort, as a versatile open-source IDS, can detect intrusions by examining packet movement across network boundaries, exploiting OpenShift manifests for container deployment.

- **Governance and Continuous Improvement Practices**

Governance in OpenShift ensures adherence to security postures while advancing technological processes and policies, foundational for maintaining a secure operational environment.

- **Auditing and Logging**: Enable comprehensive audit logging where all system events, access decisions, configuration modifications, and user activity are recorded, facilitating retrospective analysis and minimized security drift.

- **Change Management Protocols**: Integrate change management utilities within OpenShift DevOps pipelines to authenticate and approve configuration revisions systematically. This includes establishing configuration baselines and rollback procedures.

- **Security Training and Awareness**: Organizations should regularly perform security training and awareness sessions tailored specifically for teams managing OpenShift environments, enhancing their ability to identify and mitigate threats.

- **Adopt Zero Trust Architecture**: Implement the Zero Trust paradigm, mandating verified authentication and encrypted communications, irrespective of network location, ensuring that trust is based solely on tightly controlled access rights and verifiable identities.

- **Navigating Challenges in Integration**

Challenges abound when assimilating OpenShift into corporate security frameworks:

- **Legacy System Compatibility**: Aligning OpenShift with older, possibly insecure legacy systems may necessitate intermediate solutions bridging technology gaps while complying with modern security standards.

- **Scalability Concerns**: As organizations grow, scaling security configurations within OpenShift can appear daunting; employing automation tools for policy and configuration management ensures fidelity across expanding environments.

- **Cultural Shifts**: Cultural adaptation within enterprises may be required to support new and evolving security practices, driven by leadership advocating for innovation alongside risk management.

Integrating OpenShift with organizational security practices requires synchronized methodologies that resonate with core enterprise strategies. By focusing on identity management, compliance frameworks, data protection, threat detection, and governance practices, organizations can successfully synchronize OpenShift's robust capabilities with established security norms. This integration ensures resilient, secure deployment of applications within a containerized, cloud-native framework adaptable to continuous technological evolution.

7.7 Encrypting Data in Transit and at Rest

In modern enterprise environments, the protection of sensitive data is paramount. Encryption serves as a critical safeguard, ensuring data confidentiality and integrity against unauthorized access or tampering. Within OpenShift environments, encrypting data in transit and at rest forms a fundamental layer of security, helping to meet compliance standards and protect digital assets from potential threats. Understanding how encryption is implemented and managed in these contexts is essential for security practitioners aiming to bolster their infrastructure policies.

Data in transit encompasses any information that is being transmitted across networks, whether between microservices within a cluster or between external clients and services. Encrypting this data ensures that it remains confidential and is safeguarded from interception or eavesdropping attacks.

Transport Layer Security (TLS) is the most commonly used protocol for encrypting data in transit. It creates a secure tunnel over which information can be reliably exchanged without exposure to third parties.

- **TLS for External Communication**: When external clients connect to services within an OpenShift cluster, TLS ensures encrypted pathways. OpenShift's built-in routes facilitate the configuration of TLS termination, where encryption/decryption is handled at the edge, reducing the burden on backend services.

```
apiVersion: route.openshift.io/v1
kind: Route
metadata:
  name: my-secure-route
```

```
spec:
  host: secure.example.com
  to:
    kind: Service
    name: my-service
  tls:
    termination: edge
    insecureEdgeTerminationPolicy: Redirect
```

The 'tls' block configures TLS termination at the edge of the OpenShift platform, ensuring traffic is encrypted up to the defined service route.

- **Mutual TLS (mTLS) Between Microservices**: mTLS extends TLS to verify both parties' identities in communication, applying both authentication and encryption uniformly across service interactions. Istio, integrated into OpenShift, automates mTLS within service meshes, fostering trust and integrity across microservice ecosystems without individual configuration.

Secure and efficient management of TLS keys and certificates is crucial. OpenShift's secrets management allows storage of TLS keys and certificates in a secure, encrypted form, facilitating their use across deployments.

```
apiVersion: v1
kind: Secret
metadata:
  name: tls-secret
  namespace: my-namespace
type: kubernetes.io/tls
data:
  tls.crt: <base64 encoded certificate>
  tls.key: <base64 encoded key>
```

This YAML represents a TLS secret that can be referenced by applications or ingress controllers, eliminating plaintext storage and enhancing key confidentiality.

Data at rest refers to information stored on physical media. Ensuring encryption at this stage protects data even if physical security is compromised, denying illegitimate access after potential breaches.

Encryption at the storage level involves deploying encryption mechanisms directly at the file system or storage device layer, ensuring comprehensive protection across data stores.

- **Persistent Volume Encryption**: Within OpenShift, data stored in persistent volumes can leverage underlying storage systems that support encryption. By utilizing providers like AWS EBS or Azure Disks, which offer host-side or service-provider encryption, the data remains encrypted beyond the application level.

```
apiVersion: v1
kind: PersistentVolumeClaim
metadata:
  name: encrypted-pvc
spec:
  accessModes:
    - ReadWriteOnce
  resources:
    requests:
      storage: 10Gi
  storageClassName: aws-encrypted
```

It is essential to select a storage class configured for encryption to enforce security directly within cloud providers' storage services.

Databases hold crucial application data and are often susceptible targets for breaches. To protect databases within an OpenShift cluster, several encryption approaches should be considered:

- **Transparent Data Encryption (TDE)**: TDE encrypts database files at the storage level transparently to applications. Databases like PostgreSQL and Microsoft SQL Server offer built-in TDE features that integrate seamlessly within OpenShift.

- **Application-Level Encryption**: Encrypting data at the application layer before storage offers flexibility but requires key management to be tightly controlled via secure practices.

Effective encryption strategies go beyond merely implementing cryptographic algorithms. Consider these best practices for OpenShift:

1. **Use Strong Encryption Standards**: Only use well-vetted, strong encryption protocols and libraries (e.g., AES-256, RSA-2048) ensuring compliance with current security standards and practices.

2. **Comprehensive Key Management**: Deploy robust key management solutions such as HashiCorp Vault, AWS KMS, or Azure Key Vault parallel to OpenShift, fostering centralized control over encryption keys and auditing actions associated with them.

3. **Data Masking and Tokenization**: Employ data masking or tokenization for non-production environments, securing sensitive data while maintaining its usability within development or testing contexts.

4. **Regularly Update Encryption Protocols**: Stay abreast of cryptographic research and updates. Outdated ciphers should be regularly replaced to address developing vulnerabilities or better-performing alternatives.

5. **Auditing Access and Use**: Engage security information and event management (SIEM) systems to audit and record encryption usage, policy changes, and access attempts, building comprehensive logs that detect exposure or unauthorized actions.

While encryption significantly strengthens data security, several challenges deserve attention:

- **Performance Overhead**: Encryption introduces computational overhead, which can slow data transfer or processing speeds. Administrators must consider computational resource scaling to accommodate encryption's additional load.

- **Compliance and Regulatory Requirements**: Organizations must ensure that their encryption implementations align with industry-specific regulations like GDPR, HIPAA, or CCPA, often requiring encryption at specific data lifecycle stages.

- **Availability vs. Security**: Creating a balance between availability and security is essential, with encryption strategies planned in a manner ensuring constant data access while reinforcing confidentiality.

Encryption plays a pivotal role in end-to-end OpenShift security architectures, safeguarding information across infrastructural boundaries. As threat environments progress, a proactive encryption strategy equips organizations with the tools necessary to defend data integrity, confidentiality, and resilience against evolving cyber threats. Proper implementation and ongoing management of encryption practices within OpenShift ensure that sensitive data remains protected, regardless of its transit or storage state.

Chapter 8

Storage Solutions in OpenShift

This chapter provides an overview of storage options in OpenShift, highlighting the differences between persistent and ephemeral storage solutions. It details the configuration of Persistent Volumes (PVs) and Persistent Volume Claims (PVCs) for stable application storage and discusses dynamic provisioning for automating resource allocation. Integration with external storage providers such as AWS and NFS is explored to extend storage capabilities. The management of storage classes for efficient administration, along with data backup and recovery strategies, ensures data availability and integrity. Best practices for managing storage in stateful applications are also covered, emphasizing performance and consistency.

8.1 Overview of Storage in OpenShift

In OpenShift, the role of storage is critical to application deployment and management. As containerized applications become more complex and stateful, the need for robust and scalable storage solutions becomes increasingly significant. OpenShift accommodates these demands by providing a variety of storage options designed to support both ephemeral and persistent data needs, integrating seamlessly with cloud-native applications.

OpenShift platforms support two primary categories of storage: *ephemeral storage* and *persistent storage*. Each type serves different purposes, catering to the transient and permanent data requirements of applications respectively.

- **Ephemeral Storage**

Ephemeral storage is ideal for temporary data that does not need to persist beyond the lifecycle of a container. In OpenShift, this storage is typically tied to the pod's lifecycle, meaning that data stored in ephemeral volumes is deleted when the pod is terminated. This type of storage is generally used for data that can be easily recreated or fetched when needed, such as temporary caches or intermediary files in a processing pipeline.

The primary advantage of ephemeral storage is its simplicity and inherent scalability. Since it is bound to the pod, it requires minimal configuration and is automatically managed by the OpenShift platform. This makes it suitable for stateless applications or components where persistence is not a concern.

- **Persistent Storage**

Persistent storage addresses the need for data retention beyond the life of a single pod. OpenShift facilitates this through *Persistent Volumes (PVs)* and *Persistent Volume Claims (PVCs)*. PVs are storage resources within the cluster that have a lifecycle independent of any individual pod, while PVCs are requests for storage by users. The PVC acts as a bridge connecting applications with available storage resources defined by PVs.

The separation of PVs and PVCs abstracts the details of storage provision from the consumers, allowing developers to request storage without needing to know the specifics of the underlying infrastructure. This abstraction enhances flexibility and allows administrators to manage storage resources with greater control and efficiency.

```yaml
apiVersion: v1
kind: PersistentVolume
metadata:
  name: pv-example
spec:
  capacity:
    storage: 10Gi
  accessModes:
    - ReadWriteOnce
  persistentVolumeReclaimPolicy: Retain
  storageClassName: manual
  hostPath:
    path: "/mnt/data"
```

```yaml
apiVersion: v1
kind: PersistentVolumeClaim
metadata:
  name: pvc-example
spec:
  accessModes:
    - ReadWriteOnce
  resources:
    requests:
      storage: 5Gi
```

The examples above illustrate the definition of a Persistent Volume and its corresponding Persistent Volume Claim in YAML. The PV configuration defines a storage resource of 10Gi located at a specified path on the host. The PVC requests 5Gi of storage, specifying the modes through which it intends to access the data.

- **Dynamic Storage Provisioning**

Dynamic storage provisioning further extends OpenShift's capabilities by automating the creation of PVs to satisfy the requirements of PVCs. Instead of statically preconfiguring storage volumes, dynamic provisioning allows storage backend plugins to create volumes on-the-fly, according to user need. This capability reduces administrative overhead and enables more efficient resource utilization.

Provisioners are at the core of dynamic provisioning. These are backend-specific plugins that provision storage according to the demands specified in PVCs. OpenShift supports various provisioners corresponding to different storage platforms, including but not limited to AWS EBS, Azure Disk, and NFS.

- **Integration with External Storage Providers**

231

OpenShift can integrate effectively with external storage providers, ensuring flexibility and scalability required by large-scale deployments. External storage solutions extend storage capabilities beyond the cluster, incorporating resources provided by public cloud services or dedicated on-premises storage systems.

In an OpenShift environment, integration with services like AWS EBS, Google Cloud Persistent Disks, and network file systems such as NFS can be seamlessly achieved. These integrations contribute to OpenShift's deployment scalability by facilitating hybrid cloud strategies, where applications can leverage high-availability storage options without being constrained by single infrastructure limitations.

```
apiVersion: v1
kind: PersistentVolume
metadata:
  name: pv-aws
spec:
  capacity:
    storage: 20Gi
  accessModes:
    - ReadWriteOnce
  persistentVolumeReclaimPolicy: Delete
  storageClassName: aws-ebs
  awsElasticBlockStore:
    volumeID: vol-0abcd1234
    fsType: ext4
```

The AWS EBS example demonstrates how OpenShift can utilize Elastic Block Store volumes for persistent storage. By defining the volume ID and filesystem type, OpenShift can mount these volumes as PVs within the cluster, making them accessible through PVCs.

- **Storage Management Considerations**

Effective storage management on OpenShift involves several considerations beyond the basic provision of storage volumes. Users must ensure appropriate access modes, security policies, and resilience against data loss or corruption. Access modes determine the pattern in which a storage volume can be accessed by pods. Common modes include ReadWriteOnce, ReadOnlyMany, and ReadWriteMany, each offering different levels of access flexibility and concurrency.

Security considerations are equally crucial. OpenShift employs role-based access control (RBAC) to manage who can create or access PVs and PVCs. Further security enhancements can be achieved by applying encryption at rest and configuring audit logging to track access and modifications to storage resources.

Data protection strategies, such as regular backups and replication, are essential for ensuring data integrity and availability. Implementing strategies like snapshots and clones can expedite recovery in the case of data loss or service interruption.

The effective balance of storage solutions in an OpenShift cluster lays the groundwork for successful deployments. The strategic application of ephemeral and persistent storage, dynamic provisioning, and integration with external resources ensures that applications can remain agile and scalable, adapting to changing business and operational needs.

The ability to implement robust storage strategies within OpenShift is a foundational aspect of orchestrating containerized applications. Through advanced storage management capabilities, OpenShift not only supports modern software architectures but also empowers enterprises to leverage the full potential of cloud-native technologies.

8.2 Working with Persistent Volumes and Claims

In OpenShift, Persistent Volumes (PVs) and Persistent Volume Claims (PVCs) form the cornerstone of a scalable, persistent storage architecture. They provide a mechanism to decouple user storage requests from the actual storage infrastructure, allowing seamless data management regardless of its physical location. The symbiosis between PVs and PVCs facilitates stable, long-term storage necessary for stateful applications.

Persistent Volumes (PVs)

A Persistent Volume in OpenShift is a piece of storage within the cluster that has been provisioned by an administrator or dynamically provisioned using storage classes. These volumes possess a life independent of any individual pod, allowing for persistent data storage and retrieval. PVs abstract the details of the underlying storage resources, offering a consistent interface to interact with them.

PVs are defined by several key attributes: capacity, access modes, re-claim policy, and storage class. The capacity attribute specifies the amount of storage available, while access modes determine how many pods can use the volume simultaneously. The reclaim policy dictates what happens to the volume after it is released by a PVC.

```
apiVersion: v1
kind: PersistentVolume
metadata:
  name: pv-nfs
spec:
  capacity:
    storage: 50Gi
  accessModes:
    - ReadWriteOnce
    - ReadOnlyMany
  persistentVolumeReclaimPolicy: Retain
  storageClassName: nfs-class
  nfs:
    path: /var/nfs/data
    server: nfs-server.example.com
```

In this example, the PV is configured to use NFS as the underlying stor-age. The defined access modes include ReadWriteOnce (RWO) and ReadOnlyMany (ROM), enabling multiple patterns of access. The 'Re-tain' reclaim policy indicates that the PV will not be deleted once its claim is released. Instead, further manual intervention is required to clean up or re-provision the resource.

Persistent Volume Claims (PVCs)

Persistent Volume Claims are requests for storage made by users. PVCs serve as an abstraction layer that allows users to request storage with-out specifying the type or configuration of the physical storage device. A PVC effectively binds to a PV that can satisfy the requested size and access modes, providing seamless storage allocation.

```
apiVersion: v1
kind: PersistentVolumeClaim
metadata:
  name: pvc-mysql
spec:
  accessModes:
    - ReadWriteOnce
  resources:
    requests:
      storage: 5Gi
  storageClassName: nfs-class
```

In this configuration, the PVC requests 5Gi of storage with a ReadWriteOnce access mode, matching the PV's storage class. Upon creation, OpenShift finds a suitable PV that meets the criteria, binding the PVC to the PV and making the storage available for use by pods associated with the claim.

Binding and Reclaiming

The binding process between PVCs and PVs is automatic if an available PV natively satisfies a PVC's request. Once a PV is bound to a PVC, it is considered *claimed* and cannot be used by other PVCs until it is released. Release and reclaiming are crucial components in the lifecycle of a PV, determining how storage is recycled or reallocated.

The reclaim policy of a PV outlines the next steps once the PVC releases the volume. Typical policies include:

- *Retain*: Manual intervention is required to delete or repurpose the volume.

- *Recycle*: The volume is scrubbed of previous data and made available for new claims.

- *Delete*: The volume is completely deleted, and the storage is removed from the infrastructure.

Understanding the binding and reclaim mechanisms is essential for administering efficient and reliable storage under various workloads and applications.

Access Modes and Multi-Access Patterns

OpenShift's PV framework provides versatile access modes to accommodate different application needs:

- *ReadWriteOnce (RWO)*: A single node can read from and write to the volume. This mode is ideal for applications requiring exclusive access from one instance, such as a database.

- *ReadOnlyMany (ROM)*: Multiple nodes can read from the volume, but no writing is allowed. ROM is suitable for publication systems or shared libraries where concurrent reading is necessary.

- *ReadWriteMany (RWX)*: Multiple nodes can read from and write to the volume concurrently. RWX is beneficial for distributed filesystems or collaborative editing environments.

The choice of access mode impacts the architecture of the application and should align with specific use case and performance requirements.

Advanced Configuration and Dynamic Provisioning

OpenShift introduces advanced configurations through storage classes to simplify the management of PVs and PVCs. Dynamic provisioning allows for the automatic creation of PVs when a PVC requests storage, reducing administrative responsibility for pre-allocating storage resources. This capability is a game-changer for environments with fluctuating storage needs or variable workload characteristics.

Storage classes define provisioner types, parameters, and reclaim policies, effectively dictating how dynamic provisioning will occur. Below is an example of a storage class capable of dynamically provisioning PVs.

```
apiVersion: storage.k8s.io/v1
kind: StorageClass
metadata:
  name: fast-storage
provisioner: kubernetes.io/aws-ebs
parameters:
  type: gp2
  iopsPerGB: "10"
  encrypted: "true"
reclaimPolicy: Delete
```

This storage class specifies AWS EBS as the provisioner, with parameters for volume type, IOPS rates, and encryption. When a PVC requests storage using this class, OpenShift automatically provisions an EBS volume aligning with these specifications.

Security and Data Protection

Data security in OpenShift storage management is paramount, especially when sensitive and critical data is concerned. Security measures span various levels, from basic access controls to advanced encryption and data replication strategies.

Role-Based Access Control (RBAC) is integral to managing who can create, alter, or access PVs and PVCs. Implementing strict RBAC policies helps in ensuring that only authorized entities can manipulate storage resources.

Encryption is often used to protect data at rest and in transit. OpenShift supports encryption features both natively and through storage provider integrations, adding an extra layer of confidentiality to sensitive data. Furthermore, audit trails can be maintained to monitor and log access and modifications to storage resources, enhancing security postures.

Data protection also involves robust backup and restore mechanisms, supporting routine data snapshots and replicas to provide high availability and swift recovery in case of failures. Strategies like geo-redundancy enhance resilience against localized failures and disasters, strengthening overall data integrity and availability.

By understanding and leveraging the full potential of PVs and PVCs, OpenShift users can deploy resilient, stateful applications with automated, flexible storage solutions. This integral capability underscores OpenShift's capacity to host demanding, modern applications in a cloud-native, containerized environment.

8.3   Dynamic Storage Provisioning

Dynamic storage provisioning in OpenShift represents an advanced capability that supersedes traditional storage allocation and management methods. It enables the automatic creation of Persistent Volumes (PVs) to meet the storage demands defined by Persistent Volume Claims (PVCs) without manual administrator intervention. This on-demand provisioning model aligns well with cloud-native architectures, offering scalability, flexibility, and efficient resource utilization that are essential for modern application deployment.

Dynamic provisioning abstracts the complexity of storage allocation, allowing applications to request and receive storage resources as needed. This process is facilitated by storage classes, which define the characteristics and parameters for storage volumes that can be provisioned dynamically. Each storage class is associated with a provisioner, responsible for the actual allocation and management of the storage.

The architectural flow for dynamic provisioning involves these steps:

- A PVC is created, specifying the storage class it requires.

- The OpenShift controller identifies the requested storage class and invokes the associated provisioner.

- The provisioner interacts with the underlying storage back-end to create a new PV that matches the criteria set forth in the PVC and storage class.

- Once provisioned, the PV is bound to the PVC and made available to the pods that requested it.

This workflow enhances efficiency by scaling storage resources up or down based on actual usage patterns and application demands.

Storage classes in OpenShift provide a mechanism to define and categorize different types of storage provisioning attributes. These can include parameters specific to the provisioner's back-end, such as IOPS capacity, replication factors, or disk type.

```
apiVersion: storage.k8s.io/v1
kind: StorageClass
metadata:
  name: standard
provisioner: kubernetes.io/aws-ebs
parameters:
  type: gp2
  zones: us-east-1a,us-east-1b
reclaimPolicy: Retain
allowVolumeExpansion: true
```

In this storage class, AWS Elastic Block Store (EBS) is used as the provisioner, with parameters specifying a general-purpose SSD (gp2) and target zones. The inclusion of 'allowVolumeExpansion' indicates that the provisioned volume can be expanded post-creation, providing additional flexibility for scaling applications without requiring downtime or data migration.

The dynamic provisioning mechanism in OpenShift is heavily reliant on the Container Storage Interface (CSI) - a standard for exposing arbitrary block and file storage systems to containerized workloads. CSI plugins abstract different storage backends and facilitate the automation of storage-related tasks.

Each CSI plugin corresponds to a specific storage provider and implements a standard set of APIs for volume lifecycle management (create, delete, mount, unmount, etc.). This standardization allows OpenShift to support a wide variety of storage solutions, from cloud-native services like AWS EBS and Google Persistent Disks to traditional enterprise storage arrays.

Adding a new storage provisioner to OpenShift involves deploying it as a CSI driver which often comprises:

- A controller service that handles volume creation and deletion.

- A node service that manages attachment and detachment of volumes to/from nodes.

With CSI, OpenShift users can extend their storage capabilities by easily integrating with multiple cloud and on-premises storage solutions.

Once a PVC specifies a storage class, the OpenShift runtime manages the binding process. It is essential for administrators to understand this cycle to monitor and troubleshoot potential issues.

When a PVC is created with dynamic provisioning enabled, OpenShift attempts to find an appropriate storage class and initiate the provisioning of a suitable PV. If no storage class is specified in a PVC, OpenShift defaults to a predefined class or system settings. The workflow ensures that storage resources are automatically requested and allocated, relieving developers from manual interventions.

```
apiVersion: v1
kind: PersistentVolumeClaim
metadata:
  name: dynamic-pvc
spec:
  accessModes:
    - ReadWriteOnce
  resources:
    requests:
      storage: 20Gi
  storageClassName: standard
```

In this example, a PVC requests a 20Gi volume with a 'ReadWriteOnce' access mode. OpenShift dynamically provisions a PV that matches this request using the 'standard' storage class, which appropriately configures the volume's backend architecture.

Dynamic provisioning not only automates the creation of PVs but also enhances manageability over the volume lifecycle, including expansion capabilities.

Volume expansion is indispensable in scenarios of increasing application data demands. Through storage class attributes like 'allowVolume-Expansion', OpenShift allows a PVC to be resized. This process is seamless and involves the following steps:

- The user updates the 'resources.requests.storage' value in the PVC.

- OpenShift dynamically adjusts the underlying PV size based on the new request.

- The filesystem on the volume might need to be expanded manually within the node, depending on the storage backend.

Volume expansion helps in optimizing resource costs and reduces the need for manual migrations or potential downtimes.

```
apiVersion: v1
kind: PersistentVolumeClaim
metadata:
  name: dynamic-pvc
spec:
  accessModes:
    - ReadWriteOnce
  resources:
    requests:
      storage: 50Gi
  storageClassName: standard
```

By updating the 'storage' field from 20Gi to 50Gi, the request triggers OpenShift to resize the associated PV correspondingly, demonstrating the flexibility of the dynamic provisioning process.

Alongside the operational benefits, dynamic storage provisioning in OpenShift involves particular security considerations and potential challenges.

Since dynamic provisioning automates several steps typically performed by administrators, it is vital to enforce security policies encompassing who can create, bind, and expand PVCs or manage storage classes. Implementing access management through

OpenShift's RBAC and leveraging namespaces are practical measures to encapsulate permissions and control different teams' access.

Also, backup strategies and policies become critical since dynamically provisioned volumes can become crucial parts of production workloads. Integrating snapshot and data replication techniques into the system design can mitigate data risks and enhance recovery processes.

Dynamic provisioning embodies the principles required to support both traditional and modern workloads effectively. Here are some critical use cases and best practices:

- *Cloud-Native Applications*: Applications that scale horizontally benefit from dynamic provisioning's agility, automatically scaling storage in accordance with application demands.

- *Big Data Workloads*: Such workloads typically demand significant storage with varied read/write patterns. Dynamic provisioning enables pre-configured solutions for varying storage needs.

- *Database Deployment*: Databases need reliable, expandable storage in unpredictable loads. Dynamically provisioned PVs ensure that systems remain responsive without manual overhead.

Some best practices include:

- *Monitoring and Alerts*: Implementing monitoring and alerting helps track storage usage and provisioned capacity, ensuring that no unexpected depletion occurs.

- *Optimized Storage Classes*: Designing storage classes with specific application performance requirements in mind can streamline operations and ensure optimal resource alignment.

- *Regular Audits*: Conducting regular audits of storage policies to ensure compliance and alignment with evolving security postures.

Dynamic storage provisioning significantly enhances OpenShift's storage capabilities, ensuring that applications have the resources they need without undue complexity. By effectively managing the balance between operational efficiency and the flexibility of storage solutions, users can focus on deploying more strategic and dynamic application workloads.

8.4 Integrating with External Storage Providers

Integration with external storage providers in OpenShift is a powerful strategy to enhance the storage capabilities of your containerized applications. Leveraging external storage offers flexibility, scalability, and accessibility beyond the inherent limits of on-cluster storage resources. It empowers OpenShift to seamlessly incorporate diverse storage solutions from cloud providers or on-premises systems, thus enabling hybrid and multi-cloud strategies.

Rationale and Benefits

Integrating with external storage providers supports the following key objectives:

- *Scalability*: External storage systems, particularly those offered by major cloud providers, can accommodate vast amounts of data and high IOPS demands. This scalability ensures that storage resources can grow dynamically with the application needs.

- *High Availability and Reliability*: External storage providers often offer advanced features such as georedundancy, automated backups, and robust failure recovery mechanisms that enhance data availability and durability.

- *Cost Optimization*: By utilizing external storage, organizations can leverage pay-as-you-go models to optimize storage expenses, only paying for the capacity used rather than provisioning large amounts of on-premises hardware.

- *Easy Management and Access*: External storage systems typically provide user-friendly interfaces and APIs, simplifying the management of storage resources and their integration with OpenShift.

- *Data Sovereignty and Governance*: The ability to store data in specific geographic locations aids compliance with various data protection regulations.

Common External Storage Providers

Numerous external storage providers can be integrated with OpenShift, including:

- *Amazon Web Services Elastic Block Store (AWS EBS)*: A popular choice for applications requiring consistent, low-latency block storage performance.

- *Google Cloud Persistent Disks (GCP PD)*: Offers scalable solid-state and hard disk drive storage options with snapshot and replication features.

- *Azure Disks*: Provides secure, easy-to-manage disk storage for high-performance and mission-critical applications.

- *Network File Systems (NFS)*: An established protocol for shared storage solutions, suitable for applications needing cross-platform access.

Configuration Process and Prerequisites

Integrating an external provider involves several steps, each nuanced to the specific provider's interface and OpenShift's object management capabilities. It typically requires account access, credentials, and appropriate role permissions across both OpenShift and the storage provider.

- **Pre-Configuration Steps:**
    - Ensure that the OpenShift environment has network access to the external provider.
    - Obtain necessary API credentials or service accounts, and configure roles that allow OpenShift to manage the storage service.

- **Defining Storage Classes:**

– Create storage classes specific to the external provider, including parameters like volume type, size, access modes, and reclaim policies.

- **Utilizing CSI Drivers:**

  – Deploy appropriate Container Storage Interface (CSI) drivers for automatic provisioning and mounting of the external storage within OpenShift.

Practical Example with AWS EBS

For AWS EBS, integration involves deploying a CSI driver and creating a storage class to provision volumes dynamically.

```
apiVersion: storage.k8s.io/v1
kind: StorageClass
metadata:
  name: ebs-sc
provisioner: ebs.csi.aws.com
parameters:
  type: gp2
  fsType: ext4
  encrypted: "true"
reclaimPolicy: Delete
```

This configuration uses AWS's CSI driver to dynamically provision general-purpose SSD volumes. The 'encrypted' parameter ensures data at rest is securely stored. With the storage class defined, a PVC can be created as follows:

```
apiVersion: v1
kind: PersistentVolumeClaim
metadata:
  name: pvc-ebs
spec:
  accessModes:
    - ReadWriteOnce
  resources:
    requests:
      storage: 10Gi
  storageClassName: ebs-sc
```

When the PVC is applied, OpenShift automatically provisions an EBS volume according to the specified storage class parameters.

Advanced Integration Techniques

Integrating external providers might involve advanced techniques such as multi-zone or multi-region deployments and cross-provider data replication. This setup can optimize disaster recovery strategies and ensure application availability across geographic locations.

- **Multi-Zone Storage:**
    - By spanning storage volumes across multiple availability zones, applications can sustain operational disruptions within a single zone without loss of data access.

- **Cross-Region Replication:**
    - Configuring data replication across regions aids in maintaining data integrity and accessibility, even in catastrophic regional failures.

- **Provider Agnostic Interfaces:**
    - Leveraging abstraction layers or middleware that standardize interactions with different storage APIs can simplify operations and reduce vendor lock-in. Implementations can pivot between providers based on cost, performance, or regulatory needs.

Security, Monitoring, and Compliance

Securing data using external providers encompasses encryption, access control, and compliance with industry standards and regulations.

- **Encryption:** Advanced providers often support full lifecycle encryption (in transit and at rest) and key management services (KMS), essential features from a security perspective.

- **Access Control:** Role-based policies should be enforced on both OpenShift and the external storage provider platforms to restrict data handling to authorized parties. Integration with identity and access management systems (e.g., IAM in AWS) can enhance these controls.

- **Monitoring and Metrics:** Implementing monitoring through solutions that leverage provider-specific APIs (such as CloudWatch for AWS) aids in tracking storage performance and usage metrics. Monitoring can provide alerts on anomalies or breaches that require immediate response.

- **Compliance and Auditing:** Automatic logging and auditing features facilitate compliance with regulations such as GDPR, CCPA, or HIPAA. Providers often offer built-in tools to track access and modifications, which can be integrated into OpenShift logging and audit workflows.

Cost Considerations and Optimization Strategies

While leveraging external storage can be beneficial, it's important to be mindful of potential cost implications. Storage costs can be strategically managed and optimized to avoid unexpected expenses:

- **Cost Assessment and Budgeting:** Evaluate the pricing models of different providers, accounting for factors such as storage type (block, file, or object), redundancy options, and data transfer rates.

- **Long-term Storage Solutions:** Employ lifecycle policies or archival solutions (e.g., AWS S3 Glacier) for infrequently accessed data to minimize costs without losing data retention capabilities.

- **Data Transfer Economization:** Minimize excessive data transfers between regions or across providers to mitigate transfer costs. Employ caching strategies to optimize data flow efficiency.

Use Cases and Strategic Implementation

- **Hybrid Cloud Deployment:** By bridging OpenShift with external storage, applications can leverage both on-premises resources and cloud benefits, supporting seamless hybrid cloud strategies.

- **Data-Intensive Applications:** Analytics and data processing workloads often require integration with high-throughput external storage to handle extensive IO operations.

- **Backup and Disaster Recovery (DR):** Extensive integration capabilities help orchestrate sophisticated DR strategies, making it easier to automate backups and data syncs between primary and DR sites.

Integrating OpenShift with external storage providers embodies a robust approach to enhancing application scalability, resilience, and flexibility. Strategic employment of these integrations aligns with organizational objectives to modernize IT infrastructure while managing costs and enhancing user experience.

8.5   Managing Storage Classes

In OpenShift, managing storage classes is pivotal to the intelligent orchestration of storage resources. Storage classes provide a method of defining different qualities of service for storage beyond basic capacity. They enable administrators to characterize storage in ways that best fit diverse workloads ranging from simple, low-cost archiving to high-performance transactional systems.

Understanding Storage Classes

A *storage class* represents a way to describe the "class" of storage being offered. Different classes might map to quality-of-service levels, backup policies, or arbitrary policies determined by the cluster administrators. Often, this abstraction allows the separation of concerns between the resources used for managing storage and the applications consuming it.

A typical storage class in OpenShift is defined through YAML configuration, containing a provisioner that dictates how volumes of this class are dynamically provisioned. Provisioners may be backed by plugins such as those using the Container Storage Interface (CSI), enabling compatibility with multiple underlying storage systems.

```yaml
apiVersion: storage.k8s.io/v1
kind: StorageClass
metadata:
  name: fast
provisioner: kubernetes.io/aws-ebs
parameters:
  type: io1
```

```
  iopsPerGB: "10"
reclaimPolicy: Retain
allowVolumeExpansion: true
volumeBindingMode: Immediate
```

In this example, the 'fast' storage class uses AWS's Elastic Block Store (EBS) with high IOPS provisioned on 'io1' type volumes. The 'allowVolumeExpansion' field ensures volumes can be resized post-creation, while the 'reclaimPolicy' retains the persistent volume until manually handled, even after its claim is deleted.

Provisioners and Parameters

The choice of provisioner within a storage class substantively determines the backend capabilities and options available. Common provisioners include those for AWS EBS, Google Persistent Disks, and other file or block storage systems that adhere to the CSI specification.

Key parameters often configurable include:

- *Type of Storage*: Defines the storage media type, such as SSD or HDD, dictating performance characteristics.

- *Replication Factors*: Enhances data resilience by storing replicas across different nodes or datacenters.

- *Encryption*: Configuring encryption handles sensitive data storage needs securely.

- *IOPS Settings*: Tailors performance to meet application-specific requirements, critical in systems requiring guaranteed IOPS delivery.

Reclaim Policies and Binding Modes

Reclaim policies determine the lifecycle behavior of persistent volumes when released by the PVC. The policies include:

- *Retain*: Keeps the volume for manual reclamation—it preserves data, allowing users to manually clean up and reuse data.

- *Recycle*: Offers simple scrubbing and reuse of volumes. Typically intended for default, less secure environments.

- *Delete*: Automatic removal of data and volume once a PVC releases it, common with cloud environments where cost management is critical.

Volume binding modes govern when the volumes are bound to claims:

- *Immediate*: The volume is bound to the PVC as soon as it is created, regardless of pod scheduling.

- *WaitForFirstConsumer*: Defer binding until a pod using the PVC is scheduled, optimizing resource localization according to pod placement.

Managing and Monitoring Storage Classes

Effective management of storage classes in OpenShift requires visibility into how classes are being used and how they impact the workload performance and stability. This involves routine monitoring and adjustments based on observed patterns and evolving application requirements.

- **Performance Monitoring**: Utilize integrated monitoring tools or external solutions like Prometheus to gather metrics on storage performance (latency, IOPS, throughput) associated with each class.

- **Capacity Planning**: Regularly review the storage usage to forecast usage trends.

- **Policy Audits**: Conduct regular audits to verify that the storage class policies adhere to governance and compliance standards, ensuring data protection and security policies align.

Metrics and reporting platforms can help visualize data about how effectively storage classes are meeting their intended purpose, providing insight into areas requiring optimization or reconfiguration.

Use Cases in Application Scenarios

Different applications demand specific storage flavors, and defining these via storage classes simplifies the deployment and maintenance process. Here are a few typical scenarios:

249

- **Databases**: High-performance, transactional databases may require SSD-backed 'fast' storage classes with high IOPS and low latency. Backup solutions should be integrated into the class definition.

- **Archival Systems**: Data lakes or archival storage often target a 'cold' storage class leveraging cost-effective, high-capacity HDDs, typically focused on cost reduction.

- **CI/CD Pipelines**:   Development environments should use ephemeral, 'medium' performance classes where cost does not outstrip speed needs, allowing rapid build-test cycles.

Determining your storage class taxonomy boils down to understanding your organizational data footprint, application performance characteristics, and infrastructure capabilities.

Configuration and Best Practices

Maintaining a sound storage class strategy involves following best practices that account for current needs while anticipating future scale and complexity.

1. **Balance Performance and Cost**:   By understanding your workload specifics, balance premium storage use against operational cost reduction strategies—e.g., using burstable volumes only when necessary.

2. **Leverage Automation**: Use management tools to automate asset discovery and configuration enforcement, ensuring consistency across deployments.

3. **Document and Version Configurations**: Maintain comprehensive documentation around storage classes, including rationale, expected behaviors, and known-good configurations to aid troubleshooting and new environment bootstrapping.

4. **Storage as a Lifecycle**: Consider integration from provisioning and operation to eventual deprecation, aligning with data governance policies from the ground up.

This holistic approach ensures that OpenShift environments can offer diverse storage provisioning strategies that adjust quickly to technological advancement and business transformations.

Security Considerations

As with all aspects of IT infrastructure, security is paramount when managing storage classes. Properly securing storage involves multiple layers of defense:

- **Access Control**: Enforce role-based access control (RBAC) to permit only authorized groups to manage and create storage classes. Adoption of security policies that define who can create, delete, and modify storage classes is essential.

- **Data Encryption**: Wherever possible, enable data encryption both at rest and in transit. Configure the provisioner to leverage underlying storage system encryption capabilities to shield data from unauthorized access.

- **Audit and Compliance**: Ensure that all interactions with storage are logged and auditable by implementing log gathering and analysis tools to identify anomalies and unauthorized access attempts.

Managing storage classes in OpenShift forms a critical part of modern cloud-native application architectures. By providing administrators with the tools and best practices to configure, monitor, and secure storage resources, OpenShift ensures that applications receive the performance and reliability they demand, dynamically adapting to an organization's evolving landscape.

8.6 Data Backup and Recovery Strategies

Data backup and recovery strategies are crucial components of a resilient OpenShift architecture. As enterprises rely increasingly on containers to deploy critical applications, safeguarding data assets from loss, corruption, or accidental deletion becomes imperative. An effective backup and recovery plan ensures data integrity, drastically reducing downtime and mitigating the impacts of failures or disasters.

Understanding Backup and Recovery Requirements

The first step in developing a robust backup and recovery strategy is to define the requirements and objectives. This includes understanding the different types of data needing protection, such as application data, configuration files, database records, and system states. Each of these components may have specific requirements regarding backup frequency, retention periods, and recovery objectives:

- *Recovery Time Objective (RTO)*: The acceptable amount of time to restore a service after a disruption. It influences how backups are prioritized and accessed during a recovery event.

- *Recovery Point Objective (RPO)*: The maximum acceptable data loss expressed in time. It defines how frequently backups need to be taken to avoid unacceptable data loss.

- *Data Resilience and Accessibility*: Ensuring that backups are securely stored and easily accessible when needed, potentially across diverse geographic locations or storage providers to boost resilience against localized events.

- *Compliance and Regulatory Concerns*: Adherence to data regulation guidelines such as GDPR, CCPA, or industry-specific rules can dictate the methods or locations where data can be stored.

Backup Methodologies and Techniques

Several methodologies exist for implementing data backups in OpenShift, each with its advantages and intricacies. These include snapshot-based backups, application-consistent backups, and disaster recovery solutions.

- **Snapshot-Based Backups**: This involves capturing a point-in-time image of a data volume. Snapshots are critical for quickly restoring systems to a previous state and are supported by most cloud-based and modern on-premises storage providers.

```
aws ec2 create-snapshot --volume-id vol-0abcdef12 --description "Snapshot
of volume"
```

In this example, we create a snapshot of an AWS EBS volume, encompassing all the data present at the moment of capture. The process is optimized for speed and is non-intrusive, with differential snapshots ensuring only changed blocks are copied in subsequent snapshots.

- **Application-Consistent Backups**: Ensure that data is in a consistent state when backups occur. Application-consistent backups typically involve quiescing applications or databases to temporarily pause write operations during snapshot creation, guaranteeing data reliability.

- **Incremental and Differential Backups**: These lighter alternatives to full backups capture only data changes since the last backup (incremental) or the last full backup (differential). This approach streamlines the backup process and reduces storage space and time requirements.

Backup Tools and Solutions for OpenShift

Several tools and solutions are available to manage and automate backups within OpenShift. Key considerations when selecting a backup solution will include compatibility, scalability, automation capabilities, and security features:

- **Velero**: An open-source tool specifically designed for Kubernetes and OpenShift, Velero provides features such as scheduled backups, retention policies, and seamless migration of applications between clusters.

```
velero backup create app-backup --include-namespaces=my-app --wait
```

This command initiates a backup for the 'my-app' namespace, ensuring all relevant resources, persistent volumes, and configurations are securely backed up.

- **TrilioVault**: A comprehensive backup and restore platform, TrilioVault offers application-consistent backups, point-in-time

253

restoration, and multi-cloud recovery features that make it attractive to enterprises with containerized workloads.

- **Custom Scripts and Automation**: Often, organizations may tailor custom scripts to fit unique requirements, utilizing Kubernetes' built-in CLI capabilities to handle snapshots and volumes.

Recovery Strategies and Execution

When disaster strikes, efficient recovery is critical to restoring service continuity. A well-structured recovery strategy involves clear procedural steps, prioritization of services, and verification of recovered data:

- **Defining Recovery Procedures**: Create detailed documentation outlining recovery steps required for different scenarios, such as partial data loss vs. full cluster failure. This should include step-by-step guides for each service component, listing the sequence and command specifics required for restoration.

- **Prioritization and Tiering**: Determine which services are critical for recovery to restore business operations rapidly, and identify non-critical services that may be restored afterwards.

- **Regular DR Drills**: Regular testing via simulated disaster recovery drills is necessary to ensure the effectiveness of the backup and restore process. It validates the RTO and RPO, enhancing confidence in recovery capabilities.

- **Verification and Validation**: Once data is restored, validate the integrity and consistency of data to confirm successful recovery. Automation tools with built-in validation mechanisms can enhance this process's accuracy and efficiency.

Security and Compliance in Backups

Security is fundamental to backup systems, given the sensitive nature of the data. Several steps can enhance security and ensure that backups comply with necessary regulations:

- **Encryption**: Encrypt data both in transit and at rest to protect it against unauthorized access or breaches during storage and transmission.

254

- **Access Controls**: Implement strict access control policies using role-based access control (RBAC) to restrict backup management operations to authorized personnel only.

- **Audit and Log Monitoring**: Enable comprehensive logging and auditing of backup operations to ensure ongoing compliance with regulations and to detect potential unauthorized activities.

- **Geographic and Legal Considerations**: Be aware of regulations concerning cross-border data transfers, and ensure backups comply with jurisdictional requirements for where data is physically stored.

Cost Management and Optimization

Managing costs related to backup operations is crucial for maintaining budget constraints:

- **Tiered Storage**: Implement tiered storage strategies, where primary backups are kept on high-performing storage with secondary backups moved to cost-effective archival solutions.

- **Data Deduplication**: Utilize deduplication technologies to minimize storage requirements by eliminating duplicate copies of repeated data blocks.

- **Automated Cleanup Policies**: Configure cleanup policies to delete or archive obsolete or unnecessary data, reducing waste and optimizing resource usage.

- **Backup Frequency and Size Optimization**: Balance backup frequency with retained data size to maintain RPO targets efficiently without incurring excessive storage costs.

Continual Improvement and Strategy Evolution

An effective backup and recovery strategy isn't static. It requires continuous monitoring, evaluation, and improvement to keep pace with evolving business objectives and technological advancements:

- **Regular Review and Updates**: Conduct frequent reviews of backup size, performance metrics, and recovery times to ensure alignment with recovery objectives.

- **Implement Feedback Loops**: Develop feedback mechanisms from disaster recovery tests that inform enhancements to backup methodologies and recovery plans.

- **Scalable Solutions**: Ensure your backup solutions can scale with enterprise growth, supporting increasing data volumes, service expansions, and upgraded features.

By stepping beyond a mere plan into a fully integrated, continuously refined backup and recovery strategy, OpenShift users can cultivate a resilient environment that instils confidence in data security and service continuity amid potential disruptions.

8.7   Storage Best Practices for Stateful Applications

Stateful applications require special attention to storage configurations in OpenShift to ensure data consistency, availability, and performance. Unlike stateless applications, which only need temporary storage for transient data, stateful applications maintain persistent data across restarts and deployments. Successful management of storage for such applications involves strategic planning and consideration of best practices tailored to these demands.

Understanding Stateful Workloads

Stateful workloads encapsulate applications that preserve data states over transitions. These include, but are not limited to, databases, content management systems, and file storage services. Key characteristics of these workloads include the need for persistent storage, ordered transactions, and often, high availability and disaster recovery capabilities.

Given these demands, applying solutions such as persistent volumes through PersistentVolumeClaims (PVCs), leveraging StorageClasses for dynamic provisioning and defining precise access modes becomes essential for stateful application success.

Designing Storage for High Availability

Ensuring high availability for stateful applications typically involves creating redundancies and failover strategies that prevent data loss and allow seamless continuation of operations.

- Data Replication and Mirroring: Replicate data across multiple storage locations or nodes to protect against hardware failures. This can be enabled through storage plugins that support replication, allowing databases or critical application data to remain available during node disruptions.

- Geographic Redundancy: Employ geographic redundancy by storing copies of critical data or running replicas of applications across multiple data centers or cloud regions. This setup mitigates risks related to regional disasters, safeguarding continuity.

- Load Balancing and Distributed Architecture: Deploy application instances with distributed storage architectures using load balancers. This maintains performance levels and efficient data distribution across multiple storage devices.

Optimizing Performance with Appropriate Access Modes

Access modes play a pivotal role in defining how persistent volumes can be accessed by pods and hence, influence application performance and concurrency:

- ReadWriteOnce (RWO): Best suited for applications where a single instance handles read/write operations, such as many traditional databases that maintain exclusive data writes.

- ReadOnlyMany (ROM): Useful for scenarios where multiple application instances need concurrent read-access to the same dataset, for instance, deploying read replicas for scale-out querying operations.

- ReadWriteMany (RWX): Enables concurrent write access to storage across several instances. It's suitable for collaborative applications or clusters relying on shared state files.

Optimizing access modes based on application read and write characteristics enhances efficiency, reduces latency, and maximizes infrastructure utilization.

Implementing Robust Data Backup and Recovery Paths

Stateful workloads are sensitive to data corruption and require stringent backup and recovery systems:

- Regular Backups: Schedule frequent backups aligning with application RPO and RTO requirements, employing snapshot techniques for minimal disruption.

- Application-Consistent Snapshots: Coordinate with applications to enter a consistent state before backups, leveraging quiescing mechanisms to flush write buffers ensuring data validity.

```
velero create backup my-statefulset --include-namespaces=stateful-app --
    wait
```

This Velero operation initiates a backup of a specific stateful set's namespace, encapsulating all its associated persistent volumes and configurations.

- Test Recovery Procedures: Conduct recovery drills periodically to validate that backup processes meet expected recovery timelines and maintain data integrity.

Security and Compliance Considerations

Protecting stateful application data involves securing backups and enforcing compliance with regulatory mandates:

- Data Encryption: Encrypt all data at rest and in transit to prevent unauthorized visibility. Solutions may leverage underlying storage provider encryption capabilities alongside custom encryption settings in application layers.

- Access Policies: Implement stringent role-based access controls within both OpenShift and storage systems, ensuring only authorized personnel have the ability to alter storage settings or access data.

- Audit Logs and Monitoring: Enable audit logging to monitor data access patterns and detect anomalies. Regular review of logs is crucial for compliance and security posture maintenance.

Cost Management Strategies

Managing the cost associated with stateful workloads involves strategic planning and efficient resource utilization:

- Right-sizing Storage: Precisely calculate storage requirements based on application growth forecasts, opting for scalable resources that allow burst capacity when needed.

- Leveraging Storage Tiers: Utilize a combination of storage tiers for active, infrequently accessed, and archived data. This ensures high-performance storage is reserved for critical active datasets, whereas archival data inherits cost-efficient, large-capacity storage solutions.

- Efficient Use of Snapshots: Employ incremental snapshots to reduce the storage footprint by only capturing changes since the last complete backup, rather than full data duplications.

Evolving with Technological Improvements

Stateful application strategies should grow dynamically with innovations in storage technologies and methodologies:

- Adopting CSI Drivers: Stay current with advancements in CSI drivers that extend storage capabilities and feature sets, enhancing flexibility in managing different types of storage backends.

- Automation and CI/CD Integration: Integrate storage management with CI/CD workflows to automate deployment updates, configuration changes, and scaling operations aligning with continuous delivery objectives.

Case Study Example

Consider an online retail platform hosting a transactional database coupled with a catalog microservice where each element relies on stateful data management:

- *Transactional Database* requires RWX storage for write concurrency across several instances and needs automated failover

259

zones set across data regions for geo-redundancy, ensuring constant availability.

- *Catalog Microservice* demands a multimodal storage system, implementing high-performance tiered storage for active catalogue queries, integrated with bulk archival options for historic product data utilizing long-term cost-optimized solutions.

Both components must deploy cohesive backup routines, with the catalog easing versioning and history retrieval through differential snapshots, whereas the transactional database enforces minimal latency failover mirroring for continuity under peak loads.

These best practices establish a foundation for handling the nuanced demands of stateful applications within OpenShift. By implementing strategic storage plans, robust backup/recovery protocols, security enhancements, and cost management strategies, stateful workloads can be effectively managed to ensure reliable and scalable application performance. As these applications grow increasingly central to infrastructure strategies, maintaining robust storage practices remains critical to sustaining long-term operational excellence.

Chapter 9

OpenShift Pipelines and Automation

This chapter examines the role of OpenShift Pipelines, powered by Tekton, in automating continuous integration and delivery (CI/CD) processes. It guides readers through the configuration of CI/CD pipelines for seamless application deployment, integrating source control and image registries to streamline workflows. Emphasis is placed on incorporating automated testing to ensure quality and managing pipeline resources and parameters for execution control. The use of triggers to automate pipeline runs based on specific events is explored, alongside techniques for monitoring and debugging pipelines to maintain efficiency and reliability in automated deployments.

9.1 Foundations of OpenShift Pipelines

OpenShift Pipelines are an essential component of Red Hat's OpenShift Container Platform, designed to facilitate Continuous Integration and Continuous Delivery (CI/CD) processes. At the heart of OpenShift Pipelines is Tekton, an open-source framework that provides the building blocks for creating CI/CD systems. The utilization of OpenShift Pipelines streamlines automated workflows for development, testing, and deployment, integrating seamlessly with Kubernetes native solutions.

OpenShift Pipelines enable developers and operations teams to automate the complex process of managing container-based applications. This section delves deeply into the fundamental aspects of OpenShift Pipelines, explaining how they work, their components, and their significance for CI/CD automation.

Conceptual Overview

OpenShift Pipelines leverages Kubernetes constructs to facilitate CI/CD workflows in a cloud-native environment. Tekton, the underlying engine, offers flexible and extensible tools that allow the orchestration of tasks within a cluster. Tekton resources are defined through custom Kubernetes resources, enhancing their integration into modern containerized environments.

Core Components

The primary components of OpenShift Pipelines include pipelines, tasks, steps, resources, and workspaces. Understanding these components is crucial for building efficient and robust CI/CD workflows.

- **Pipelines:** At the highest level, a pipeline represents the sequence of tasks to be executed. It is a logical flow described as a 'Pipeline' resource that encapsulates various stages of CI/CD processes—from code building to deployment.

- **Tasks:** A task is a collection of steps defined as a 'Task' resource. Each task specifies a discrete operation within the pipeline, such as compiling code, running tests, or deploying applications. Tasks are reusable components that can be shared across different pipelines.

- **Steps:** Each task consists of one or multiple steps, executed sequentially. Steps are individual units of execution where each step often corresponds to invoking a specific command or script within a container. The steps are specified in a 'Task' resource as a series of container images and commands.

262

- **Resources:** Resources in OpenShift Pipelines are inputs and outputs necessary for task execution. Common resources include Git repositories, Docker images, and cluster configurations. The 'PipelineResource' object in Tekton defines these resources, allowing tasks to interact with external systems.

- **Workspaces:** Workspaces are shared file storage locations accessible to tasks during pipeline execution. Workspaces facilitate the sharing of data between multiple tasks within a pipeline run, enabling efficient data management and persistence.

Configuring a Pipeline

Configuring an OpenShift Pipeline involves defining these components in YAML format, reflecting the declarative nature of Kubernetes resources. The following example illustrates a simple pipeline configuration that encompasses application building and testing.

```
apiVersion: tekton.dev/v1beta1
kind: Pipeline
metadata:
  name: simple-ci-pipeline
spec:
  tasks:
    - name: build-task
      taskRef:
        name: build-to-image
    - name: test-task
      taskRef:
        name: run-tests
      runAfter:
        - build-task
```

Pipeline Execution

The execution of a pipeline is initiated via a 'PipelineRun' resource, which specifies the pipeline and its parameterization for a particular execution instance. This mechanism allows pipelines to be triggered manually or automatically, adapting to different use cases such as on-demand builds or integration with version control systems.

```
apiVersion: tekton.dev/v1beta1
kind: PipelineRun
metadata:
  generateName: simple-ci-pipeline-run-
spec:
  pipelineRef:
    name: simple-ci-pipeline
```

Upon execution, Tekton manages the lifecycle of tasks within the pipeline, ensuring dependencies between tasks are respected through the 'runAfter' specification. Logs from pipeline runs are made available, facilitating monitoring and debugging.

Integration with Source Control

To achieve fully automated workflows, OpenShift Pipelines can be integrated with source control systems such as Git. This integration allows for pipelines to be automatically triggered based on code changes, contributing to a streamlined CI/CD process.

A common approach involves defining a 'PipelineResource' for a Git repository, which tasks can use to clone the source code during execution.

```
apiVersion: tekton.dev/v1alpha1
kind: PipelineResource
metadata:
  name: source-repo
spec:
  type: git
  params:
    - name: url
      value: "https://github.com/example/repo.git"
```

Pipeline tasks can then access this resource, enabling them to perform operations such as building the application with the latest code.

Role in CI/CD Automation

OpenShift Pipelines enhance CI/CD processes by reducing manual intervention and enabling consistent, repeatable builds and deployments. These pipelines facilitate a DevOps culture, encouraging collaboration between development and operations teams.

CI/CD automation involves several practices that OpenShift Pipelines support, including:

- **Continuous Integration:** By automatically triggering builds and tests whenever new code is committed, organizations can detect integration issues early, ensuring code changes do not disrupt application functionality.

- **Continuous Delivery:** Pipelines streamline deployment processes, facilitating the delivery of application updates to staging or production environments. OpenShift Pipelines provide the necessary tooling and structure to automate deployments while maintaining control over the process.

- **Continuous Deployment:** In scenarios where deployments are automated to production, OpenShift Pipelines help in managing the deployment funnel, ensuring quality gates are met and deployments occur without human intervention.

Scalability and Flexibility

One of the distinguishing features of OpenShift Pipelines is their scalability, derived from their Kubernetes-native implementation. Pipelines can be scaled by leveraging Kubernetes primitives such as pods and nodes, ensuring they are able to handle large volumes of tasks efficiently without degradation of performance.

Additionally, pipelines offer extensive flexibility through the use of custom tasks and resources, allowing organizations to tailor pipelines to fit their unique workflows and integration requirements. This customization is supported by Tekton's pluggable architecture, encouraging extension and enhancement to meet evolving technology stacks.

Security Considerations

Security is integral to CI/CD processes, and OpenShift Pipelines address this by allowing fine-grained Role-Based Access Control (RBAC). This ensures that tasks and pipelines execute with appropriate permissions, reducing the risk of unauthorized access or modifications.

Furthermore, tasks run in isolated containers, enhancing security by keeping task executions encapsulated. This containerized execution model fits well within security policies adhering to least privilege principles.

OpenShift Pipelines, through their integration with Tekton, present a comprehensive solution for managing CI/CD workflows in modern Kubernetes environments. The configuration of pipelines, tasks, and resources, as explored, underscores their significance in promoting automation, scalability, and security.

The architecture inherent within OpenShift Pipelines supports both standard and complex workflows, addressing diverse application lifecycle stages. Through proper integration with associated tooling, these pipelines enable efficient, reliable, and secure application deployment methodologies, reinforcing the foundational principles of DevOps.

Managing the transition from traditional software release cycles to automated, cloud-native CI/CD processes requires an understanding of these crucial aspects of OpenShift Pipelines, laying the groundwork for innovative and streamlined software development practices.

9.2 Building a CI/CD Pipeline

The development of a Continuous Integration and Continuous Delivery (CI/CD) Pipeline within OpenShift involves a meticulous approach that intertwines various components of the infrastructure to automate the building, testing, and deployment of applications. The ability to construct a robust CI/CD pipeline is crucial for modern software development, enhancing efficiency and reducing time-to-market for updates and features.

Building a CI/CD pipeline in OpenShift comprises several stages, beginning with the design and configuration of tasks and resources, progressing to the integration of testing procedures and deployment strategies. Understanding each stage is invaluable for creating pipelines that are automated, reliable, and maintainable.

Pipeline Architecture

A CI/CD pipeline in OpenShift is architected using Tekton, which provides the abstractions necessary for managing complex workflows. The architecture hinges on defining a sequence of tasks that reflect the stages of a typical software lifecycle: source retrieval, build, test, and deploy.

Design Considerations: The design of a pipeline should consider the modularity and reusability of tasks. Tasks should be designed to accomplish specific units of work and be reusable across different pipelines or projects. This aligns with the principles of DRY (Don't Repeat Yourself) and modular programming, enhancing maintainability and reducing overhead.

Essential Components

- **Tasks and Steps:** As previously discussed, a task encompasses a group of steps that execute sequentially. When building a pipeline, tasks are the primary units of computation and carry out specific functions such as code compilation, testing, and artifact creation. Steps within these tasks are defined as individual containers, each performing specific commands or scripts.

- **Pipeline Resources:** Resources such as Git repositories and Docker images are vital inputs and outputs for task operations. These resources are declared using 'PipelineResource' objects in YAML format, serving as interfaces with external systems or tools.

- **Workspaces:** Workspaces facilitate data sharing across tasks within a single pipeline execution. For instance, the result of a build task might be a binary or Docker image that needs to be available for a subsequent deployment task.

Developing a Simple Pipeline

To illustrate the development of a pipeline, consider a scenario where an application is built, tested, and deployed. The following is a step-by-step guide to creating a pipeline using YAML definitions.

First, define the tasks required for the pipeline. A build task is responsible for compiling the code and creating a container image, while a test task runs unit and integration tests on the codebase.

```
apiVersion: tekton.dev/v1beta1
kind: Task
metadata:
  name: build-task
spec:
  steps:
    - name: build
      image: maven:3.6.3-jdk-8
      command:
        - mvn
      args:
        - clean
        - package
```

```
apiVersion: tekton.dev/v1beta1
kind: Task
metadata:
  name: test-task
spec:
```

```
steps:
  - name: test
    image: maven:3.6.3-jdk-8
    command:
      - mvn
    args:
      - test
```

With these tasks defined, the next step is to encapsulate them within a pipeline.

```
apiVersion: tekton.dev/v1beta1
kind: Pipeline
metadata:
  name: ci-pipeline
spec:
  tasks:
    - name: build
      taskRef:
        name: build-task
    - name: test
      taskRef:
        name: test-task
      runAfter:
        - build
```

The defined pipeline sequences the build and test tasks, ensuring that the test task is only initiated if the build task completes successfully.

Triggering Pipelines

Executing the pipeline is accomplished through a 'PipelineRun'. This resource specifies the pipeline to be executed and configures any parameters needed for the run.

```
apiVersion: tekton.dev/v1beta1
kind: PipelineRun
metadata:
  generateName: ci-pipeline-run-
spec:
  pipelineRef:
    name: ci-pipeline
```

Automating the pipeline run is an essential facet of CI/CD, and OpenShift Pipelines support integration with webhooks from version control systems to trigger pipeline runs on specific events, such as code commits or pull requests.

Incorporating Advanced Features

Building on the basic pipeline, advanced features can be introduced to enhance the functionality and efficiency of CI/CD:

- **Parameterization:** Pipelines can be parameterized to accept user-defined inputs at runtime, enabling greater flexibility. Parameters are defined within the pipeline and referenced in tasks.

```
apiVersion: tekton.dev/v1beta1
kind: Pipeline
metadata:
  name: param-pipeline
spec:
  params:
  - name: git-url
    type: string
    description: "The URL of the git repository"
  tasks:
  - name: fetch-repo
    taskSpec:
      params:
      - name: git-url
        type: string
      steps:
      - name: clone
        image: alpine/git
        script: |
          git clone $(inputs.params.git-url)
```

- **Parallelism and Concurrency:** Pipelines can run tasks in parallel, improving overall execution time. This is achieved by removing dependencies that enforce serial execution (e.g., 'runAfter'), allowing independent or parallel tasks to be defined without these dependencies.

- **Error Handling:** Robust error handling is vital for production pipelines. Tekton supports mechanisms like 'finally' tasks, which execute at the end of a pipeline regardless of prior task success or failure. These are useful for cleanup operations or sending notifications.

Securing CI/CD Pipelines

Security is a fundamental concern at every stage of the CI/CD process. Securing the pipeline involves several practices:

- **Secure Credentials Handling:** Secrets, such as API keys and passwords, should be managed via OpenShift's built-in secret management capability. Tasks can access secrets securely without exposing sensitive data.

```
apiVersion: tekton.dev/v1beta1
kind: Task
metadata:
  name: deploy-task
spec:
  steps:
    - name: deploy
      image: deploy-tool
      env:
      - name: AUTH_TOKEN
        valueFrom:
          secretKeyRef:
            name: api-token
            key: token
      command:
      - deploy-tool
      args:
      - --deploy
```

- **RBAC Policies:** Role-Based Access Control (RBAC) should be employed to restrict access to pipeline resources, ensuring only authorized users can modify or trigger pipeline runs. This ensures adherence to the principle of least privilege.

- **Image Security Scanning:** Integrating container image scanning tools into the pipeline can automate the identification of vulnerabilities in images, ensuring that only secure, compliant images make it to production environments.

Continuous Improvement and Feedback Loops

To nurture a continuous improvement culture, pipelines can be configured to provide immediate feedback to stakeholders through integration with notification services. This involves sending alerts for build failures, performance regressions, or security vulnerabilities. Feedback loops facilitate the early identification and resolution of issues, promoting the incremental enhancement of application quality and performance.

The detailed development and integration of these elements culminate in a CI/CD pipeline that not only automates software development workflows but also fosters agile practices, encourages collaboration, and supports the rapid iteration of software products. OpenShift Pipelines provide the scaffolding required to implement these processes at scale, adapting to the diverse needs of modern software development teams.

9.3 Integrating Source Control and Image Registries

The integration of source control and image registries within OpenShift Pipelines is a cornerstone of the Continuous Integration and Continuous Delivery (CI/CD) process. These integrations form the backbone of automated workflows, enabling seamless source code management and application deployment. They ensure that software artifacts are built from the latest code and are securely stored and verified before being deployed to production environments.

Source Control Integration   Source control systems, such as Git, play a fundamental role in CI/CD pipelines by hosting the codebase and recording its version history. They enable collaborative software development and are pivotal in triggering automated pipeline runs based on code changes. This section explores the mechanisms by which OpenShift Pipelines integrate with source control systems and the configurations necessary to achieve this integration.

Connecting to Git Repositories   Integrating Git within an OpenShift Pipeline involves utilizing 'PipelineResource' definitions, which specify details about the Git repository and enable tasks to interact with the version-controlled codebase. A common setup involves cloning the repository at the beginning of the pipeline to access the latest code for building and testing.

```
apiVersion: tekton.dev/v1alpha1
kind: PipelineResource
metadata:
  name: source-repo
spec:
  type: git
  params:
  - name: url
    value: "https://github.com/example/repo.git"
  - name: revision
    value: "main"
```

This configuration specifies the URL and branch (or tag) of the repository to clone. Using this resource, tasks within the pipeline can pull the code required for subsequent operations.

Automating Pipeline Execution with Webhooks Webhooks are critical for automating pipeline executions in response to events within the source control system, such as commits or pull requests. The Git system sends an HTTP request to a specified endpoint with the details of the event that occurred, which in turn triggers the pipeline.

OpenShift Pipelines can integrate with tools like Tekton Triggers to configure such webhook-driven events. Tekton Triggers listen for incoming webhook requests, parse the payload, and initiate the corresponding pipeline run.

```
apiVersion: triggers.tekton.dev/v1alpha1
kind: TriggerBinding
metadata:
  name: trigger-binding
spec:
  params:
  - name: gitrevision
    value: "$(body.head_commit.id)"
  - name: gitrepositoryurl
    value: "$(body.repository.url)"
---
apiVersion: triggers.tekton.dev/v1alpha1
kind: EventListener
metadata:
  name: event-listener
spec:
  triggers:
  - bindings:
    - name: trigger-binding
    template:
      name: pipeline-template
  serviceAccountName: pipeline
```

This example illustrates a 'TriggerBinding' that extracts information from the payload and an 'EventListener' that listens for events and triggers a pipeline run using specified bindings.

Image Registry Integration Integrations with image registries are equally vital as they manage the lifecycle of container images, which are the artifacts produced by pipeline builds and deployed in Kubernetes clusters. A robust pipeline should automatically build, tag, and push images to a registry following a successful code build, and facilitate pulling these images for deployment.

Configuring Image Resources   Similar to source control integration, OpenShift Pipelines utilize 'PipelineResource' definitions for container images. These resources enable tasks to interact with image registries, supporting both the building and pushing of images.

```
apiVersion: tekton.dev/v1alpha1
kind: PipelineResource
metadata:
  name: image-resource
spec:
  type: image
  params:
  - name: url
    value: "quay.io/username/repository"
```

Using the image resource, a task can perform operations such as building a Docker image from a Dockerfile and pushing it to an image registry.

Building and Pushing Docker Images   Building and pushing a Docker image involves adding specific steps within a task definition that utilizes container tools like Buildah or Kaniko. These tools enable the building of images without a running Docker daemon, which is advantageous for Kubernetes-native environments.

```
apiVersion: tekton.dev/v1beta1
kind: Task
metadata:
  name: build-and-push-image
spec:
  params:
    - name: pathToDockerFile
      type: string
      description: The path to the Dockerfile
      default: "/workspace/source/Dockerfile"
    - name: imageName
      type: string
      description: The name of the image to build and push
  steps:
    - name: build-and-push
      image: gcr.io/kaniko-project/executor:latest
      args:
        - "--dockerfile=$(inputs.params.pathToDockerFile)"
        - "--destination=$(inputs.params.imageName)"
```

The above task utilizes Kaniko to build a Docker image and push it to the specified image registry. Kaniko allows building container images efficiently within a Kubernetes environment by resolving all dependencies from the local environment.

Ensuring Secure Integrations   Security considerations are imperative when integrating source control and image registries. These measures ensure that the pipeline executions adhere to best practices and that artifacts remain secure throughout the CI/CD process.

Managing Credentials Securely   In order to clone private repositories or push images to secured registries, pipelines must authenticate with source control and registry services. Secrets in OpenShift are used to store sensitive information securely and provide it to pipeline tasks through environment variables.

```
apiVersion: v1
kind: Secret
metadata:
  name: git-credentials
type: kubernetes.io/basic-auth
data:
  username: <base64-encoded-username>
  password: <base64-encoded-password>
```

This secret is created with base64-encoded credentials and can be mounted in tasks that require access to private resources.

Image Vulnerability Scanning   It's essential to integrate image vulnerability scanning tools within the pipeline to identify and mitigate potential security risks in container images. These tools can automatically scan for vulnerabilities post-build and notify the development team if issues are detected.

An example of leveraging Clair or Trivy can be integrated into the task as an additional step before pushing images to the registry. Integrating such security checks enforces compliance with security policies proactively.

Implementing Best Practices Several best practices should be adhered to when integrating source control and image registries to enhance efficiency, reliability, and security:

- **Immutable Tags:** Use immutable tags in image registries to ensure that each image can be traced back to a specific state of code. Immutable tagging supports rollback and auditability.

- **Branch-based Workflows:** Configure pipelines to track multiple branches for parallel development streams. This allows development, staging, and production environments to automatically pull the correct versions of application containers.

- **Monitoring and Logging:** Implement logging and monitoring for pipeline activities, Git operations, and registry interactions. Observability ensures that errors or irregular patterns are detected and remediated timely.

Facilitating a DevOps Culture By effectively integrating source control with image registries, organizations can foster a DevOps culture that emphasizes collaboration, automation, and a rapid feedback loop. This integration allows for:

- **Continuous Feedback:** Teams receive immediate feedback on code changes, from build errors to test failures and deployment readiness, promoting a cycle of continuous improvement.

- **Cross-functional Collaboration:** Developers, operations, and security teams can work closely with integrated tools and workflows, reducing silos and encouraging shared responsibility.

- **Enhanced Operational Efficiency:** Automation of repetitive tasks enhances efficiency and allows teams to focus on innovation and problem-solving.

In constructing these integrations, OpenShift Pipelines with Tekton provides the essential capabilities to orchestrate complex workflows across source control and image registries, ensuring that applications are tested, built, and deployed in a secure, consistent, and efficient manner.

9.4 Automating Tests and Quality Assurance

Automating tests and quality assurance within an OpenShift Pipeline is critical to maintaining high application standards and ensuring reliable software delivery. A well-designed automated testing framework enables rapid feedback on code changes, minimizes human error, and supports continuous integration and deployment.

This section explores the nuances of automating testing processes within CI/CD pipelines, leveraging OpenShift Pipelines to enforce quality assurance (QA) at various stages of the software development lifecycle. It delves into strategies, tools, and configurations to streamline testing operations.

- **Importance of Automated Testing:** Automated testing is fundamental to efficient CI/CD pipelines, enabling teams to catch defects early in the development process. It validates functionalities, detects regressions, and provides developers with timely feedback. Automation reduces the manual effort required for testing, making it scalable and repeatable across different environments and iterations.

- **Types of Testing:** Various types of testing can be automated, including unit tests (checking the smallest parts of the application), integration tests (verifying combined modules work together), and end-to-end tests (ensuring the entire application functions correctly from a user perspective). Each type serves a different purpose and provides a unique value in the QA process.

- **Integrating Testing into Pipelines:** A pivotal step in the pipeline is integrating automated tests. This integration is typically accomplished by adding tasks to the pipeline that execute test scripts or frameworks, analyze results, and make informed decisions on whether to halt or proceed with the deployment.

- **Unit Testing:** Unit tests are structured to run at the earliest stage of the pipeline. This ensures any foundational issues in the

code are identified and addressed before further processing, helping maintain code quality and stability.

```
apiVersion: tekton.dev/v1beta1
kind: Task
metadata:
  name: unit-test-task
spec:
  steps:
    - name: run-unit-tests
      image: maven:3.6.3-jdk-8
      script: |
        mvn test
```

Here, the 'run-unit-tests' step engages Maven to execute the unit tests,
leveraging the project's Maven configuration.

- **Integration Testing:** Integration tests are typically executed
  after the unit tests, focusing on interactions between different
  components or services within the system. These tests often require the application (or its relevant components) to be running
  in a testing environment.

```
apiVersion: tekton.dev/v1beta1
kind: Task
metadata:
  name: integration-test-task
spec:
  steps:
    - name: start-services
      image: docker/compose:1.27.4
      script: |
        docker-compose up -d
    - name: run-integration-tests
      image: maven:3.6.3-jdk-8
      script: |
        mvn verify
    - name: stop-services
      image: docker/compose:1.27.4
      script: |
        docker-compose down
```

In this example, services are started via Docker Compose, enabling the
integration tests to run in a live-like environment against the necessary
components.

- **End-to-End Testing:** End-to-end tests require a complete operating environment and often make use of specialized tools like

Selenium or Cypress to simulate user interactions with the application.

```
apiVersion: tekton.dev/v1beta1
kind: Task
metadata:
  name: e2e-test-task
spec:
  steps:
    - name: run-e2e-tests
      image: cypress/base:10
      script: |
        npx cypress run
```

This task utilizes Cypress to execute tests detailed within the Cypress testing framework, simulating user behavior to validate the application's functionality as a whole.

- **Test Data Management:** Effective test data management is crucial for consistent results across runs. Automated tests should have access to scenarios representative of production conditions while avoiding data-related flakiness or inconsistency.

- **Data Environments:** Managing separate environments with tailored datasets can ensure tests remain isolated, reproducible, and authentic. Staging environments that mirror production conditions with sanitized data often serve as a suitable basis for testing.

- **Test Data Initialization:** Tasks can include steps to initialize databases or mock external services to provide predictable and controlled responses during testing.

```
apiVersion: tekton.dev/v1beta1
kind: Task
metadata:
  name: setup-test-data
spec:
  steps:
    - name: init-database
      image: mysql
      script: |
        mysql -h db -u user -p password < /workspace/data/init.sql
```

This task initializes a SQL database with predefined data to establish a known state before executing further tests.

- **Quality Gates and Metrics:** Integrating quality assurance practices into a pipeline involves defining quality gates— thresholds or standards which code must meet or exceed before advancing. Metrics might measure test coverage, code quality, or performance criteria.

- **Analyzing Test Results:** Task results should be parsed and analyzed to assess pass/fail conditions. This can be implemented with reporting tools that consolidate results and identify trends over time. Open source tools like SonarQube can provide insights into code smells, vulnerabilities, and test coverage.

```
apiVersion: tekton.dev/v1beta1
kind: Task
metadata:
  name: sonar-analysis-task
spec:
  steps:
    - name: sonar-analysis
      image: sonarsource/sonar-scanner-cli
      script: |
        sonar-scanner -Dsonar.projectKey=my_project -Dsonar.sources=src
```

- **Setting Quality Gates in SonarQube:** Quality thresholds can be configured within SonarQube to enforce standards like minimum test coverage, ensuring that the feedback loop in CI/CD highlights areas needing improvement.

- **Executing Parallel Testing Strategies:** Parallel testing optimizes pipeline runtimes by distributing tests across multiple environments, reducing the bottleneck of long test execution times.

- **Parallelizing Unit Tests:** Many testing frameworks support parallel execution of unit tests, allowing for significant reduction in execution time. Ensure the underlying code and data structures are thread-safe before implementing parallel testing.

- **Distributed Testing Frameworks:** Distributed testing setups, such as Selenium Grid, enable running tests across multiple browsers or devices. This aids in cross-browser testing, ensuring a consistent user experience across platforms.

279

- **Advanced Testing Techniques:** In advanced pipelines, techniques such as behavior-driven development (BDD), performance testing, and canary releases enhance test and quality assurance practices.

- **Behavior-Driven Development (BDD):** BDD frameworks like Cucumber facilitate writing tests in a language akin to natural speech, enhancing collaboration between technical and non-technical stakeholders.

```
apiVersion: tekton.dev/v1beta1
kind: Task
metadata:
  name: bdd-test-task
spec:
  steps:
    - name: run-bdd-tests
      image: java:8
      script: |
        mvn test -Dcucumber.options="--tags @runTest"
```

- **Performance Testing:** Performance metrics are crucial for assessing application robustness under load. Tools like JMeter can be integrated to execute simulated load scenarios.

```
apiVersion: tekton.dev/v1beta1
kind: Task
metadata:
  name: performance-test-task
spec:
  steps:
    - name: run-performance-test
      image: jmeter
      script: |
        jmeter -n -t test-plan.jmx -l results.jtl
```

- **Canary Releases:** Incorporating deployment strategies such as canary releases allows testing with a small subset of users, assessing real-world performance and user interaction prior to full-fledged rollout.

- **Enhancing CI/CD with Testing Automation:** By embedding robust testing and QA practices within the CI/CD pipelines, organizations can achieve:

- **Faster Time to Market:** Automated regression suites detect issues early, reducing the cycle time from development to deployment, and enabling more frequent releases.

- **Higher Quality and Reliability:** Consistent automated testing improves overall application quality and reliability, reducing bug rates in production environments.

- **Increased Developer Productivity:** By automating repetitive toils, developers spend less time on manual testing and more on innovative feature development.

OpenShift Pipelines, when coupled with comprehensive testing strategies, lay the foundation for effective quality assurance processes. This integration ensures that all code changes are thoroughly vetted, resulting in resilient, reliable software systems that delight users and stakeholders alike.

9.5 Managing Pipeline Resources and Parameters

Efficient management of resources and parameters in OpenShift Pipelines is integral to building flexible and maintainable CI/CD workflows. Resources and parameters allow pipelines to be dynamically configured and adapted to different contexts, maximizing their reusability and scalability across various development environments and projects.

This section explores the structured management of pipeline resources and parameters, providing insights into their configurations and functionalities. It demonstrates how to harness these elements to control and customize pipeline executions effectively.

Pipeline Resources Pipeline resources in OpenShift, powered by Tekton, represent the inputs and outputs of pipeline tasks. These resources facilitate interactions between the pipeline and external systems, such as version control repositories or container registries, enabling smooth data flow.

Types of Pipeline Resources   Pipeline resources are categorized based on their functions and interactions with external entities. The key types include:

- **Git Resources:** Managed as PipelineResource objects, Git resources reference repositories containing source code. They are pivotal for tasks that require access to the latest codebase revisions.

```
apiVersion: tekton.dev/v1alpha1
kind: PipelineResource
metadata:
  name: my-git-repo
spec:
  type: git
  params:
    - name: url
      value: "https://github.com/example/project.git"
    - name: revision
      value: "main"
```

- **Image Resources:** Represent Docker images used within tasks or as build outputs and pushed to registries for deployment.

```
apiVersion: tekton.dev/v1alpha1
kind: PipelineResource
metadata:
  name: my-image
spec:
  type: image
  params:
    - name: url
      value: "docker.io/myrepo/myimage"
```

- **Storage Resources:** Used for handling files or artifacts and interacting with storage services like AWS S3 or GCP Storage.

```
apiVersion: tekton.dev/v1alpha1
kind: PipelineResource
metadata:
  name: my-storage
spec:
  type: storage
  params:
    - name: location
      value: "gs://my-bucket/path"
    - name: type
      value: "gcs"
```

282

Customizing Pipeline Resources Custom resources can be created to suit unique workflows not covered by predefined resource types. These are defined similarly and incorporated into pipeline tasks as needed, expanding the possibilities for task interactivity.

Defining and Using Parameters Parameters play a pivotal role in making pipelines dynamic and configurable. They allow task and pipeline behaviors to be modified at runtime, responding to variable conditions or stakeholder requirements.

Defining Parameters Parameters are defined within the Pipeline or Task resources, specifying potential inputs that can be passed during execution.

```
apiVersion: tekton.dev/v1beta1
kind: Pipeline
metadata:
  name: my-pipeline
spec:
  params:
    - name: image-tag
      type: string
      description: "The tag for the built image"
      default: "latest"
steps:
  ...
```

Parameters are declared with a name, type, description, and possibly a default value, which is used if no value is provided at runtime.

Utilizing Parameters in Tasks Tasks can reference these parameters within their execution environment, adapting task behavior based on provided values.

```
apiVersion: tekton.dev/v1beta1
kind: Task
metadata:
  name: build-image-task
spec:
  params:
    - name: image-tag
      type: string
  steps:
    - name: build-image
      image: gcr.io/kaniko-project/executor:latest
      args:
```

```
- "--destination=docker.io/myrepo/myapp:$(params.image-tag)"
```

Here, the image-tag parameter is injected into the task at runtime, allowing for dynamic image tagging based on pipeline executions.

Configuring Pipeline Runs with Parameters Pipeline runs incorporate parameter values, defining the configuration for that specific execution. This enables customization of each pipeline execution without altering the pipeline definition.

```
apiVersion: tekton.dev/v1beta1
kind: PipelineRun
metadata:
  generateName: my-pipeline-run-
spec:
  pipelineRef:
    name: my-pipeline
  params:
    - name: image-tag
      value: "v1.0.0"
```

This configuration overrides the default parameter value with v1.0.0, tailoring the pipeline run.

Advanced Management Techniques Managing resources and parameters effectively involves advanced techniques that elevate pipeline capabilities, facilitating complex workflows while maintaining maintainability.

Conditional Execution Conditional executions allow pipelines to adapt based on parameter values or resource states, enhancing their flexibility.

```
apiVersion: tekton.dev/v1beta1
kind: Task
metadata:
  name: deploy-conditionally-task
spec:
  ...
conditions:
  - lastTransitionReason: "Success"
    execute:
      test "$(params.deploy-env)" == "production"
```

Incorporating conditions accommodates dynamic decision-making processes, whether to deploy or not based on the environment parameter.

Using Workspaces for Enhanced Resource Management

Workspaces are a powerful addition that allow resources to persist between tasks. They accommodate file sharing and persistent storage needs within a pipeline execution context.

```
apiVersion: tekton.dev/v1beta1
kind: Task
metadata:
  name: process-data-task
spec:
  workspaces:
    - name: shared-data
  steps:
    - name: load-data
      image: busybox
      script: "cp /source/data.csv /workspace/shared-data/"
    - name: process-data
      image: myapp/data-processor
      script: "process /workspace/shared-data/data.csv"
```

With the shared workspace, data produced by the load-data step is available for processing in successive steps or tasks.

Ensuring Secure Management of Resources and Parameters

Secure management prevents unauthorized access or mishandling of sensitive details:

Secrets Handling   Sensitive information such as credentials or API tokens should be encapsulated within Kubernetes Secrets, ensuring secure access through controlled environments.

```
apiVersion: tekton.dev/v1beta1
kind: Task
metadata:
  name: access-secret-task
spec:
  ...
  steps:
    - name: use-secret
      image: alpine
      env:
        - name: MY\_SECRET
          valueFrom:
```

285

```
        secretKeyRef:
            name: my-secret
            key: secret-key
        script: "echo $MY_SECRET"
```

This task demonstrates secure consumption of a secret stored in Kubernetes, maintaining confidentiality throughout pipeline executions.

Promoting Reusability and Modularity Designing modular pipelines with parameters fosters reusability across distinct projects and environments:

- **Reusable Task Libraries:** Create and maintain task libraries—collections of tasks designed to execute common operations (e.g., deployment, testing) with parameterized configurations, promoting DRY principles.

- **Parameterized Pipelines:** Structure pipelines with parameters that allow similar workflows to be invoked across different branches, environments, or setup requirements without duplicating effort.

By adeptly managing resources and parameters, OpenShift Pipelines achieve a high degree of configurability and adaptability, empowering development and operations teams to automate complex workflows while ensuring streamlined processes. These elements, poised for secure integration and reusability, underlie the strength and flexibility of Tekton-powered pipelines, integral to scalable and maintainable CI/CD systems.

9.6 Using Triggers for Automated Pipeline Execution

Automation of pipeline executions using triggers represents a significant advancement in Continuous Integration and Continuous Delivery (CI/CD) operations within OpenShift Pipelines. Triggers facilitate event-driven pipeline runs, allowing dynamic responses to changes in the development and operational environments, such as code commits or updates to external systems.

Understanding and implementing triggers effectively can drastically improve the responsiveness and efficiency of CI/CD pipelines, enhancing agility and enabling rapid iteration in the software development lifecycle.

Understanding the Role of Triggers Triggers in OpenShift Pipelines, powered by Tekton, provide a mechanism for initiating pipeline executions based on specific events or conditions. They operate within the broader ecosystem of event-driven architecture, allowing pipelines to react promptly to changes that impact the software delivery process.

- **Event Sources:** Triggers are typically configured to respond to webhooks from various services, such as Git repositories, Continuous Integration servers, or external APIs. These webhooks send notifications when particular events occur, such as a new commit, a pull request, or a tag creation.

- **Benefits of Using Triggers:** By automating pipeline executions, triggers reduce manual intervention, minimize potential delays, and ensure consistency and reliability in the build and deployment processes. They support a more seamless, continuous delivery model, where updates can be released automatically based on pre-defined conditions.

Components of Trigger Configuration A robust triggering mechanism in OpenShift relies on several key components, each configured to facilitate seamless event-driven actions.

- **TriggerTemplates:** Defines how a pipeline or task should be executed when triggered. This includes the references to the pipeline and any parameters to be passed upon execution.

```
apiVersion: triggers.tekton.dev/v1alpha1
kind: TriggerTemplate
metadata:
  name: pipeline-trigger-template
```

287

```
spec:
  params:
  - name: gitrevision
    description: The git revision
  - name: gitrepositoryurl
    description: The URL of the git repository
  resourcetemplates:
  - apiVersion: tekton.dev/v1beta1
    kind: PipelineRun
    metadata:
      generateName: build-and-deploy-
    spec:
      pipelineRef:
        name: my-pipeline
      params:
      - name: git-revision
        value: $(params.gitrevision)
      - name: git-url
        value: $(params.gitrepositoryurl)
```

- **TriggerBindings:** Interprets event payloads and extracts values to populate parameters in the TriggerTemplates.

```
apiVersion: triggers.tekton.dev/v1alpha1
kind: TriggerBinding
metadata:
  name: pipeline-trigger-binding
spec:
  params:
  - name: gitrevision
    value: $(body.head_commit.id)
  - name: gitrepositoryurl
    value: $(body.repository.url)
```

- **EventListeners:** Acts as HTTP endpoints that listen for events and instantiate the appropriate TriggerBindings and TriggerTemplates, effectively serving as the entry point for all externally triggered events.

```
apiVersion: triggers.tekton.dev/v1alpha1
kind: EventListener
metadata:
  name: pipeline-event-listener
spec:
  serviceAccountName: pipeline
  triggers:
  - binding:
      name: pipeline-trigger-binding
    template:
      name: pipeline-trigger-template
  serviceAccountName: pipeline
```

288

The combination of these components allows for the automation of pipeline interactions based on incoming events from integrated systems.

Configuring Webhooks with Source Control Systems   One of the most common implementations of triggers is through webhooks associated with Git repositories. Configuring these webhooks ensures pipelines are automatically executed upon code changes.

- **Webhook Setup in GitHub or GitLab:** Webhooks in source control systems require pointing to the EventListener address. When setting up webhooks in GitHub or GitLab, specify the target URL to be the entry point exposed by the EventListener.

```
POST /pipeline-event-listener HTTP/1.1
Host: <event-listener-host>
Content-Type: application/json
{
  "ref": "refs/heads/main",
  "head_commit": {
    "id": "abcd1234"
  },
  "repository": {
    "url": "https://github.com/example/project"
  }
}
```

This payload serves as input to the configured EventListener, facilitating pipeline execution with extracted parameters through the TriggerBinding.

Advanced Triggering Strategies   To further enhance the flexibility and capability of automated triggers, several strategies can be employed, allowing pipelines to adapt to complex scenarios and requirements.

- **Conditional Triggering:** Conditions can be incorporated into EventListeners or TriggerTemplates to decide whether a pipeline should be triggered. This can be based on the event payload's content, ensuring pipelines run only when certain criteria are met.

289

```
apiVersion: triggers.tekton.dev/v1alpha1
kind: EventListener
metadata:
  name: conditional-event-listener
spec:
  triggers:
  - triggerRef:
      name: pipeline-trigger
    interceptors:
    - cel:
        filter: "body.ref.endsWith('refs/heads/main')"
```

Here, pipelines are only triggered for events on the 'main' branch, using CEL (Common Expression Language) for condition evaluation.

- **Chained Triggers:** Pipelines can be chained by configuring the completion of one pipeline to trigger another. This is beneficial in large workflows where sequential stages need execution.

```
apiVersion: tekton.dev/v1beta1
kind: TaskRun
metadata:
  generateName: stage-one-run-
spec:
  taskRef:
    name: stage-one-task
  resources:
    outputs:
    - name: trigger-pipeline
      resourceRef:
        name: next-pipeline-trigger
---
apiVersion: tekton.dev/v1alpha1
kind: EventListener
metadata:
  name: chained-trigger-listener
spec:
  triggers:
  - already defined TriggerTemplate
```

The output of one task or pipeline can include artifacts or parameters that cascade to subsequent executions.

- **Multi-Event Triggers:** Pipelines can be configured to respond to multiple distinct events, each potentially originating from different systems or part of diverse workflows. This flexibility supports complex microservices architectures or federated devops systems.

290

Event-Driven Architecture Influence in CI/CD   Event-driven architectures have become increasingly prevalent, promoting decoupled and asynchronous systems where components react to events similarly to how human-driven triggers are processed. Applying such paradigms within CI/CD accentuates several key benefits:

- **Scalability and Modularity:** Triggers allow pipelines to scale independently of the systems that initiate them. This modularity improves fault tolerance, as the failure or unavailability of one service or component does not directly impact the overall pipeline arrangement.

- **Reduced Complexity and Maintenance:** By listening for specific events, pipelines avoid unnecessary executions, reducing resource consumption and promoting efficient utilization of computing power. This simplicity extends to maintenance routines which become less involved, focusing efforts on refining critical, high-use cases.

- **Facilitated Real-Time Processing:** By immediately responding to events such as code pushes or issues being opened, automated triggers encourage immediate adaptation and response, implementing rapid CI/CD cycles conducive to agile development practices.

Implementing Security Measures for Triggers   Security in automated triggers is paramount to protect against unauthorized pipeline executions and ensure integrity across deployments:

- **Authentication and Authorization:** EventListeners can be secured with authentication mechanisms, ensuring only authorized systems can trigger them. This may involve using service accounts, tokens, or integration with identity provider systems.

- **Secured Communication Channels:** Employ HTTPS and encryption for all webhook and event communication to prevent data leaks and intercepting. This ensures integrity and confidentiality for all transmitted data.

- **Input Sanitization and Validation:** Implement validation of incoming event payloads to guard against injection attacks or malformed data. Triggers should incorporate checks for expected structures, types, and content.

9.7 Pipeline Monitoring and Debugging

Monitoring and debugging are critical aspects of managing Continuous Integration and Continuous Delivery (CI/CD) pipelines in OpenShift. A well-structured monitoring and debugging process ensures pipelines run efficiently, errors are swiftly identified and resolved, and the overall health of software delivery processes is maintained at optimal levels.

This section delves into the effective strategies and best practices for monitoring and debugging OpenShift Pipelines, providing insights into tools and methods to enhance observability, diagnose issues, and achieve higher reliability and performance in pipeline executions.

Importance of Monitoring in Pipelines

Regular monitoring of CI/CD pipelines is essential for maintaining software quality and operational efficiency. Monitoring provides visibility into pipeline runs, helping teams to track performance metrics, identify bottlenecks, and preemptively address potential issues.

Key Metrics to Monitor: Understanding which metrics to monitor can make a significant difference in proactive issue detection. Key metrics include:

- Pipeline Run Duration: Insight into the total time taken for pipeline completion, helping identify stages with delayed executions.

- Task Success Rates: Ratio of successful task completions against failures, a vital indicator of pipeline stability.

- Resource Utilization: Tracks CPU, memory, and storage usage during pipeline tasks to ensure resources are adequately provisioned.

- Event Logging: Comprehensive logs that capture detailed execution information and uncover patterns indicative of underlying problems.

Monitoring Tools and Techniques

A variety of tools and techniques can be leveraged to monitor OpenShift Pipelines, helping teams keep track of performance and operational health.

Prometheus and Grafana: Integrate Prometheus as a monitoring tool to collect real-time metrics from OpenShift clusters and pipelines, utilizing Grafana for visualization. These platforms facilitate the creation of dashboards that display critical pipeline metrics and trends.

```
scrape_configs:
  - job_name: 'tekton-pipeline'
    static_configs:
      - targets: ['<tekton-metrics-server>:8080']
```

Kibana and Elasticsearch: Use Elastic Stack (Elasticsearch, Logstash, and Kibana) for managing logs and visualizing data. These tools aggregate and index logs from pipeline runs, making it easier to conduct comprehensive searches and generate insights.

OpenTelemetry: Integrate OpenTelemetry for distributed tracing, capturing trace data that reflects interactions between various pipeline components and external systems.

Debugging Pipeline Failures

Effective debugging of pipeline failures requires structured approaches and well-defined workflows to quickly identify and resolve issues, minimizing downtime and ensuring consistent deployment success.

Log Analysis: Access logs generated by pipeline runs to diagnose and troubleshoot problems. Tekton pipelines maintain logs that document step-by-step execution details, offering insights into errors or anomalies during runs.

```
kubectl logs pod/<pipeline-pod> --container=<container-name>
```

Event and Error Reporting: Employ structured error reporting to capture information regarding failed tasks and events. It's important to document not only what failed but also contextual information around the failure.

Pipeline Visualization: Use visualization tools to map out pipeline workflows, converting abstract definitions into diagrams that help understand dependencies and interactions, thus aiding in recognizing failure points.

Advanced Monitoring Techniques

Advanced monitoring strategies enable deeper pipeline insights and enhance the overall effectiveness of monitoring systems.

Anomaly Detection: Implement machine learning-driven anomaly detection algorithms to recognize deviations from established pipeline behavior patterns, enabling proactive identification of potential issues that may require preemptive intervention.

Custom Metrics and Alerts: Define custom metrics specific to pipeline performance objectives and set up alerts for threshold breaches. This targeted monitoring can be more effective than generic alert mechanisms by focusing on critical indicators.

```
apiVersion: monitoring.coreos.com/v1
kind: PrometheusRule
metadata:
  name: pipeline-alerts
  namespace: monitoring
spec:
  groups:
  - name: pipeline-metrics
    rules:
    - alert: LongRunningPipelines
      expr: pipeline_run_duration_seconds > 300
      for: 5m
      labels:
        severity: critical
      annotations:
        summary: "Pipeline running for more than 5 minutes"
```

Rate Limiting and Throttling: To manage excessive load and ensure fair resource distribution, implement rate limiting within pipeline access and execution controls. This reduces inadvertent resource strain during peak usage.

Implementing Security in Monitoring and Debugging

Monitoring processes must ensure compliance with security best practices, protecting data integrity and privacy.

Secure Authentication: Require authentication for accessing monitoring dashboards and logs, employing secure protocols and role-based access control (RBAC) to enforce strict permissions.

Data Encryption: Encrypt data at rest and in transit, ensuring all collected logs, metrics, and traces are securely stored and transmitted, protecting against unauthorized access or interception.

Anonymization and Redaction: Implement data anonymization and redaction strategies in logs and traces to safeguard sensitive elements, like user information or secret keys.

Developing a Robust Monitoring Culture

Building a culture of proactive monitoring within teams extends beyond tool implementation. It requires fostering shared goals around observability, transparency, and ownership in pipeline management.

Cross-functional Collaboration: Encourage collaboration between development, operations, and security teams in building and maintaining monitoring systems. This brings diverse perspectives into dashboard creation, alert configuration, and response playbooks.

Continuous Training and Evaluation: Provide ongoing training to ensure teams understand tools and methodologies. Regularly evaluate monitoring outcomes and adapt strategies to meet evolving technological environments and business needs.

Multifaceted Benefits of Effective Monitoring and Debugging

Well-executed monitoring and debugging strategies afford numerous benefits, contributing significantly to organizational performance:

Early Problem Detection: Monitoring provides early warning signals that enable prompt intervention before issues escalate, reducing downtime and safeguarding application performance.

Enhanced Decision Making: Data-driven decisions supported by accurate monitoring insights improve operational strategies and resource management, aligning technical execution with organizational objectives.

Optimized Resource Utilization: Continuous performance monitoring optimizes resource allocation, ensuring minimal wastage and supporting scalability without compromising pipeline efficiency.

Ultimately, monitoring and debugging form the bedrock of resilient CI/CD practices, ensuring that pipelines operate smoothly, swiftly navigate challenges, and deliver consistent value. Implementing comprehensive, strategic approaches to monitoring empowers organizations to maintain high levels of agility, reliability, and quality in their software delivery processes. Through enhanced visibility and controlled feedback loops, OpenShift Pipelines maximize the efficacy of continuous integration and deployment endeavors, transforming routine operational management into a strategic advantage.

Chapter 10

Advanced OpenShift Features and Troubleshooting

This chapter delves into advanced OpenShift features, including the use of Custom Resource Definitions (CRDs) and the Operator Framework for extending platform capabilities and automating application lifecycle management. Strategies for integrating OpenShift within hybrid cloud environments are discussed to enhance deployment flexibility. The chapter offers insights into performance tuning and optimization, resource quota management, and enforcing limits to ensure efficient operation. It also addresses common issues and their resolutions through effective troubleshooting and diagnostic techniques, leveraging OpenShift logs and metrics to maintain cluster health and application performance.

10.1 Leveraging Custom Resource Definitions (CRDs)

Kubernetes is a powerful orchestration tool that allows developers to deploy, manage, and scale containerized applications. One of the key features of Kubernetes is its extensibility, which is most commonly achieved via Custom Resource Definitions (CRDs). CRDs enable users to define their own resource types, thereby expanding the Kubernetes API to suit specific application needs. OpenShift, built on top of Kubernetes, fully supports CRDs, offering an adaptable platform where tailored solutions can be implemented for diverse application complexities.

Custom Resource Definitions allow users to extend Kubernetes capabilities by defining custom objects without modifying core components or requiring any updates to the Kubernetes API server. This ability to incorporate new kinds of objects provides immense flexibility, enhancing the Kubernetes ecosystem to cater to specific workflows and applications.

- To gain a comprehensive understanding of CRDs, it is crucial to dissect their core components and functionality.

- A CRD comprises several key elements: apiVersion, kind, metadata, and spec. These elements define the API group and version, specify the kind of resource, include metadata such as the name and namespace, and describe the custom specification of the resource, respectively.

A simple example of a CRD is provided below, illustrating the creation of a custom resource for managing MySQL databases. This simple YAML file defines a custom resource called MySQLDatabase.

```
apiVersion: apiextensions.k8s.io/v1
kind: CustomResourceDefinition
metadata:
  name: mysqldatabases.example.com
spec:
  group: example.com
  names:
    kind: MySQLDatabase
    listKind: MySQLDatabaseList
```

298

```
    plural: mysqldatabases
    singular: mysqldatabase
  scope: Namespaced
  versions:
   - name: v1
     served: true
     storage: true
     schema:
       openAPIV3Schema:
         type: object
         properties:
           spec:
             type: object
             properties:
               storageSize:
                 type: string
```

The YAML snippet above defines a new custom resource definition for a MySQLDatabase. Notably, it includes the fields required under the spec block, such as storageSize, an essential property for managing database storage requirements.

Creating a CRD is just the first step in making use of custom resources. The next vital step involves creating instances of this resource. An example of creating a MySQL database instance using the defined CRD can be seen below.

```
apiVersion: example.com/v1
kind: MySQLDatabase
metadata:
  name: mydatabase
spec:
  storageSize: "20Gi"
```

This YAML file instantiates a MySQLDatabase object named mydatabase. The spec portion adheres to the schema defined earlier in the CRD, specifically regarding the storageSize property.

Utilizing CRDs permits the encapsulation of complex operational patterns within a single resource, allowing users to interact with Open-Shift in a more intuitive and domain-specific manner. OpenShift leverages these custom definitions to support more intricate deployment and application management schemes. By facilitating custom API extensions, developers craft resources that handle specific tasks or configurations autonomously.

```
$ kubectl apply -f mysql-crd.yaml
customresourcedefinition.apiextensions.k8s.io/mysqldatabases.example.com created
```

```
$ kubectl apply -f mydatabase.yaml
mysqldatabase.example.com/mydatabase created
```

Once the CRD and its instances are applied in a cluster, users can manage their custom resources just as they would native Kubernetes resources. Access to the resources can be managed using standard Kubernetes Role-Based Access Control (RBAC) policies, further integrating CRDs into existing security and operational frameworks within OpenShift environments.

An insightful advantage of CRDs is the simplicity with which they can be utilized to craft resource-specific custom controllers, typically leveraging the Kubernetes Operator pattern. Operators embody powerful Kubernetes abstractions that go beyond simple automation tasks to manage complex application lifecycle events.

Creating a Kubernetes Operator involves developing a controller that interacts with CRDs. Controllers listen for resource state changes and react accordingly, often by updating other resources or modifying the state of the cluster to achieve the desired state stipulated by the custom resource definition.

Consider a custom controller for the MySQLDatabase CRD. In the Go programming language, a general structure for an Operator that watches MySQLDatabase objects and manages database deployment would involve boilerplate code and the control loop mechanism. Here's a simplified example of a reconciliation loop in such an Operator:

```go
// Reconcile reads that state of the cluster for a MySQLDatabase object and makes
//     changes based on the state read
func (r *MySQLDatabaseReconciler) Reconcile(req ctrl.Request) (ctrl.Result, error) {
  ctx := context.Background()
  log := r.Log.WithValues("mysqldatabase", req.NamespacedName)

  // Fetch the MySQLDatabase instance
  var mySQLDB examplev1.MySQLDatabase
  if err := r.Get(ctx, req.NamespacedName, &mySQLDB); err != nil {
    log.Error(err, "unable to fetch MySQLDatabase")
    return ctrl.Result{}, client.IgnoreNotFound(err)
  }

  // Perform operations for the MySQLDatabase resource
  // e.g., deploy a MySQL instance, manage lifecycle, etc.

  return ctrl.Result{}, nil
}
```

In this brief Go snippet, the custom Operator establishes a reconciliation loop. It fetches the relevant `MySQLDatabase` instance and implicitly defines conditional logic to manage the application's lifecycle, such as initializing or scaling MySQL deployments based on the custom resource's current state.

The use of CRDs, combined with Operators, embodies the idiomatic operating model for applications on Kubernetes. This model enables the extension of Kubernetes with custom application management logic. With CRDs serving as the foundational mechanism, users can create bespoke API-centric workflows to address specific business needs or operational constraints.

As users continue to refine their deployment strategies, understanding the impact of CRDs on resource management, scaling policies, and interaction patterns becomes increasingly pivotal. Efficient schema designs, as well as a thoughtful approach to handling versioning and lifecycle management of CRDs, can lead to robust system operations in OpenShift environments.

Custom Resource Definitions are instrumental for OpenShift users aiming to build sophisticated infrastructure-centric solutions. Their flexibility not only fosters innovation but also empowers users to leverage Kubernetes as a comprehensive platform for addressing tailored application requirements, ultimately enhancing operational efficiency and developmental agility.

10.2 Operator Framework and Building Custom Operators

In the Kubernetes ecosystem, Operators stand out as a powerful pattern for managing complex applications. An Operator extends Kubernetes' capabilities by encapsulating knowledge on deploying, operating, and scaling applications, thereby automating tasks and operational processes traditionally managed by human operators. The Operator Framework provides a suite of tools and libraries to streamline the development and management of Operators, simplifying integration and lifecycle management in OpenShift environments.

Operators leverage the Kubernetes extensibility ability, primarily using Custom Resource Definitions (CRDs) to define new types of resources and manage these resources effectively. They inherently encode domain-specific knowledge, enabling Kubernetes to manage stateful applications in a declarative manner, solving problems specific to running applications at scale.

One of the core components of building an Operator is the Operator SDK (Software Development Kit). The Operator SDK assists developers by providing scaffolding, boilerplates, and automation tools to produce Operators in a more structured and consistent format. Operators can be developed using various programming languages, but the SDK mainly supports Go, Ansible, and Helm, each catering to different levels of complexity and operational needs.

The lifecycle of an Operator consists of several stages, including the planning, development, deployment, and ongoing management of the Operator. Each stage is pivotal to ensuring that the Operator serves its intended purpose of automating a robust application management process.

Planning the Operator

During the planning phase, it's crucial to determine the scope and requirements for the Operator. This involves identifying the capabilities and resources that will be managed by the Operator and defining the application's lifecycle, including deployment, snapshotting, scaling, upgrades, and failure recovery sequences. The planning phase must clarify the interactions between the custom resources and the controller logic for managing those resources.

A well-planned Operator should include considerations for configuration management, monitoring, logging, authentication, and authorization for seamless integration within the Kubernetes ecosystem.

Developing the Operator

Once the planning phase is complete, the development of the Operator begins. Utilizing the Operator SDK significantly simplifies this process. Consider a basic Go-based Operator for managing a simple application, possibly a complex stateful database service.

First, the initial scaffolding for the Operator can be created using the

SDK CLI. Here is a command that initializes a new Operator project:

```
$ operator-sdk init --domain=example.com --repo=github.com/example/mysql-
    operator
```

This command sets up the initial structure for the Operator. Following this, specific APIs and controllers need to be created for the custom resource definitions and associated logic:

```
$ operator-sdk create api --group=database --version=v1alpha1 --kind=MySQL
```

The 'create api' command generates the necessary modules to define new Kubernetes resources ('MySQL') under an API group ('database') and version ('v1alpha1'). This step automates boilerplate code generation, which is essential to managing the CRDs and the custom logic for orchestrating the application's lifecycle.

The core business logic for an Operator resides within the Reconcile function in the controller code. This function inspects the current state and desired state of the cluster and then takes appropriate actions to drive the current state to match the desired state.

Here's an illustration of the reconciling pattern using a simplified reconcile function in Go:

```
func (r *MySQLReconciler) Reconcile(req ctrl.Request) (ctrl.Result, error) {
    ctx := context.Background()
    log := r.Log.WithValues("mysql", req.NamespacedName)

    // Fetch the MySQL instance
    var mysql examplecomv1alpha1.MySQL
    if err := r.Get(ctx, req.NamespacedName, &mysql); err != nil {
        log.Error(err, "unable to fetch MySQL")
        return ctrl.Result{}, client.IgnoreNotFound(err)
    }

    // Manage cluster state and deploy MySQL resources
    // Add your custom logic here

    return ctrl.Result{}, nil
}
```

In this cycle, the reconciliation loop constantly checks for changes, processing events in the cluster, and acting based on the specifications outlined in the CRD.

Deploying the Operator

Once the Operator is developed, it should be meticulously tested and

303

packaged for deployment. Typically, Operators are distributed and run as containers within a Kubernetes cluster, encapsulated with all necessary dependencies.

The Operator Lifecycle Manager (OLM) is another part of the Operator Framework that eases the deployment and management of Operators in OpenShift. OLM provides facilities like dependency management, versioning, and updates, ensuring Operators are kept up-to-date with minimal manual intervention.

To deploy an Operator through OLM, users define a cluster service version (CSV), which specifies metadata about the Operator, including its version, dependencies, and available APIs. A typical CSV file might look as follows:

```
apiVersion: operators.coreos.com/v1alpha1
kind: ClusterServiceVersion
metadata:
  name: mysql-operator.v0.1.0
spec:
  displayName: MySQL Operator
  description: A simple MySQL Operator
  version: 0.1.0
  install:
    strategy: deployment
    spec:
      deployments:
        - name: mysql-operator
          spec:
            replicas: 1
            selector:
              matchLabels:
                name: mysql-operator
            template:
              metadata:
                labels:
                  name: mysql-operator
              spec:
                containers:
                  - name: operator
                    image: my-registry/mysql-operator:v0.1.0
```

Deploying this CSV in OpenShift integrates the Operator into the cluster, where it then manages its children custom resources according to the logic defined during development.

Ongoing Management

After deployment, it is critical to manage the Operator effectively. This includes observing its impact on resource utilization and performance.

Operators should be monitored for health and availability to ensure they perform as expected and guarantee the stability of the applications they manage.

Routine updates and upgrades form the backbone of ongoing management, ensuring the software, vulnerabilities, and operational processes remain current and secure. Using OLM, these updates can often be rolled out with minimal interruptions to service.

The integration of Operators into the OpenShift ecosystem provides streamlined workflows and improvements in operational efficiency, making application lifecycle management significantly less error-prone and more scalable. With the innate capability to embed domain knowledge into code, Operators empower OpenShift to act as an automated operations engineer, autonomously managing complex systems according to best practices.

Overall, the development and utilization of Operators require a comprehensive understanding of both the applications being managed and the Kubernetes platform. As Kubernetes and OpenShift continue to evolve, Operators will remain at the forefront of cloud-native application management, offering a structured, reliable means of encapsulating complex operational intelligence into repeatable processes.

10.3 Integrating OpenShift with Hybrid Cloud Environments

The increasing adoption of cloud platforms has ushered in a new era of computing, where hybrid cloud environments have become a vital component of enterprise IT architecture. These environments combine on-premises infrastructure with public and private cloud resources to balance security, performance, cost, and compliance needs. OpenShift, as a robust Kubernetes distribution, provides a versatile platform to seamlessly integrate with hybrid cloud environments, offering consistent management, scalability, and deployment flexibility across diverse architectures.

Integrating OpenShift with hybrid cloud environments involves several key considerations, including networking, identity and access management, data synchronization, and workload distribution. Each of these areas requires a nuanced understanding to ensure that Open-Shift not only operates efficiently within each part of the hybrid cloud but also enhances overall system reliability and performance.

Networking in Hybrid Cloud Environments

Networking forms the backbone of any hybrid cloud strategy, as it dictates the ability of different cloud components to communicate efficiently and securely. OpenShift provides robust networking capabilities that can be extended across hybrid cloud infrastructures. This includes facilitating communication between OpenShift and external services, allowing seamless integration of applications and data regardless of their physical location.

One approach to ensuring efficient networking in a hybrid cloud setup is the deployment of software-defined networking (SDN) technologies. OpenShift uses Open Virtual Networking (OVN) as its default SDN, enabling it to manage complex networking policies across diverse environments.

A typical example includes configuring an OpenShift cluster to connect with Azure's Virtual Network service, providing an integrated setup where on-premises data centers and Azure resources can interact freely. The following command outlines a method to configure Azure's virtual network peering with an OpenShift cluster:

```
$ az network vnet peering create \
  --name myVnetPeering \
  --resource-group myResourceGroup \
  --vnet-name myVnet \
  --remote-vnet /subscriptions/abc12345/resourceGroups/myOtherRG/providers/
     Microsoft.Network/virtualNetworks/myOtherVnet \
  --allow-vnet-access
```

This command creates a peering connection that enables seamless communication between Azure virtual networks and OpenShift deployments, thus forming a cohesive hybrid network architecture.

Identity and Access Management (IAM)

Identity and access management is another crucial aspect of hybrid cloud integration, addressing how authentication and authorization are managed across multiple environments. OpenShift supports diverse IAM solutions such as LDAP, OAuth, and Active Directory, easing the process of identity synchronization across on-premises and cloud setups.

An example of integrating OpenShift with an enterprise identity provider like LDAP involves configuring it within the cluster using a file defined in YAML format. Here's a simplified configuration:

```
apiVersion: config.openshift.io/v1
kind: OAuth
metadata:
  name: cluster
spec:
  identityProviders:
  - name: LDAPProvider
    mappingMethod: claim
    type: LDAP
    ldap:
      url: ldaps://ldap.example.com:636/ou=users,dc=example,dc=com?uid
      bindDN: uid=admin,ou=users,dc=example,dc=com
      bindPassword:
        name: ldap-bind-password
      insecure: false
      ca:
        name: ldap-ca
```

By defining this configuration, OpenShift authenticates users against the specified LDAP directory service, thereby providing consistent identity verification throughout the hybrid infrastructure.

Data Synchronization

Robust data synchronization is critical in hybrid cloud environments to maintain consistency and integrity across various data sources and applications. With OpenShift, enterprises can utilize tools like OpenShift Container Storage (OCS) to manage data across different cloud services. Tools such as Apache Kafka and Amazon S3 integration can provide advanced solutions for data replication and storage synchronization.

For instance, employing Kafka for synchronized messaging between OpenShift deployments in different locations ensures real-time data flow between cloud services. Interconnecting these services aids in maintaining data continuity and availability despite geographic barriers.

A Kubernetes-centric method to define storage on OpenShift using Persistent Volumes (PVs) and Persistent Volume Claims (PVCs) might be structured in YAML as follows:

```
apiVersion: v1
kind: PersistentVolume
metadata:
  name: my-pv
spec:
  capacity:
    storage: 100Gi
  accessModes:
    - ReadWriteOnce
  persistentVolumeReclaimPolicy: Retain
  storageClassName: my-storage-class
  hostPath:
    path: "/data/my-db"

---

apiVersion: v1
kind: PersistentVolumeClaim
metadata:
  name: my-pvc
spec:
  accessModes:
    - ReadWriteOnce
  storageClassName: my-storage-class
  resources:
    requests:
      storage: 100Gi
```

These configurations enable OpenShift to utilize hybrid cloud storage solutions, achieving both high availability and reliability.

Workload Distribution and Scalability

Hybrid cloud environments benefit from OpenShift's capacity to dynamically distribute workloads based on balancing load requirements and resource availability. Multi-cloud architectures powered by OpenShift can scale applications horizontally, providing resources as demand fluctuates.

OpenShift facilitates workload distribution through its autoscaling features, which can automatically scale services in response to CPU or memory usage patterns. Configuring a Horizontal Pod Autoscaler (HPA) exemplifies a powerful method to address dynamic workload demands:

```
apiVersion: autoscaling/v2
kind: HorizontalPodAutoscaler
metadata:
```

```
  name: my-app
spec:
  scaleTargetRef:
    apiVersion: apps/v1
    kind: Deployment
    name: my-app-deployment
  minReplicas: 2
  maxReplicas: 10
  metrics:
  - type: Resource
    resource:
      name: cpu
      target:
        type: Utilization
        averageUtilization: 50
```

This YAML file configures an HPA to automatically adjust the number of replicas for a deployment named 'my-app-deployment', responsive to CPU utilization.

OpenShift's ability to integrate with automated CI/CD pipelines further augments workload distribution by facilitating rapid application updates and deployment in hybrid environments. These pipelines ensure seamless version rollouts across multiple cloud services while authenticating each step and maintaining configuration integrity.

Security Considerations

Security is a pivotal consideration when building hybrid clouds, and OpenShift incorporates comprehensive security measures, including regulated control policies, network segmentation, and progressively layered defenses. These measures provide robust resistance to a range of vulnerabilities, including distributed denial-of-service (DDoS) attacks, unauthorized access, and data leaks.

Security configurations are managed via NetworkPolicies and Role-Based Access Control (RBAC), controlling traffic flow and access permissions respectively. Here is a NetworkPolicy example allowing ingress traffic only from a specific namespace:

```
apiVersion: networking.k8s.io/v1
kind: NetworkPolicy
metadata:
  name: my-app-access
  namespace: my-app-namespace
spec:
  podSelector:
    matchLabels:
      app: my-app
```

```
ingress:
  - from:
    - namespaceSelector:
        matchLabels:
          name: allowed-namespace
    ports:
    - protocol: TCP
      port: 8080
```

This configuration illustrates how NetworkPolicies can ensure that only accepted traffic is allowed to communicate with sensitive applications.

Additionally, integrating OpenShift with hybrid clouds necessitates careful governance and compliance measures, requiring organizations to adopt practices such as continuous security monitoring and audits.

The integration of OpenShift with hybrid cloud environments presents limitless opportunities for innovation and efficiency. By strategically leveraging these multi-domain environments, organizations can enjoy enhanced scalability, security, interoperability, and technological agility, ultimately advancing their cloud-native applications toward the enduring fulfillment of complex business objectives.

10.4 Performance Tuning and Optimization

Optimizing the performance of an OpenShift cluster is a multifaceted task that involves fine-tuning resource management, network configurations, and application deployment strategies. High-performance clusters are crucial for enterprises aiming to achieve maximum efficiency and reliability in handling their workloads. This section delves into the strategies and techniques available for enhancing OpenShift's performance, ensuring optimal resource utilization, and achieving consistent application response times.

Effective performance tuning begins with a holistic approach, considering both the workload characteristics and the underlying infrastructure. The primary areas of focus include:

- Resource allocation and scheduling

- Networking configurations

- Application deployment strategies

- System monitoring and auditing

Each of these components plays a significant role in overall performance, and concerted efforts in all areas yield the best outcomes.

Resource allocation and scheduling are critical for maintaining high performance. Kubernetes' underlying scheduling capabilities serve as the basis for resource management within OpenShift, ensuring optimal placement of containers based on resource requests, limits, and node characteristics.

To begin, a clear understanding of resource requests and limits is essential. Resource requests define the minimum CPU and memory required by a pod, influencing scheduling decisions, whereas resource limits cap the maximum resources a pod can consume. Efficient use of requests and limits can prevent resource contention and starvation. The following YAML snippet demonstrates specifying resource requests and limits for a deployment:

```
apiVersion: apps/v1
kind: Deployment
metadata:
  name: my-app
spec:
  replicas: 3
  template:
    spec:
      containers:
      - name: my-app-container
        image: my-app-image:v1
        resources:
          requests:
            memory: "256Mi"
            cpu: "500m"
          limits:
            memory: "512Mi"
            cpu: "1"
```

In this configuration, the application my-app requests 256MB of memory and 0.5 CPU units per pod, with limits set to 512MB and 1 CPU unit. This setup balances resource allocation with capacity planning, safeguarding against resource exhaustion.

311

Node labeling provides another layer of resource management. By assigning labels to nodes and including node selectors in pod specifications, OpenShift ensures that workloads are matched with nodes best suited to handle them. Consider this example of using node selectors:

```
apiVersion: apps/v1
kind: Deployment
metadata:
  name: example-deployment
spec:
  replicas: 5
  template:
    spec:
      containers:
      - name: myservice
        image: myimage:latest
      nodeSelector:
        performance: high
```

In this scenario, the node selector performance: high directs the deployment to nodes specifically labeled for high performance, ensuring that latency-sensitive applications receive adequate resources.

Additionally, OpenShift's support for CPU and GPU management allows for exploitation of hardware-specific capabilities, maximizing throughput for compute-intensive tasks. Access to these resources is controlled via device plugins or hardware accelerators, seamlessly integrating high-performance computing into the cloud-native ecosystem.

Optimized network configurations are vital for maintaining application responsiveness and throughput. OpenShift's networking layer, based on Open Virtual Networking (OVN) and Calico, provides a flexible foundation for achieving high-performance networking.

To optimize cluster networking, it's important to manage pod-to-pod, pod-to-service, and external communication efficiency. Network Policies can be employed to enforce Egress and Ingress rules, governing traffic flow to minimize latency and maximize bandwidth.

Below is an example of a Network Policy enforcing ingress controls to a web application:

```
apiVersion: networking.k8s.io/v1
kind: NetworkPolicy
metadata:
  name: allow-ingress
  namespace: web-app-namespace
spec:
```

```
podSelector:
  matchLabels:
    app: web-app
policyTypes:
- Ingress
ingress:
- from:
  - podSelector:
      matchLabels:
        component: frontend
    ports:
    - protocol: TCP
      port: 80
```

This Network Policy restricts ingress traffic to only those pods labeled frontend on TCP port 80, reducing the risk of network congestion.

Furthermore, employing Horizontal and Vertical Pod Autoscalers (HPA/VPA) dynamically aligns resource utilization with real-time application demands, facilitating efficient utilization of network resources. For instance, an HPA configuration may automatically adjust the replica count based on observed CPU utilization.

Here is a YAML configuration for employing a Horizontal Pod Autoscaler:

```
apiVersion: autoscaling/v2
kind: HorizontalPodAutoscaler
metadata:
  name: example-autoscaler
spec:
  scaleTargetRef:
    apiVersion: apps/v1
    kind: Deployment
    name: example-deployment
  minReplicas: 2
  maxReplicas: 10
  metrics:
  - type: Resource
    resource:
      name: cpu
      target:
        type: Utilization
        averageUtilization: 50
```

This configuration dynamically scales the example-deployment deployment from 2 to 10 replicas based on CPU utilization metrics.

Careful consideration of application deployment strategies contributes significantly to performance optimization. OpenShift supports strategies such as Blue-Green and Canary deployments, enabling seamless application updates with minimal downtime and rapid rollback capabilities.

Blue-Green deployment involves coordinating two identical environments—one live and one staging. The staging environment is thoroughly tested before traffic is rerouted from the live environment, minimizing disruptions. Canary deployments incrementally update a small percentage of the production environment, monitoring performance and stability before full-scale rollout.

Below is a basic representation of a Blue-Green deployment strategy using OpenShift routes:

```
apiVersion: route.openshift.io/v1
kind: Route
metadata:
  name: my-app
spec:
  host: myapp.example.com
  to:
    kind: Service
    name: my-app-green
    weight: 100
  alternateBackends:
  - kind: Service
    name: my-app-blue
    weight: 0
```

At any given point, traffic can be redirected between my-app-blue and my-app-green, reducing risk during updates.

Effective performance monitoring and auditing form the cornerstone of continuous optimization. Utilizing tools like Prometheus, Grafana, and OpenShift's built-in monitoring stack, operators can gain real-time visibility into cluster health and performance metrics.

Prometheus's robust querying language allows for creating sophisticated monitoring alerts, while Grafana offers rich visualization dashboards tailored to performance metrics. With OpenShift Monitoring, users have pre-configured integrations to monitor CPU, memory, and network usage, as well as application-specific metrics.

Here is an example of a basic Prometheus alerting rule for CPU usage:

```
groups:
- name: OpenShift CPU Alerts
  rules:
```

```
- alert: HighCPUUsage
  expr: sum(rate(container_cpu_usage_seconds_total[1m])) by (pod) > 0.75
  for: 5m
  labels:
    severity: warning
  annotations:
    summary: "High CPU usage detected"
    description: "CPU usage of pod {{ $labels.pod }} is above 75\% for more than 5
        minutes."
```

This Prometheus rule triggers an alert if any pod exceeds 75% CPU utilization for 5 consecutive minutes, providing timely notification of potential performance issues.

Continuous auditing of resource allocations, configurations, and application logs contributes to maintaining optimal performance and provides insight into potential areas for improvement.

By integrating these performance tuning and optimization strategies, OpenShift environments can achieve greater efficiency and resilience, empowering enterprises to host scalable, responsive applications that effortlessly align with fluctuating workloads and evolving business requirements.

10.5 Understanding and Managing Quotas and Limits

Efficient resource management is essential in any Kubernetes-based system, with OpenShift being no exception. Properly configuring quotas and limits ensures a balanced allocation of resources, prevents resource contention, and promotes fair usage among various projects and teams. Quotas and limits are fundamental to maximizing utilization, enhancing performance, and maintaining scalability and stability across the OpenShift environment.

In OpenShift, quotas and limits play a crucial role in managing the compute resources of the cluster. They serve distinct yet complementary purposes: quotas enforce constraints on resource allocation at the cluster level, while limits dictate per-container resource usage within those allocations. The precise application of quotas and limits facilitates predictable resource consumption patterns and mitigates risks associated with over-provisioning.

- **Quotas in OpenShift**

Resource quotas are applied on a namespace level, controlling aggregate resource consumption across all resources within that namespace. They act as a gatekeeper to ensure that no single team or application monopolizes cluster resources. Implementing effective resource quotas demands thorough analysis, taking into account projected workload requirements and balancing resource demands against overall capacity.

To create a quota, administrators define a 'ResourceQuota' object, specifying the total amount of CPU, memory, persistent storage, or other compute resources permissible for all pods within a namespace. Resource quotas are articulated in YAML format, as demonstrated below:

```
apiVersion: v1
kind: ResourceQuota
metadata:
  name: compute-quota
  namespace: team-a-namespace
spec:
  hard:
    requests.cpu: "10"
    requests.memory: "20Gi"
    limits.cpu: "20"
    limits.memory: "40Gi"
    persistentvolumeclaims: "10"
    pods: "20"
```

This YAML configuration caps the namespace 'team-a-namespace' to a maximum of 10 CPUs and 20Gi memory for resource requests, while allowing CPU limits up to 20 and memory limits to 40Gi. Additionally, it restricts the number of PersistentVolumeClaims and pods to 10 and 20, respectively.

Quotas uphold the principle of preventing "noisy neighbor" effects—whereby one workload disproportionately affects others by over-consuming resources—by providing a framework for distributing finite resources fairly. By enforcing such quotas, OpenShift ensures a harmonious sharing of cluster resources and prevents resource depletion.

- ## Limits in OpenShift

While quotas address resource usage at the namespace level, limits operate within a more granular context—governing individual container resource usage. Limits prevent a single container from consuming excessive resources, potentially impairing the performance of other workloads sharing the same node.

Defining limits within OpenShift involves creating a 'LimitRange' object, which imposes restrictions on the minimum and maximum CPU and memory resources assignable to a container and thus influences scheduling decisions. Consider the following YAML description of a 'LimitRange' object:

```
apiVersion: v1
kind: LimitRange
metadata:
  name: container-limits
  namespace: team-a-namespace
spec:
  limits:
  - type: Container
    max:
      cpu: "2"
      memory: "2Gi"
    min:
      cpu: "100m"
      memory: "256Mi"
    default:
      cpu: "500m"
      memory: "512Mi"
    defaultRequest:
      cpu: "200m"
      memory: "256Mi"
```

This example enforces a maximum limit of 2 CPUs and 2Gi of memory per container. The minimum is set to 100m CPU and 256Mi memory. The default resources are set to 500m CPU and 512Mi memory, ensuring that resource requests align with imposed defaults.

By using 'LimitRange', OpenShift maintains a predictable allocation of compute resources, thus optimizing scheduling efficiency and maximizing node occupancy. These controls form the basis for elastic scalability and significant cost efficiency gains.

- ## Strategies for Managing Quotas and Limits

Implementing quotas and limits requires a strategic approach. Default quotas and limits align with broader organizational policies, while specific configurations should be informed by applications' unique performance footprints. A diligent assessment of historical resource utilization data, anticipated workload growth, and specific project requirements is imperative.

• Monitoring and Adjusting Quotas:

Regular monitoring and review of resource usage are integral to recalibrating quotas and limits in response to changing circumstances. Prometheus and Grafana provide an effective mechanism for tracking utilization against quotas, identifying potential bottlenecks, and refining policies based on empirical data.

An example Prometheus rule to alert for nearing quota exhaustion is shown below:

```
groups:
- name: QuotaAlerts
  rules:
  - alert: CPUQuotaExceeding
    expr: |-
      sum(namespace_resource_quota{type="hard", resource="limits.cpu"})
      > (0.9 * sum(namespace_resource_quota{type="used", resource="limits.cpu"}))
    for: 10m
    labels:
      severity: warning
    annotations:
      summary: "Namespace CPU quota nearing"
      description: "More than 90% of CPU quota limits are nearing utilization in
          namespace {{ $labels.namespace }}."
```

This alert provides advance notification when CPU consumption approaches the quota threshold, empowering administrators to perform proactive resource adjustments.

• Balancing Quotas Across Projects:

Optimizing the distribution of quotas demands inter-project benchmarking and adjustments based on actual throughput and operational necessity. Ensuring equitable allocation results in improved overall system performance and user satisfaction.

• Automation and Reporting:

Automating resource adjustments with tools like Jenkins or Ansible can streamline quota management processes and reduce manual oversight. Coupled with comprehensive reporting, automation frameworks offer near-real-time insights into resource usage patterns, enabling swift resolution of imbalances.

- **Challenges and Best Practices**

Managing quotas and limits in OpenShift is not without its challenges, and adhering to best practices is essential for effective resource management. Key challenges include:

- **Interactive Workload Unpredictability:**

Dealing with highly variable workloads can render static quotas and limits suboptimal. Monitoring traffic patterns and implementing dynamic scaling strategies like Horizontal Pod Autoscalers can mitigate such challenges.

- **Application Performance Variability:**

Resource constraints can inadvertently degrade performance if not properly configured, especially for compute-intensive applications. Undertaking performance profiling and advanced capacity planning ensures accurate resource estimates.

- **Resource Fragmentation:**

Poorly defined limits can result in resource fragmentation, where isolated containers reserve but underutilize resources, leading to inefficient resource usage. Regular pruning of inactive or underused resources and reallocation aligns usage with active demands.

Adopting best practices ensures the smooth implementation and management of quotas and limits, as outlined below:

1. **Comprehensive Requirements Analysis:** Gauge workloads with precise specificity before configuring resource policies, incorporating both average and peak usage forecasts.

2. **Empirical Evaluation:** Base limit and quota adjustments on rigorous and ongoing measurement of system usage, leveraging telemetry data from monitoring tools.

3. **Scalable Architectures:** Design applications to support elasticity, with scalable microservices architectures and decoupled components fostering adaptive resource management.

Ultimately, configuring quotas and limits in OpenShift is an iterative process combining foresight, analysis, and adaptability. By acknowledging evolving resource needs and recalibrating strategies accordingly, organizations can maintain a well-functioning, agile OpenShift environment that maximizes overall performance and operational efficiency.

10.6 Troubleshooting Common OpenShift Issues

The dynamic nature of OpenShift environments, with their interplay of microservices and containers, invariably leads to a variety of operational challenges. Mastery in troubleshooting these issues is essential for maintaining the reliability, performance, and security of OpenShift clusters. This section delves into strategies for addressing prevalent OpenShift issues related to networking, storage, application deployments, and node performance, along with systematic debugging approaches.

- Networking Issues

Networking problems in OpenShift can stem from multiple sources, such as incorrect configurations, DNS resolution errors, or impaired communication pathways among services. Effective troubleshooting begins with a systematic examination of network configurations and connectivity across pods and services.

- Common Symptoms:

- Pod-to-pod communication failures
- Inaccessibility of services or routes
- DNS resolution errors

Commencing with DNS issues, ensure that core DNS services are functioning correctly by verifying the configuration and availability of the 'coredns' pods using:

```
$ oc get pods -n openshift-dns
```

If DNS pods are not running, inspect the events to identify the root cause:

```
$ oc describe pod <dns-pod-name> -n openshift-dns
```

In cases of pod communication failures, leveraging OpenShift's built-in debugging tools such as 'oc exec' to ping other pods aids in confirming inter-pod network connectivity:

```
$ oc exec <pod-name> -- ping <target-pod-ip>
```

When debugging route accessibility, validate route configurations to ensure correct hostname, path, and termination policies, utilizing the command:

```
$ oc describe route <route-name>
```

Misconfigurations can be rectified by editing route definitions and by verifying the associated service and deployment statuses to confirm that necessary endpoints are exposed and reachable.

- Storage Issues

Storage challenges often arise from misconfigured Persistent Volumes (PVs) or Persistent Volume Claims (PVCs), resulting in data persistence problems, inadequate storage provisioning, or access errors.

- Common Symptoms:

  - Pod stuck in 'ContainerCreating' state due to volume attachment errors

- PersistentVolumeClaims remaining in 'Pending' state
- Insufficient or incorrect capacity provisioning

Diagnosing storage issues starts with examining the events and statuses of the PVCs:

```
$ oc get pvc <pvc-name>
$ oc describe pvc <pvc-name>
```

If PVCs persist as 'Pending', ensure sufficient capacity exists in available PVs, and that PVs are correctly configured with matching storage class, access modes, and capacities:

```
$ oc get pv
$ oc describe pv <pv-name>
```

Troubleshooting volume mount issues often involves reviewing pod event logs for clues to misconfiguration and ensuring that node hosts have access to the underlying storage backend.

Editing the PVC configuration might involve specifying the appropriate storage class or resizing claims if additional capacity is required. For example:

```
spec:
  resources:
    requests:
      storage: "20Gi"
  storageClassName: "custom-sc"
```

For advanced cloud storage integrations, ensure that provisioners are correctly configured as per the cloud provider's guidelines.

- Application Deployment Issues

Deployment issues typically result from errors in application configurations, container images, or pod resource definitions, affecting application startup, behavior, and availability.

- Common Symptoms:
  - Pods failing to start or entering a 'CrashLoopBackOff' state
  - Applications returning unexpected errors or not responding

– Image pull errors

The first step in diagnosing deployment issues involves inspecting the pod logs for error messages:

```
$ oc logs <pod-name> --previous
```

For 'CrashLoopBackOff' conditions, determining root causes such as failed command invocations, misconfigured environment variables, or missing dependencies is critical.

Analyzing the deployment descriptors for entity correctness □ verifying configurations, ports, volumes, and environmental setups □ can illuminate discrepancies needing adjustment:

```
$ oc describe deployment <deployment-name>
```

Image pull errors typically yield insights from event logs showing authorization failures or nonexistent image references. Confirm connectivity to the Docker registry and validate image tags and credentials used for pulling:

```
$ oc get events -n <namespace>
```

For authentication with private repositories, create and apply image pull secrets, linking them to the service accounts used by the pods:

```
$ oc create secret docker-registry <secret-name> \
  --docker-server=<registry-server> \
  --docker-username=<user> \
  --docker-password=<password> \
  --docker-email=<email>

$ oc patch serviceaccount default -p \
  '{"imagePullSecrets": [{"name": "<secret-name>"}]}'
```

• Node Performance Issues

Node issues within OpenShift can manifest as degraded application performance, resource exhaustion, or nodes becoming 'NotReady'. These problems often stem from resource saturation, configuration disparities, or system faults.

• Common Symptoms:

- Nodes reporting 'NotReady' status
- Elevated response times or unresponsive applications
- High CPU/memory consumption

Begin by examining node status to check connectivity, health, and resource availability:

```
$ oc get nodes
$ oc describe node <node-name>
```

Check node conditions for disk pressure, memory pressure, or network partition errors and assess whether nodes meet adequate resource requirements.

Analyze the resource utilization metrics using 'top' or Prometheus monitoring to identify nodes with high consumption levels:

```
$ oc adm top nodes
```

For nodes marked 'NotReady', assess underlying kubelet and systemd logs to investigate errors related to failed services or daemons:

```
$ journalctl -u kubelet
$ journalctl -xe
```

Node reboots or system updates may rectify transient issues. Persistent issues might require scaling node resources, tuning system configurations, or adjusting application workloads for efficient distribution.

The confluence of these troubleshooting strategies with suitable monitoring and alerting systems fortifies the resilience of an OpenShift environment. Further integration with automated CI/CD pipelines and configuration management tools refines problem-solving efficiency, securing dependable service delivery in dynamic cloud-native ecosystems.

10.7 Using OpenShift Logs and Metrics for Diagnostics

Effectively diagnosing issues within OpenShift environments demands a comprehensive approach to monitoring and logging. These systems capture a wealth of information relevant to the performance, health, and security of clusters. By harnessing OpenShift's integrated logging and metrics, administrators can enhance visibility into cluster operations, resolve issues efficiently, and gain insights to preemptively address potential threats.

OpenShift's integrated observability stack includes tools such as Prometheus for metrics collection, Grafana for visualization, and Elasticsearch, Fluentd, and Kibana (EFK) for log management. This section explores the practicalities and methodologies for leveraging these tools to diagnose and address both routine and complex issues that may arise within OpenShift clusters.

The Role of Logging in OpenShift

Logs provide a sequential record of events that occur within the OpenShift platform, delivering insight into application behavior, system performance, and error conditions. There are multiple levels of logs relevant to diagnostics:

- **Application Logs:** Captured by the containers, detailing application-specific activities and potential issues.

- **System Logs:** Generated by the Kubernetes control plane components and node operating systems.

- **Audit Logs:** Record administrative actions and are critical for compliance and security auditing.

Fluentd serves as OpenShift's default log aggregator, collecting and forwarding logs to external systems such as Elasticsearch, where they can be indexed and queried.

To view logs for a particular pod, the following command can be used:

```
$ oc logs <pod-name>
```

For ongoing log monitoring, a streaming log view can be initiated:

```
$ oc logs <pod-name> -f
```

Logs for an entire deployment can also be captured, providing broader insight when diagnosing distributed or interrelated system behaviors:

```
$ oc logs dc/<deployment-config-name>
```

OpenShift's EFK stack facilitates advanced log analysis. For example, Kibana provides powerful querying capabilities that can filter and investigate logged events across many nodes and applications. Consider the following Kibana query to find all error logs generated within the last 24 hours by 'myapp':

```
Kubernetes.labels.app.keyword: "myapp" AND log_level: "ERROR" AND @timestamp >= now-24h
```

Through these insights, tendencies in applications' performance and stability can be identified and addressed.

Harnessing Metrics with Prometheus and Grafana

Metrics are quantifiable data points that measure aspects of system and application performance. OpenShift uses Prometheus to scrape and store time-series data, providing critical insights into resource consumption, latency, and other operational metrics.

Prometheus employs a robust querying language, PromQL, enabling intricate queries of metrics data. For example, to calculate the average CPU usage per pod over the past 5 minutes, the following PromQL query would be useful:

```
avg(rate(container_cpu_usage_seconds_total{image!="",namespace="default"}[5m]))
    by (pod)
```

Grafana complements Prometheus by enabling graphical visualization of metrics data, which helps identify trends and anomalies quickly. Creating dashboards that visualize these metrics supports continuous monitoring and rapid identification of performance issues.

For instance, setting up an alerting rule in Grafana to notify administrators the moment CPU usage exceeds threshold levels for more than 10 minutes could be implemented as follows:

- Navigate to 'Alerting' in Grafana and create a new alert.

- Set the condition with a Prometheus query:

```
max_over_time(cpu_usage{namespace="default"}[10m]) > 0.8
```

- Define alert notifications via email, webhook, or other channels.

Through strategic use of Prometheus and Grafana, operators can gain valuable insights, mitigate risks, and make informed decisions to optimize resource positioning and performance.

Centralized Logging and Monitoring Strategy

In a distributed system like OpenShift, a centralized logging and monitoring strategy ensures seamless correlation of events and metrics. By adopting a unified observability pipeline, administrators bolster their management tactics and amplify responsiveness to system perturbations.

EFK Stack:

- **Elasticsearch** serves as the search and analytics engine, ingesting and indexing logs for retrieval.

- **Fluentd** acts as the log collector, parsing and forwarding logs from numerous sources to Elasticsearch.

- **Kibana** offers visualization capabilities, allowing for query, analytical, and dashboard functionalities.

Deploying the EFK stack in OpenShift is streamlined through the use of predefined templates and operators that automate cluster integration.

For setting it up programmatically:

```
$ oc new-app elasticsearch-operator
$ oc create -f logging-es.yaml
$ oc create -f logging-fluentd.yaml
$ oc create -f logging-kibana.yaml
```

Prometheus and Grafana:

In an OpenShift cluster, monitoring applications rely on Prometheus to collect metrics data, enabling visualization and reporting in Grafana, streamlining the diagnostics process.

For deployment, utilize Operators:

```
$ oc apply -f prometheus-operator.yaml
$ oc apply -f grafana-operator.yaml
```

Set up services and resources, including defining ServiceMonitors and Alerts based on manual or dynamic discovery of services requiring monitoring.

Diagnostic Workflows

Efficient diagnostics in OpenShift follow robust methodologies aimed at identifying root causes and implementing mitigations swiftly.

Workflow for Applications:

- **Detection:** Initiate with metrics-driven insights capturing anomalies in application performance metrics, such as response times or error rates.

- **Gathering Logs:** Aggregate pertinent logs from impacted pods and correlate with metrics to uncover error sources.

- **Analysis:** Utilize Kibana to conduct detailed log searches and assess frequency and triggers of anomalies.

- **Resolution:** Implement changes—adjust configurations, scale resources, apply patches—and utilize monitoring to validate stability.

Workflow for Infrastructure:

- **Monitor Nodes:** Employ Grafana dashboards focused on infrastructure metrics—CPU, memory, disk throughput—to detect patterns indicative of node-level issues.

- **Audit Resource Usage:** Investigate usage patterns, exercising Prometheus queries to validate potential resource contention.

- **Correlate Data:** Use intersectional insights from application, network, and system logs to locate systemic faults.

- **Remediate:** Employ orchestration or configuration adjustments, followed by an observability cycle to confirm resolution efficacy.

By embedding these workflows into day-to-day operations, organizations can improve system availability and reliability.